NAZI UFOs

NAZI UFOs

The Legends and Myths of Hitler's Flying Saucers in WW2

S.D. Tucker

FRONTLINE
BOOKS

An imprint of
Pen & Sword Books Ltd
Yorkshire – Philadelphia

FRONTLINE
BOOKS

First published in Great Britain in 2022 by

Frontline Books
an imprint of Pen & Sword Books Ltd,
47 Church Street, Barnsley, S. Yorkshire, S70 2AS

ISBN 978 1 39907 156 7

A CIP catalogue record for this book is available from the British Library.

Typeset in Chennai, India
by Lapiz Digital Services.

Printed and bound by CPI Group (UK) Ltd, Croydon, CR0 4YY

Pen & Sword Books Ltd incorporates the imprints of Pen & Sword Archaeology, Atlas, Aviation, Battleground, Discovery, Family History, History, Maritime, Military, Naval, Politics, Social History, Transport, True Crime, Claymore Press, Frontline Books, Praetorian Press, Seaforth Publishing and White Owl

For a complete list of Pen & Sword titles please contact

PEN & SWORD BOOKS LTD
47 Church Street, Barnsley, South Yorkshire, S70 2AS, England
E-mail: enquiries@pen-and-sword.co.uk
Website: www.pen-and-sword.co.uk

Or

PEN AND SWORD BOOKS
1950 Lawrence Rd, Havertown, PA 19083, USA
E-mail: Uspen-and-sword@casematepublishers.com
Website: www.penandswordbooks.com

Contents

Introduction

Jerry–Built Saucers?

War is the father of all things.

Adolf Hitler, German politician and inventor of flying saucers

Beginning in 1946, the year after he had supposedly shot himself dead through the skull in a Berlin bunker to escape the imminent advance of the Red Army, no less an individual than Adolf Hitler (1889–1945) began mailing out a long-running series of letters to persons living in the rural eastern US states of Kentucky, Tennessee and West Virginia. These letters – in which Adolf strangely billed himself as 'the Furrier' rather than 'the Führer', or else allowed the name of his new wife, 'Eva Hitler', or his latest Chief of Staff, 'General Kannengeiser', to appear in their evil master's stead – came soliciting donations for a cunning new Nazi plot to enslave the US, the world and finally the galaxy itself.

It turned out Hitler had been taken alive after all, and had then somehow escaped and fled across the Atlantic to the US, from where his latest communications, written in the kind of barely literate English you might expect from a non-native speaker, made their recipients a tempting offer: in return for cash donations in the form of postal orders, Adolf would consider pushing General Kannengeiser aside and making each donor his official 'Furrier #2'. As Hitler would accept individual sums as low as $5 for his cause, this represented quite a bargain.

Hiding out in a top-secret location somewhere in the enemy heartland, Hitler had established no fewer than 116 underground factories across Kentucky and Idaho, with his 36,000-strong army of German revolutionaries slowly but surely digging tunnels towards Washington where he would later establish his 'new kingdom'. Within these subterranean lairs, Adolf's scientists were busily manufacturing atom bombs and an indestructible fleet of 'invisible spaceships which make no sound' with which to defeat the

US. If those in receipt of the Furrier's begging letters had not already seen or heard such wonders buzzing through their local skies, then this only showed just how invisible and silent these craft were – the ideal vehicles, Hitler maintained, to launch a 'surprise attack' on the White House.

Authorities were first tipped off about this rebellion when Adolf's most generous supporter, a 70-year-old Virginia stonemason with the good, solid old Teutonic name of G.A. Huber, dropped dead. Huber's family did not expect to inherit much from their apparently penniless relative, living as he did in a pathetic wooden shack. Yet the reason Huber was so destitute was because he had blown his $10,000 life savings on aiding Hitler's future coup. A 1947 Gallup poll showed 45 per cent of Americans believed Hitler was still alive, with newspapers full of wild tales to that effect, and Huber, described as being in 'poor physical and mental health', had taken it upon himself to investigate the fugitive Führer's whereabouts personally. After Huber's death, around 200 handwritten begging letters from Hitler were found in his hovel, together with stacks of money order receipts filed away as proof of Huber's purchase of the eventual role of Deputy-Furrier.

Alerted to the existence of this looming totalitarian plot, a heroic postal inspector named W.W. Lewis managed to lure Adolf into a post office in Middlesboro, Kentucky, to pick up a vital new money order worth as much as $15 towards conquering the universe. As soon as Hitler cashed the cheque on 11 August 1956, he was arrested, despite the dictator's shrewd disguise – that of a 61-year-old black man, surely the last identity you would ever expect to have been assumed by history's most notorious white supremacist. Once safely behind bars, the dark-skinned prisoner had to admit he was not the Furrier at all, but a former coalminer and part-time Baptist mountain-preacher turned mail-order fraudster named William Henry Johnson (b.1895).

Hearing rumours Hitler was hiding in Kentucky, G.A. Huber had met with Johnson, who lied that he knew Adolf himself, offering to become a 'go-between' linking the two men. Lined up to be 'Furrier #3' behind Huber was the Tennessee handyman Charlie Brown who, despite his name, had hardly been sending Johnson peanuts. Around $1,000 had been squeezed from Charlie by promising him a 'royal palace' and his 'choice among . . . virgins', with a forced child-bride to be sourced from the families of the future Nazi diplomatic corps once Washington had been obliterated. So eager was Charlie for his reward that, when contacted by Inspector Lewis, he had only

8 cents and a single can of beans left to live off, having just mailed Hitler his final $20. Adolf was so impressed by Brown's sacrifices that he wrote to Huber admitting he may make Charlie 'assistant world-ruler [alongside yourself] for his bravery act last week (in sending me money)'.

Sometimes, Brown was brave enough to send Hitler other things via the US Postal Service too, specifically a natty sports-coat and pair of size 11 white shoes, it being 'necessary for Adolf to dress sporty so he won't be recognised' when goose-stepping around town. Yet Hitler also had use of an 'invisible cab' to go with his invisible spaceships, so you would have thought no camouflage was necessary. Charlie very much wanted to meet Adolf, but this would blow the demonstrably non-white Johnson's cover, even if he donned full Nazi field-uniform and a fake moustache, and every time a rendezvous was arranged, it was irritatingly thwarted at the last moment by Adolf falling suddenly ill or becoming trapped in his room by FBI agents. However, as Hitler's future close assistant Charlie Brown was black too, perhaps the Nazi Party was now an equal opportunities employer. Furrier #1 implied that by taking a German 'diplomat virgin' for his wife 'our coloured friend Brown' could put a drop of beneficial white Aryan blood into his offspring, thus helping 'hand down German rulers [to the blacks] to rule their race'.

William Henry Johnson had high hopes for the potentially bottomless nature of both his fellow human beings' gullibility and their wallets, signing some letters in the neo-Nazi non-name of A. von Boguslowski in apparent mockery. Given that he sometimes slipped up and signed letters in his own real name too, Johnson could easily have been mocked himself. Johnson hoped his captors would prove equally stupid, claiming to legal authorities that, as a top undercover private detective, he had perpetrated the scam at the behest of a group of shadowy Chicago-based intermediaries but that, once he had amassed enough proof, he intended to turn double-agent and warn the FBI about all the hidden Nazi spacecraft factories. However, his story was inconsistent. One time, he said the Chicago firm was headed up by G.A. Huber's cousins, another time he said he had been recruited on his doorstep by 'a man named Hoover', presumably the FBI chief J. Edgar Hoover (1895–1972), who was, illogically, Hitler's true Deputy-Führer. In court, he showed off a large home-made badge reading 'Secret Service', claiming to have graduated from a 'Chicago Secret Service correspondence school' for spies, on whose behalf he was tracking Nazis.

When arrested, Johnson had provided a written confession that 'I am guilty of everythings', but added he would only admit so if the police guaranteed his case would not make the newspapers, so his Baptist congregation wouldn't discover their preacher was a criminal. If no such deal was forthcoming, Johnson warned he would have to pretend to be not guilty instead. But as he also confessed he was 'a poor guilty criminal' and that if his victims had been 'crazy enough to send me money, I had been crazy enough to spend it', it is difficult to see how he could deny culpability. Further armed with the knowledge he had a previous 1951 conviction for postal fraud, a jury took only 15 minutes to find Johnson guilty and Hitler received three concurrent three-year sentences (though not to be served in Landsberg Prison this time) from presiding judge, H. Church Ford – much to the disgust of loyal black Nazi Charlie Brown, who, such was his devotion to the cause, actually testified on the false Führer's behalf. He was impressed that, after being arrested, Hitler had charitably returned $800 of the $1,000 he had previously stolen to build his space fleet.[1]

* * *

The Kentucky Hitler Hoax appears to show that, as early as 1946, a mere year after German defeat, there was already an imaginative connection being made between the ostensibly unconnected fields of Nazism and what we now call UFOs. Actually, however, Johnson's initial acts of fraud predate the very idea of a UFO as such entirely. The word 'UFO' was first used by the newly formed US Air Force (USAF) in the late 1940s and early 1950s, then popularised through Project Blue Book, an official investigation of the subject headed up by USAF Captain Edward J. Ruppelt (1922–59) from 1952 onwards. Blue Book's dry adoption of the term 'Unidentified Flying Object' was intended in a literal non-committal sense, as indicating some unknown item witnessed in the sky, not as a technical-sounding synonym for 'alien spaceship', as we tend to presume today. Ruppelt, who claimed personal credit for devising the phrase, hoped it might replace the hitherto ubiquitous label 'flying saucer', as the majority of reports investigated by him were not of classic disc-shaped objects at all, and also as a wilfully banal-sounding means of distancing the subject from sensational Hollywood sci-fi b-movies of the era like *Earth vs the Flying Saucers* and *Invasion of the Saucer-Men*.[2]

This earlier term 'flying saucer' had gained currency in the immediate wake of the first widely publicised UFO sighting, that made by the private pilot and travelling fire-safety equipment salesman Kenneth Arnold

(1915–84) when flying over Washington State's Cascade Mountains at around 3.00 p.m. on 24 June 1947, on the look out for wreckage of a missing C-46 Marine Corps transport plane. During this search, when 'the sky and air was as clear as crystal', Arnold saw 'a bright flash as if a mirror were reflecting sunlight at me' bounce off his plane. Towards Mount Rainier, he then spied 'a chain of nine peculiar aircraft' flying at 'a terrific speed' from which the sun kept reflecting.

These 'peculiar aircraft' were the first ever flying saucers. Yet they were not saucers at all. Although Arnold later concluded that UFOs were not machines but shoal-like 'groups and masses of living organisms' native to Earth's upper atmosphere and able to change their shapes and densities at will, his initial thought was that the objects were secret aerial weapons, possibly tail-less jet planes or 'guided missiles, robot-controlled'. He thought them unmanned, as 'the human body simply could not stand' the speed they flew at, estimated initially at 1,200mph. These proto-drones may well have been the work of enemy powers, reasoned Arnold – not Nazis, but Russians.

In a written report to US military authorities, Arnold later warned that 'used as an instrument of destruction, in combination with our atomic bomb, the effects [of these craft] could destroy life on our planet'. Accordingly, immediately after his sighting Arnold flew to the nearest FBI office in Oregon but found it closed. Unlike secret agents, the news never sleeps, so he instead got warning out to the nation by giving a post-flight interview to reporters Bill Bequette (1917–2011) and Nolan Skiff of the *East Oregonian* newspaper, talking of having witnessed nine objects whizzing through the sky in an 'erratic' high-speed manner compared with being 'like a saucer would [move] if you skipped it across the water'. If only Arnold had made the more familiar comparison with a pebble being skimmed over a lake, not a saucer, the consequent mess of verbal confusion may not have arisen.

The nine objects were not circular at all, but roughly crescent-shaped, with later sketches resembling Batman's patented 'batarang' device, sprung free from his famous utility belt. In a 26 June radio interview, Arnold preferred to describe them as looking 'like a pie-plate that was cut in half with a sort of convex triangle in the rear'. Arnold's initial urgent news was delivered just before presses rolled, however, so his story was written up in a mad rush, before appearing on the newspaper's front page under the heading 'Impossible! Maybe, But Seein' Is Believin', Says Flier'. And Arnold himself was widely believed; as a responsible self-employed businessman, experienced licensed air rescue pilot, deputy US Marshal and all-round solid citizen, he seemed the very definition of a reliable witness. Unlike his supposedly circular saucers themselves, Arnold seemed much too square and straight to be doubted.

Paraphrasing Arnold's words in compressed fashion, the *East Oregonian* fatefully stated that the objects were 'saucer like', an evocative phrase understandably taken to mean the aerial phantoms were saucer shaped, which they were not. In a follow-up report on 26 June, Bill Bequette clarified that Arnold had actually described the objects as 'somewhat bat-shaped', but the damage was already done. Other newspapers quoted Arnold describing his mystery objects as 'crescent-shaped' or 'half-moon shaped, oval in front and convex in the rear', but by 27 June the specific phrase 'flying saucers' was already in print, coined by several different journalists independently.

Arnold later employed other metaphors to the effect that the objects, which had flown in a kind of reverse-echelon formation like migrating birds, really moved more like 'speed-boats on rough water, or similar to the tail of a Chinese kite that I once saw blowing in the wind', but the image had stuck, and so we do not speak of people having seen 'flying speedboats' or 'alien kite-ships'. Arnold also described them as looking 'boomerang-shaped' or even 'tadpole-shaped', rather suggesting he wasn't entirely certain quite what he had seen. Nonetheless, in the immediate wake of Arnold's mis-reported sighting, thousands of witnesses came forward to report spotting their own circular saucers in US skies too, a class of objects conspicuously absent from the popular imagination prior to this date.

Then again, ufology is full of peculiar ambiguities, and it does appear there were a handful of purported sightings of odd disc-shaped things whizzing over the US from April 1947 onwards, from several different states. However, these accounts only gained meaningful publicity in the wake of Arnold's words, and you would guess some witnesses were re-interpreting what they had seen in light of Arnold's sighting of 24 June, or else inventing them wholesale. The initial opinion of Arnold on this subsequent copy-cat cascade was sceptical; if this 'lot of foolishness' continued at this rate, 'it wouldn't be long before there would be one of these things in every garage'.

Maybe so. By 19 August, a Gallup opinion poll showed nine out of ten Americans had heard the phrase 'flying saucers', a great rate of brand-name recognition for such a newly launched consumer product. The only known specific pre-1947 verbal comparison of an unknown aerial item to a saucer occurred in 1878 when a Texan farmer, John Martin, reported an orange object 'the size of a large saucer' in the sky – but again, Martin did not say it was saucer like in shape at all, only in size. One 1946 Iowa newspaper spoke of what would now be termed a UFO, but which was described at the time as both 'a great white bird' and 'a bomb', things every bit as dissimilar as a boomerang and a tadpole.[3] The term 'flying saucer' became so ubiquitous less because of its physical accuracy than because it allowed the public to place their otherwise potentially unrelated and unclassifiable encounters with unusual things in the atmosphere within a convenient and catchy new verbal and conceptual category. By 1948, Arnold was writing an article, 'The Truth About Flying Saucers', for the first ever issue of *FATE* magazine, soon to become the US' leading paranormal periodical, which came with a hugely inaccurate yet highly striking cover painting showing his plane encountering not flying tadpoles but a pair of giant 'classic' flying saucers emerging from within a cloudbank. Arnold could not have objected too much to the misrepresentation, as when his article was expanded into book-length form in 1952 as *The Coming of the Saucers*, this very same illustration was recycled on the dust jacket.[4] Personally, I have no idea what Kenneth Arnold actually saw that day over the Cascade Mountains, whether mundane or genuinely mysterious. Odd things seen skimming through the skies are not purely a media invention; but flying saucers, strictly speaking, self-evidently are.

* * *

Once Kenneth Arnold had accidentally given birth to the flying saucer, a second new bastard-child was then sired: that of the Nazi flying saucer, a genuine historical – or ahistorical – anachronism. Although Nazi Germany ceased to exist in 1945, flying saucers did not begin to exist until 1947, and so all talk of such things are by definition backwards mental projections. Like the plain vanilla saucers themselves, ones bearing swastikas were also a concocted, media-spawned fantasy; the notion that the Third Reich might have possessed top-secret super weapons which would have been unleashed to wreak anti-gravity, laser spitting death upon a defenceless world had the war only been strung out by Hitler for a few months more was a sci-fi horror story of great potency. As such, it has sold a lot of books, films and newspapers down the years, beginning as quickly as 28 June 1947, only one day after the very term 'flying saucers' itself first began troubling the headlines, when a story appeared in the *Seattle Times* speculatively linking Arnold's objects with wartime Nazi tech.[5]

Naturally, several con men exploited this fortuitous confluence of media tropes for personal gain during the decade or so following the war, and not only in the US. Rivalling William Henry Johnson's tale for strangeness was that of the one-time Nazi spy-ring leader Niels Christian Christensen (a cover name stolen from a dead Danish athlete, his real identity being Josef Jacob Johannes Starziczny). Arrested and imprisoned, in 1948 the secret agent disingenuously offered to spill the beans about Arnold's saucers to his captors. Christensen had been recruited by the Nazi counter-intelligence agency, the Abwehr, and dispatched to Rio de Janeiro in 1941 to establish hidden radio networks transmitting information about British merchant shipping, allowing vessels leaving Brazilian ports to be easily targeted and torpedoed by U-boats. The subsequent sinking of Brazilian-flagged supply ships alongside the British-flagged ones led to a public outcry and police were soon on the look out for German agents.

The careless Christensen made three key mistakes. First, he personally went into a store and ordered a wave-meter part suitable for use only in powerful transmitters of the kind ordinary people would never need. Alerted by the shopkeeper, officers were easily able to trace Christensen due to his second rookie error, that of openly installing a large antenna on the roof of his own house like a big neon sign saying 'NAZIS ARE HERE'. Thirdly, he wrote himself a helpful list of his fellow conspirators as an aide-memoir, which was discovered during a raid, unravelling the whole spy ring. Arrested, tortured and interrogated, confessions were soon elicited from the Abwehr recruits and sentences handed down, including thirty years behind bars for Christensen himself.

Apprehended in March 1942, the not-so-secret agent was silent until 5 November 1948, when an interview appeared in mass-circulation Rio evening newspaper *Diário da Noite*, concerning the saucers first seen by Kenneth Arnold the previous summer. The prisoner confirmed these were wartime German creations, radio-controlled drones intended for aerial reconnaissance and anti-aircraft purposes. Being an inventor himself, trained at the University of Breslau with a hundred or so patents to his name, who had used his time in prison to invent a new form of 'dehydrator and atomiser' for food, Christensen offered to gift the Brazilian Army Hitler's old saucer patent for free. If given access to some 'young engineers', he could build Brazil a working disc with a top speed of 1,000kmph within a mere ninety days and for a low, low cost of only 400,000 cruzeiros, he said.

As Christensen had personally invented the craft's design himself 'without any help from anyone' he did not see why this task should prove especially difficult. It would be easy to gather materials, as the propeller driven drone was made of simple aluminium and its silent-running engine powered by nothing more exotic than oil and alcohol. The disc could also carry 'explosive bombs' (are there any other kind?), even atom bombs, which could be detonated remotely. Whilst proclaiming he would gift Brazil his invention for free, 'requiring nothing in exchange for the patent', the subtext was that all Christensen really asked for in return was his freedom. He didn't get it, at least not immediately, but *Diário da Noite* did give him some twenty articles, between December 1948 and January 1949, to make his case.

Although General Álvaro Fiúza de Castro (1889–1971), Chief of Staff of the Brazilian Army, later denied ever having heard from the man, Christensen kept on popping up in the national press throughout the next decade, insisting he be taken seriously. Yet every time Christensen made the papers, his claims became more grandiose. His spy saucer grew into an actual spaceship, capable of dousing enemy planes in flammable materials, and it transpired he had now worked on it directly during 1939–40 back in the Third Reich, where prototypes had later been successfully built in his absence before all the blueprints were stolen by Russian troops in 1945. So, if the Communists already had these things, surely Brazil needed to have them too, for the sake of national security? 'What I want to make very clear is that these discs do not come from other planets,' Christensen explained. In fact, they were not even discs at all, this being an optical illusion created by the actions of the propeller and the escape of burning propulsion gases during flight.

In June 1952 the ex-Nazi's wife wrote to the US military, pleading for Washington to ensure her husband's extradition to the West, as the Russians were dangerous and 'only one spaceship could destroy another'. By that August the prisoner was indeed walking free, as were many other local Abwehr members arrested alongside him. Yet Christensen's release had little to do with US intervention.

In return for filling up their pages, Christensen was given a sympathetic write-up by *Diário da Noite*, journalists complaining of his 'sadness and his silence' at being condemned to 'thirty years of seclusion', when the war was now long over. Honourably, Christensen pledged to go on living amongst the Brazilian people, 'perfecting their scientific knowledge' and placing himself 'at the disposal of the Brazilian Government in every way'. So, with his 'exemplary behaviour sheet' and his vow to have 'renounced Nazism', why had he not yet been granted any pardon? A 'mysterious force' kept him in prison, the paper implied, possibly some Supreme Court minister with a grudge. This was surely 'a crime that is committed against national interests' Christensen wailed, with it being better for Brazil to follow the wise example of Argentina, whose fascism-flirting leadership had happily allowed several ex-Nazi scientists to help develop their post-war aerospace industries.

The real way the captured Abwehr members got released early was by exploiting a legal loophole. They were all convicted under a specific anti-spy measure formally signed into Brazilian law on 1 October 1942, but most, including Christensen, had been arrested prior to this date, making their convictions arguably unsafe. Appeals Court judges were thus obliged to review or reduce the sentences, generally letting the Nazis free. During his final interviews, Christensen was awaiting his own Appeals Court appearance, and clearly wanted mass public exposure to create pressure for a ruling in his favour too, a tactic which succeeded. Upon being freed a whole two decades early in August 1952, the former spy, good to his word, remained in Rio where he filed patents for a new kind of 'internal combustion engine' that November, presumably intended for use in saucers. This didn't make him rich, though, so Christensen, the 'king of espionage' as he rather charitably became known, had to settle for opening a humble radio-repair shop instead.

On 24 December 1954, *Diário da Noite* discovered another easy column-filler, the Yugoslavian 'electro-radiologist' Voislav Todorovic, who claimed to have been forced to build his own saucer under the direction of a German scientist called Huber Strauss, whilst held captive for five years in a Nazi concentration camp. It was magnetic and radio-controlled, being intended as a catapult-launched spy drone to seek out enemy infantry. Todorovic was trying to make a larger disc for troop transport, when his workshop was bombed by the Allies. So grateful was he to Brazil for then giving him asylum that Todorovic was prepared to reproduce his wartime forced labour for the nation's benefit. If the air force would set him up with a lab, he'd fix them up a mini-saucer in a mere eight months, quicker than you could gestate a baby.

Did anyone really believe such claims? One man who feared they might was Brazilian dentist Sebastião Fernandes Lima, who in March 1950 contacted another Rio newspaper, *A Noite*, to complain about the undue prominence their rival publication had been giving to Christensen's claims, which were a stain on national pride. Far from being a German invention, did journalists not know that flying saucers were Brazilian in origin, like all the best things in life? According to Lima, he had filed a patent for an aerial disc with the Ministry of Labor in 1948 which would have flown with entirely silent turbines operated using 'a new theory of force' and 'the same principle as the gyroscope', with its construction being far 'less expensive than any of these Flying Fortresses' of the Second World War US aerial bombing fleet. Armed with his 1948 patent, Lima warned he could legally prevent the manufacture of rip-off saucers by Christensen 'or any other foreigner', Nazi or no Nazi. The dentist must not have been aware that saucers had already been invented the year prior to this by the sickeningly all-American Kenneth Arnold.[6]

* * *

Is there any genuine evidence that the Nazis actually did have a real-life flying saucer building or investigation programme during the war years of 1939–45, or was the whole thing merely the post-war invention of opportunistic con men like Niels Christian Christensen and William Henry Johnson? In 1970 *Le Livre Noir Du Soucupes Volantes* (*The Black Book of Flying Saucers*) by Henry Durrant was published in France, containing sensational information about a top-secret German study group called Sonderburo-13, apparently established by worried Nazis to look into their own pre-Kenneth Arnold UFO sightings during the war, as part of something code-named 'Project Uranus', supposedly directed by a Professor Georg Kamper.

If true, this rather undermines my present argument that flying saucers were essentially a post-war invention of the US media – but was it true? No, but Durrant's juicy morsel was still repeated by subsequent UFO authors like Britain's well-known Timothy Good (b.1942), in his best-selling 1987 work *Above Top Secret*. Alas, it turned out that Durrant had invented the whole thing as a test to see who would just copy out his lie wholesale without having checked up on any of the pseudo-facts it described first, akin to map-makers deliberately including tiny mistakes in their charts to protect them from plagiarists.

Nonetheless, Project Uranus is now an established part of UFO lore, billed as 'the Nazi Project Blue Book', with an entire spurious case history behind it. The Project's first case allegedly came in 1942 when Luftwaffe pilot Hauptman Fischer reported seeing a 'flying whale' over Norway; Sonderburo-13 dismissed this as the result of temporary madness caused by the harsh Scandinavian snows. In 1944, meanwhile, a ballistic missile trial at Kummersdorf military test centre was reputedly monitored by a 'strange spherical orb' in the sky, before film footage of the event was quickly seized by Kamper's agents. Their purpose seems to have been either to cover up an alarming ET presence in Nazi skies, or to disguise sightings of experimental German saucers as being glimpses of aliens by spreading disinformation – tasks which must have been easy, as all these 'cases' were invented many years after the war had actually ended anyway, as was the Sonderburo itself.[7]

It is a cautionary tale, and yet in Good's defence the whole area of ufology is by definition a fringe topic, and fringe writers – including myself – who dip into its waters almost always operate on limited budgets, generally on a part-time basis. I haven't been able to rigorously double-check all my sources at first hand myself. I can't read French, so haven't personally ascertained that a fake account of Project Uranus does indeed appear in Durrant's *Le Livre Noir Du Soucupes Volantes* for Good to have been tricked by at all; I'm just taking this particular factoid on trust, from sources generally deemed to be reliable.

There are bound to be some errors of both fact and interpretation in this present book, too. I am 100 per cent sure that my main thesis is water-tight – as my main thesis is 'there are no Nazi spaceships', it is unlikely not to be – but presume at the outset that a certain number of (hopefully) small errors will creep in, especially when dealing with sources taken from other languages I don't speak, primarily German. Some of the key original texts of the Nazi UFO mythos have yet to be fully translated from Hitler's native tongue, for much the same reason Derek Acorah's autobiography has yet to appear in Sanskrit. But what if my own inevitable slips end up entering into the subsequent literature on these topics too?

When the US' most prominent purported alien abductee Whitley Strieber (b.1945) began researching ufology in earnest, he met with the following paradoxical situation: 'I found myself in a minefield. Real documents that seemed to be false. False documents that seemed to be real. A plethora of "unnamed sources". And drifting through it all, the thin smoke of an incredible story.'[8] And, with the incredible, never ending story of the Nazi UFO legend, the smoke of truth is thin indeed. Although there is no such thing as a 'Nazi UFO', from small and dubious beginnings the idea that there really were such things has now grown into a mass-media legend, being spread across the whole world through books, TV shows and, in particular, by an absolute plethora of worthless websites online. In a companion text to this present volume, *The Saucer and the Swastika: The Dark Myth of Nazi UFOs*, I track in detail the mutation of what was initially a fairly narrow narrative – the false idea that the Germans built fully functional spaceships during the Second World War, as chronicled in these present pages – into a much more byzantine mix-and-match grab bag of total fantasy in which the Nazis developed amazing paranormal powers and became involved with allied races of white supremacist aliens from other star systems, before hatching a series of fiendish conspiratorial plots to conquer mankind, having failed to do the job properly the first time around.

The motives of the persons who have helped concoct this never ending torrent of total nonsense are various. Some are outright neo-Nazis, hoping to lure gullible sci-fi fans into their way of extremist political thinking by using sensational tales of UFOs as bait. Others, disillusioned by a drab, bland and boring post-war world of democracy, peace and prosperity in the US and Western Europe, have sought to find spiritual solace in the more exciting idea of Nazi space travel, developing entire religious cults based around the adventurous notion. Some are just in it for the attention it brings them. And, of course, yet others are simply nuts. Being a wholly fictional topic, Nazi ufology can be more-or-less whatever you want it to be, for more-or-less whatever reason you want it to be so.

Once the legend was successfully launched, the liars who launched it could not control what other subsequent liars then did with their own original lies, especially once the limitless rumour mill machine that is the Internet came along. If you had told William Henry Johnson or Niels Christian Christensen about the wider narratives which would ultimately be spun from early Nazi UFO stories like theirs, they would surely not have believed you. This whole subject has by now grown into an elaborate exercise in fiction by collage, like using scissors to cut all the mis-matching pieces of several unrelated jigsaw puzzles up to force-fit them together into the particular shape you so desire. Splice three separate jigsaw elements of lion's head, goat's body and dragon's tail in the correct order and you can easily spawn a ufological chimera of your very own. For a lucky few who get their colourfully ultra-credulous 'documentaries' about all this broadcast on The History Channel, there might even be some money in it. And all because a man in a plane didn't actually see some saucers skimming over a mountain top one day . . .

Sceptical ufologists of something known as the 'psychosocial school' would describe the muddle unleashed by Kenneth Arnold's inaccurately reported words of 1947 as one of 'cultural tracking'; an excellent illustration of UFOs being basically imaginary entities, mere mental projections made onto unusual looking but entirely explicable atmospheric and aerial phenomena like passing satellites and twinkling stars, made under the influence of prevailing media conditioning and cultural trends. According to this notion, witnesses perceive and interpret unfamiliar cloud-clipping sights in terms of things they already recognise, and have been 'trained' to see by prevailing cultural priming; in past centuries, odd lights in the sky may have been mis-read as dragons, gods or angels, not then inconceivable things like starships. However, so-called 'nuts-and-bolts' ufologists, who interpret such visions literally as being actual visiting alien spacecraft, would disagree, naturally, as would the minority who view UFOs as somehow paranormal or interdimensional in nature, and I actually think such people may at times have a point.

Whilst personally feeling the psychosocial school represents the general answer to the UFO mystery, it can prove reductive when applied to precise elements of certain specific cases. When UFOs leave behind apparent physical traces, like ostensible landing marks or radiation burns, it seems hard to attribute them purely to the effects of mass media and culture. A certain small-ish proportion of reports do indeed currently stand as unexplained – although that is far from automatically proclaiming that aliens or demons lie behind them. Nonetheless, in this present text, I shall adopt an almost total perspective of hard-line scepticism, as the specific sub-genre of ufology with which it deals is a wholly specious one. There may well be such things as UFOs; but there are definitely no Nazi ones. If there were, the Germans would surely have won the war, would they not?

Some readers may think the book stands as an exercise in debunking a topic so self-evidently ludicrous it doesn't even deserve to be debunked, but this is not so. A surprisingly sizable number of apparent adults do believe in the literal reality of the whole Nazi-UFO nexus, in spite of its embarrassingly obvious non-tenability, and for a wide variety of reasons. Given this, I think the topic does deserve to be picked apart, and to do so this present text mostly travels back in time to the very beginnings of the legend, in order to see precisely how it was that the myth was born. Essentially, it tells the tall tales of a series of fake 1940s and 1950s saucer inventors, largely from the wartime Axis powers of Germany, Austria and Italy, and their implausible claims of having built Hitler some literal, physical, nuts-and-bolts craft to use as wonder weapons against the otherwise unbeatable Allied air armadas of the US and Great Britain.

In honour of their alleged true origin, should Unidentified Flying Objects therefore really be labelled by their worldwide witnesses as being Unbekanntes FlugObjekt, as they are in Germany? Or, even better, should the letters 'UFO' instead be re-understood as actually standing for Unidentified Fascist Objects rather than Unidentified Flying Ones? No, but determining precisely why not proves a far more intricate exercise than you may expect. It turns out Adolf Hitler has even more to answer for than we thought he did. So does Kenneth Arnold.

Chapter One

No Foos Without Fires: Strange Lights and Silver Christmas-Tree Decorations Hanging Over Nazi Germany

During the Second World War itself, nobody ever reported seeing any Nazi flying saucers – how could they, if the war ended in 1945 and the concept itself only came into being in 1947? Nonetheless, once the imaginative seed had been planted, researchers combed through wartime records to see if they could unearth a pre-history for the subject. This proved easy, and the notion of the 'foo-fighter' was born and subsumed effortlessly into the new and growing field of ufology. These foos were initially painted as being Nazi secret weapons, although others soon guessed they may have been extraterrestrial in origin. Foo-fighters did definitely exist – although only in the same way that UFOs existed prior to Kenneth Arnold and Project Blue Book. The glowing, globular foos were most likely a bundle of potentially somewhat unrelated aerial and meteorological phenomena, later gathered together under the same conceptual canvas to give people an intelligible way to think about such things.

The term is usually traced back to the US comic-strip star Smokey Stover, whose adventures appeared daily in the *Chicago Times* from 1938 onwards, Smokey having first blazed a trail through its Sunday edition in 1935. Stover, created by cartoonist Bill Holman (1903–87), was a madcap firefighter who, prone to comic malapropism, gormlessly described himself as a 'foo-fighter' instead, when out quenching blazes in his impossible two-wheeled 'Foo-Mobile'. Holman's creation proved highly popular stateside, with fan-led 'Foo Clubs' being founded, and Smokey later being painted as amateur nose-art on US bombers by troops.

Quite what 'foo' itself actually means is debatable. It could be a silly mis-pronunciation of the French word 'feu', meaning fire, or it may be a verbal slip for 'faux', meaning 'fake', or 'fou', meaning 'mad'. It could mean 'fuel', with Smokey thought daft enough to try and extinguish a fire with petrol.

Bill Holman himself said he found the word written on the bottom of a Chinese figurine one day, liked the sound of it, and obsessively kept writing it everywhere in his strip, not only in speech bubbles but on signs, menus and car registration plates.

Some Allied combatants later called Japanese fighter pilots foo-fighters, on account of their kamikaze-like manoeuvres, this term then being extended towards the similarly erratically moving luminous sky balls. Others said it was used by sceptics simply to mean 'phooey!' in relation to reports of proto-UFOs, thus to dismiss their alleged witnesses as 'foo-ls'. Then again, British troops reportedly used the term 'FOO WAS HERE' as a graffiti tag, equivalent to the more famous 'KILROY WAS HERE' meme, 'FOO' perhaps meaning 'Forward Observation Officer'. It could also have become mixed up with the sweary military acronym FUBAR, as in 'Fucked Up Beyond All Recognition/Repair', itself possibly derived from the German 'furchtbar', or 'terrible'.[1] Yet most such explanations are clearly just what lexicographers term 'back formations', or retrospective guesses about the precise nature and history of the word, performed some time after the fact of its actual appearance. The same thing would soon happen with foo-fighters themselves, when people began using hindsight to deduce they were Nazi secret saucer weapons or Martian mini-probes after the war.

Smokey's main catchphrase was 'Where there's foo there's fire!', an intentionally ridiculous logic-loop and, if 'foo' was indeed a slip for the French 'feu', then, like many an idiot savant, with this circular motto the tautology spouting Stover proved himself an ontological genius of the first order. Wherever there was a foo-fighter, there was really only some feu, for that is stereotypically what they were: unusual balls of light or other fiery shapes encountered by Allied aircrews in the skies over German-occupied Europe, singularly or in formation, generally nocturnally. During the day, they could appear more like silvery spheres. Possibly these were two separate phenomena, or possibly they were metallic by day, luminous by night, like certain atmospheric plasmas. Occasionally, foos possessed both metallic and luminous qualities simultaneously, as with the 'shiny silver ball of several feet in diameter and shining by its own incandescence' reported by one astonished crew on a raid over Frankfurt on 4 February 1944.[2] They often came across as seeming as though they were intelligently controlled, mirroring planes' movements perfectly, something potentially explained by them being an electromagnetic phenomenon attracted towards an aircraft's metal bodywork. Or were foos early remote-controlled drones? Whilst the Nazis did make substantial advances in guided rockets and glider bombs, 1940s radio-control techniques of the sort which would have been needed to steer full-blown drones depended on a clear line of sight being maintained between operator and device, impossible in high-altitude night-flying conditions in which bomber crews most frequently sighted foos.

When RAF pilots reported them back to the Air Ministry, officials logged and labelled them in neutral tones simply as 'night phenomena' and 'balls of fire'. British crews themselves preferred to call them 'The Light' or 'The Thing', or else improvised labels randomly; the 1943 logbook entry of an RAF Squadron Leader P.H.V. Wells told only of a 'screaming dog-fight with the Light'. One RAF squadron newsletter spoke more whimsically of 'weird and wonderful apparitions', 'the latest species of wizardry' and 'this Loch Ness Monster' of the skies. A 1942 British intelligence report dismissed them as 'freaks' of a one-off nature, being 'only reported on isolated occasions'. Canadian fliers sometimes called them 'scarecrows' as whilst they looked threatening, in actuality they seemed harmless enough. Unlike a fire, a foo did not kill.[3] If you had asked most Allied pilots during the war if they had seen a foo-fighter, they would no more have known what you were talking about than if you had asked someone as late as 23 June 1947 if they had ever seen a flying saucer. For non-Americans, the lights only gained their now familiar label after the conflict was over and people were on the hunt for earlier, pre-Kenneth Arnold evidence of UFOs in the archives. Yet this does not mean people were not seeing them.

As British UFO scholar Andy Roberts has shown, radiant airborne balls of light were seen by pilots throughout the Second World War, not just in its latter stages, and not simply over Germany, as is often blithely stated in texts about the subject. Soliciting letters from ex-RAF men through appeals in aviation and military magazines, Roberts proved such things had been spotted throughout the war years, in every theatre of conflict. The oft-repeated assertion they were almost entirely a phenomenon of German skies during the late 1944/early 1945 period was, he concluded, a 'false fact of the foo-fanciers' faith' being pushed by writers who just wanted you to believe that where there were foos there were by definition also fascists (or aliens nervously monitoring warmongering mankind's offensive aerospace capabilities, maybe).[4] In fact, many foo-fighters were witnessed zooming over the Far East during the war in the Pacific, too, mitigating against the whole 'Nazi secret weapon' interpretation. Although frequently printed alongside misleading captions implying otherwise, the most iconic photo of foo-fighters in alleged action actually shows bright blobs of light accompanying Japanese Takikawa-Kawasaki 98 fighters over the Suzuka Mountains in 1945, nowhere near one of Hitler's presumed hidden weapons labs dug deep inside the impregnable mountainsides of the Third Reich. Furthermore, according to the physicist R.V. Jones (1911–97), wartime Assistant Director of Intelligence (Science) for Britain's Air Ministry and author of the classic 1978 memoir *Most Secret War*, captured German night-fighter crews admitted having been bothered by foos as well, which, if true, also tends to discredit the Nazi secret weapon idea.[5]

* * *

It is obvious foo-fighters existed before 1944, the usually cited year of their birth, just not *as* foo-fighters. It would be truer to say foos were only named in print in 1944, than to say they only appeared then. The first immediately recognisable widespread media reports concerning foos stemmed from a pair of Allied military press releases of 13 December 1944, picked up in papers like the *New York Times* the next day as follows:

Floating Mystery Ball Is New Nazi Air Weapon

SUPREME HEADQUARTERS, Allied Expeditionary Force, Dec. 13 – A new German weapon has made its appearance on the western air front, it was disclosed today. Airmen of the American Air Force report that they are encountering silver-coloured spheres in the air over German territory. The spheres are encountered either singly or in clusters. Sometimes they are semi-translucent.

SUPREME HEADQUARTERS, Dec. 13 (Reuters) – The Germans have produced a 'secret' weapon in-keeping with the Christmas season. The new device, apparently an air-defence weapon, resembles the huge glass balls that adorn Christmas trees. There was no information available as to what holds them up like stars in the sky, what is in them, or what their purpose is supposed to be.[6]

By 15 December, follow-up stories speculated such devices may have been designed to interfere with radar, radio or bomb-targeting. Journalist C.E. Butterworth of Associated Press guessed that, as 'the balls are described as silver in colour', this would indicate they were 'of a metallic nature' rather like the 'lightweight, tinfoil-like strips of material' which could be loosed by the enemy to deflect radio waves. Perhaps, said Butterworth, these strips when dropped from planes had proved 'not too satisfactory' to the Nazis as 'gravity soon drew them to earth', and so 'the silver balls, particularly if made of some light material, would have greater buoyancy and thus stay aloft longer and maintain a more extended interference period.'[7] The Nazis' two most advanced aerial weapons, the V-1 'Buzz-Bomb', a semi-guided airborne cruise missile, and the long-range V-2 ballistic missile, had just been launched against London in June and September 1944 respectively, lending immediate weight to the idea that more such strange contraptions might linger in the airspace over the remnants of Nazi-occupied Europe, even giant floating Christmas baubles of obscure function.

Such stories did not yet lend any specific name to these unusual shiny balls, though. How, then, did the foos become foos? The December 1945 issue of the *American Legion Magazine* carried an article by Lieutenant Colonel Jo Chamberlin called 'The Foo-Fighter Mystery', which provided the most generally accepted answer. Chamberlin's duties partly involved the penning of public relations pieces for various magazines, with all fees being donated to war widows and orphans. In spring 1945 he took a visit to the 415th Night-Fighter Squadron (NFS), based in France, where many of the foo-reports had originated. Here, Chamberlin interviewed aircrews, finding that the foo-fighter was not christened until as late in hostilities as November 1944 by an unnamed member of the 415th who, discussing the odd luminosities his fellow fliers had been reporting of late in the mess hall, decided to christen them after his favourite comic strip.[8] Later interviews by the US folklorist Jeffery A. Lindell revealed a fuller version of this story which had proved rather less suitable for publication. The unnamed airman was in fact Chicago-born radar operator Lieutenant Donald J. Meiers who, agitated after being chased by a red ball of fire during a nocturnal mission, pulled a Smokey Stover comic from his back pocket during an intelligence debriefing and shouted, 'It was another one of those fuckin' foo-fighters!' then stormed off. This outburst stuck, with the foos' original name, as used by the men of the 415th, actually being the triply alliterative 'fuckin' foo-fighters'. By February, following media reports and proliferating barrack-room gossip, this new slang term had spread amongst other US aircrews in Europe, somewhat replacing earlier descriptive phrases like 'Kraut Fireballs/Meteors'.[9] On

31 December 1944, Associated Press' Robert C. Wilson had already called in on the 415th NFS, intending to write a story based around the gimmick of being in the skies over Germany just as midnight struck and a hopefully Nazi-free New Year was rung in with a chorus of bomb blasts on deserving targets below. Icy conditions prevented this, so Wilson found himself conducting a more general series of on-ground interviews, the results of which appeared in most major US newspapers on 2 January, gaining a front-page story in the *New York Times* headed 'Balls of Fire Stalk US Fighters in Night Assaults Over Germany'. That the term 'foo-fighter' was presumed by sub-editors to be at this point unfamiliar to readers can be seen in the specific phrasing of other headlines of this date. The *Chicago Tribune*'s 'Mystery Flares Tag Along with US Night Pilots; Yanks Call Nazi Weapon a Foo-Fighter' showed that even the home city of Smokey Stover himself thought the novel name needed some explaining.[10] The tag was introduced into the wider US lexicon by Wilson in his opening sentence: 'The Nazis have thrown something new into the night skies over Germany – the weird, mysterious "foo-fighters", balls of fire which race alongside the wings of American Beaufighters flying intruder missions over the Reich.' Defining any given foo as being 'eerie' and an unknown 'sky-weapon', Wilson added that they 'accompany planes for miles' and 'appear to be radio-controlled from the ground'. As 'it is not in the nature of the fire-balls to attack planes', it was possible the foos were 'designed to be a psychological weapon', he wrote.

Wilson also introduced a useful visual template for what other US airmen could expect to report should they, too, ever encounter one. 'None saw any structure on the fire-balls', Wilson wrote, with Lieutenant 'fuckin' foo-fighters' Donald J. Meiers quoted as explaining that:

> There are three kinds of these lights we call 'foo-fighters' . . . One is red balls of fire which appear off our wing-tips and fly along with us, the second is a vertical row of three balls of fire which fly in front of us and the third is a group of about fifteen lights which appear off in the distance – like a Christmas-tree up in the air – and flicker on and off . . . A foo-fighter picked me up at 700 feet and chased me 20 miles down the Rhine Valley . . . I turned to starboard and two balls of fire turned with me. We were going 260 miles an hour and the balls were keeping right up with us. On another occasion when a foo-fighter picked us up, I dived at

360 miles an hour. It kept right off our wing-tips for a while and then zoomed into the sky. When I first saw the things, I had the horrible thought that a German on the ground was ready to press a button and explode them. But they didn't explode or attack us. They just seem to follow us like Will-o'-the-Wisp.[11]

At last, the foos had truly taken flight! But how seriously did readers take them? Wilson's story was expanded on by the leading US periodical *Time*, which described the foo as an 'apparition', with 'baffled' scientists dismissing such 'flares' as a probable 'illusion' caused by 'an afterimage of light which remained in the pilots' eyes after they had been dazzled by flak-bursts', or perhaps examples of the atmospheric phenomenon of St Elmo's Fire. Whilst providing various 'solemn' theories about how the foos, if they really were new Nazi tech, might have worked, *Time* prefaced this with a sarcastic comment about 'front-line correspondents and arm-chair experts' having 'a Buck Rogers field day' with their own similar guesses, thus illustrating how the only links between foos and outer space at this time were made purely in jest.

Whilst by 2003 Harold Augsperger, the commanding officer of the 415th, could openly entertain the opinion the foos he and his men had seen decades earlier were of ET origin, this would not have been the case in 1944/45. 'If it was not a hoax or an optical illusion, it was certainly the most puzzling secret weapon that Allied fighters have yet encountered', opined *Time*; but the implication seemed very much that it *was* a hoax or optical illusion.[12]

* * *

There was unquestionably a lot of talk about foo-fighters amongst US aircrews heading into the war's final year, but this could be partly a media artefact, not evidence they were truly multiplying. Once foo stories started popping up in reliable newspapers, aircrews could have felt able to report what they had seen without being laughed at or chided for wasting superiors' time – although some pilots did consider certain airy and light-hearted media dismissals of their experiences as being 'a personal attack on their integrity'.[13] On 8 May 1945, though, VE Day arrived and the war in Western Europe ended, followed by final Allied victory over Japan on 2 September. Together with the Axis powers, it seemed the foo-fighters had also been defeated, as they disappeared from headlines too. Presumably newspapers now had better things to report on than funny lights in the sky. By the time his foo story hit the presses on 2 January 1945, Robert C. Wilson was already busy covering the advance of the 7th Army through northern France, his mind and that of his readers moving on with the troops.[14] If it had not been for the post-1947 birth of ufology, you have to imagine the foos would have remained as neglected obscurities, known of and cared about by almost no one. Thus, in accidentally creating the flying saucer, Kenneth Arnold in a way unintentionally invented the foo-fighter too.

Take an interview which appeared in the *Nashville-Tennessean Magazine* just in time for Hallowe'en 1966, whose first sentence ran as follows: 'It wasn't until 1947, when the stories about flying saucers hit page one, that Nashville's Joe Thompson Jr gave much thought to those strange objects he saw in World War II.' During the conflict itself, Thompson, a former photo-reconnaissance pilot, had heard talk of strange objects resembling footballs or even 'a smashed beer can', which were initially thought some variant of German barrage balloon. Thompson saw some himself over the Rhine Valley; they appeared 'made of aluminium'.

He told the squadron intelligence officer when he got back to base, but the man didn't care, so Thompson 'let it drop'. After all, 'they were not bothering us', so the foos 'just didn't seem important' to crews at the time: 'What was important was to complete the mission and stay alive.' It was only during post-war civilian life, when he became 'something of a buff' on the subject of saucers, that these wartime experiences gained any backwards-looking significance. Following UFO talks Thompson gave, audiences 'would come up and wonder excitedly if the foo-fighters could have been sent from somewhere in space to observe the war in Europe and, possibly, to gauge the threat of V-2 weapons to their own world.'[15] Yet pilots didn't wonder that at the time.

Even Jo Chamberlin's lengthy *American Legion Magazine* article was also soon forgotten, before being resurrected by the British fortean writer Harold T. Wilkins (1891–1960) for a 1951 piece in the US paranormal magazine *FATE*, 'The Strange Mystery of the FOO-FIGHTERS', in which he essentially just rewrote his predecessor's interviews with the men of the 415th NFS, a tradition which has since continued, with most subsequent major accounts of the foos' history shamelessly cannibalising Chamberlin's somewhat novelistic narrative, complete with invented dialogue. It is in Chamberlin's work you can first find many of the key basic foo facts of chronology which have since been taken largely for granted, such as that they initially appeared over

German skies during the war's latter stages, and that they suddenly vanished following its end, when German factories and research stations were raided by the Allies.

Post-1947, Wilkins was now able to argue this latter fact proved foo-fighters were probably of ET or paranormal origin, as 'in no such station was the slightest clue discovered even hinting that the Nazi technicians had invented and then flown these mysterious blazing balls'. As such, the foos' operators 'would appear to hail from some phenomenal world of a different wavelength of visibility of our own' as 'whoever these etherian beings are [they] can operate controlled machines which suddenly appear from nowhere, fly at vertiginous speeds, and as suddenly vanish into thin air' like William Henry Johnson in an invisible Nazi taxi.

Yet actually the foos were still here. Wilkins saw one himself at 6.20 p.m. on 2 November 1950, 'a yellow luminous ball' which appeared over Bexleyheath, flying 'silently, with no gas or spark-emission' before disappearing into clouds. One month later in Cornwall a blue light shaped 'like a sausage' sped across the sky, Wilkins further reported. Wilkins also cited various cases from the past, such as two 'bright globular lights, blazing like stars' witnessed over Inverness in 1848, to imply the foos had always been with us, and always would be.[16] In 1991, folklorist and former USAF electronic warfare systems analyst Jeffery A. Lindell made his own investigation, also concluding that shining aerial phantoms had always been with us, but that foos per se were simply a new form of 'technological folk-belief' in which 'technology is rapidly replacing the supernatural' as an explanation for strange lights seen in the sky. Lieutenant Meiers had specifically compared his own fuckin' foo-fighters to Will-o'-the-Wisps in 1945, with Wills, like their cousins the Jack-o'-Lanterns, being fairies, devils or spirits who appeared in the form of fiery balls of light after dark, misleading night wanderers foolish enough to follow them to their doom in swamps.

Often explained as misperceptions of ignited marsh gas – a sceptical line also sometimes tried as regards UFOs – these fiery fairies had many alternative titles. The French called them 'feu follet', or 'fiery lunatics/fairies', in Latin they were 'ignis fatuus', 'foolish fires' or 'ignis erraticus', 'erratic fires', whilst the Dutch called them 'dwaalicht' or 'wandering stars', all of which sound like close synonyms for the 'foolish fighters' witnessed during the war years. Will and Jack are generally now labelled illusions, a word derived from the Latin 'illudere', meaning 'to play with or mock', and Lindell noted that 'almost all' the pilots he interviewed said the lights 'seemed to play with them'.[17] Perhaps the foos just appealed to the reading public's general appetite for tales of mystery. Jo Chamberlin, telling of Lieutenant Meiers' first encounters with the foos 'roaming the night skies on either side of the Rhine River north of Strasbourg' in November 1944, described this location as something from a fairytale, being 'for centuries the abode of sirens, dwarfs, gnomes and other supernatural characters that appealed strongly to the dramatic sense of the late A. Hitler', a fan of Wagnerian operas based on ancient Germanic myths. However, the land of the Brothers Grimm had by 1944 become 'no [opera] stage but a grim battleground'; a place which, you might argue, stood in dire need of re-enchantment. Will-o'-the-Wisp's return wearing a costume of hard silvery steel armour, complete with unearthly glow like that of Hamlet's father, came just in time to become a new tutelary spirit of the military-industrial age; also like ghosts, the foos did not show up on radar.[18]

* * *

In 1951 Harold T. Wilkins told his better informed US readers that 'probably not one English person in a million knows what is meant by "foo-fighters" or has ever heard of them', but later things were to change.[19] Today, there is a popular US rock band named after the things, who evidently expect their global fan-base to understand their name perfectly. The Foo Fighters were founded in 1995 by drummer Dave Grohl (b.1969), whose first tracks were solo efforts in which he played all the instruments himself. Wanting to remain anonymous, Grohl desired a name which misleadingly made him sound like a group, not an individual, and, reading a lot of UFO books at the time, settled upon 'The Foo-Fighters', something he now regrets as 'it's the stupidest fucking band name in the world'.[20] I disagree. Grohl's plan may have failed, but in principle he was correct to identify that the term is capable of acting as a bewildering disguise. The category of 'foo-fighter' may be something of a false one, as descriptions of the specific phenomena to which the label is applied are rather diverse, not unlike identifying a shark and a minnow simply as 'fish'.

A search provides the following brief catalogue of claimed wartime foos, reported from theatres of battle worldwide, from air, sea and land: 'two fog-lights flying at high speed that could change direction rapidly'; 'some strange globe glowing with greenish light, about half the size of the full moon'; 'like a flare in appearance, travelling horizontally over the sea'; 'a brilliant star, high in the dark sky . . . [which] began to swell like a balloon and come closer'; 'a sphere, hovering above me, motionless and silent, at least five times as bright as the most brilliant star'; 'white, egg-shaped and brilliant'; 'a glowing globe . . . [of] cloudy glass with a light inside'; 'crystal balls, clear, about the size of basketballs'; 'a huge red light'; 'rockets . . . with a fiery head and blazing stern'; 'a gold-coloured ball with a metallic finish'; 'reddish-orange balls about the size of baseballs . . . [which] appeared to break up into four or five fragments that flew in all directions'; 'a brilliant point of light'; 'large orange glows'; 'a red ball leaving a trail of yellow/ red flames and black smoke'; 'a meteor . . . reddish-orange in colour . . . emitting a burst giving off a green star'; 'five or six red and green lights in a "T"-shape'; 'a cherry-red light . . . about five times as big as the largest star and perhaps a fifth a size of the moon . . . [which] would contract and expand every few seconds, rhythmically'; 'like a great ball of fire . . . their colour was very subdued, not blazing like a torch'; 'a glowing red object shooting straight up'; 'burning particles . . . [like] a big swarm of bees milling around'; 'large numbers of projectiles . . . resembling schools of flying fish'; 'a number of white balls . . . tennis balls made of cotton wool'; 'two airborne objects . . . changing from a cherry-red to an orange, and to a white light which would die out and become cherry-red again . . . in day-light seen to be bright silver in colour'; '100 balls of orange fire'; 'one orange ball and one green one'; 'lights [which] made distinct lines somewhat like arrows'; 'airborne white lights . . . [which] were staggered evenly verti-cally'; 'a rotating white beacon'; 'a hot bar of steel about a half-inch wide and about a foot long'; 'round, speedy balls of fire'; and, in an early and edible-sounding alternative to flying saucers, 'flying hot-cakes', followed along by 'coloured air-waves' 30ft long and 6ft wide.[21] Somewhat dissimilar though they may have been, these various UFOs – for in the literal, Project Blue Book sense of that term, that is what they were, *Unidentified* Flying Objects – were certainly eerie and alarming, and the natural conclusion was that they were Nazi secret weapons. Arguing against this explanation, though, is the fact that they weren't very good. Not once did they ever so much as open fire on an Allied plane or sidle up nearby and detonate. All they did was pulse about pointlessly; they didn't even shoot back when fired upon. A puzzled December 1944 RAF Operational Research Section report, bearing the studiously non-committal title 'A New Phenomenon', assessed their operational ineffectiveness thus:

The phenomenon is seen as a light, moving very fast. The general consensus of opinion is that no shape can be seen and no aircraft identified, and that the objects do not fire; when fired at by the bombers a large proportion of them burst into flames or explode. Some have been seen to explode spontaneously or dive to the ground and it is therefore assumed that they are self-destroying. No bombers have been damaged or, so far as is known, even rocked by the explosion of these bodies. A tentative opinion is that they may be robot projectiles, possibly of the V-1 type, probably launched from the air into the bomber-stream . . . [but] there is no evidence of any aircraft destroyed or even damaged by one of them.[22]

To account for this powder puff nature, some argued they were unarmed reconnaissance drones, or psychological warfare devices intended to put pilots off and make them blunder into flak, barrage balloons or aerial mines. A 1942 British Air Ministry report dismissed the possibility the unknown lights themselves could be aerial mines, as some feared, on the twin grounds that '(a) no aircraft is known to have sustained damage from them and (b) it is thought that the whole object of an aerial mine would be defeated if its position were indicated by such a luminous object.' Then again, there was always the possibility that, if the foo tailed the plane like a magnet, as some pilots testified, then waiting German anti-aircraft batteries on the ground could use it as a handy luminous target, or what might be termed a 'sticky spotlight'.[23]

If foos were mobile electromagnetic disruptors intended to scramble enemy engines, as some have also speculated, then it appears that they never succeeded – unless the crews of the planes thus downed never lived to tell the tale. The closest non-invented account of something like this actually occurring was reported by one Sergeant Leonard H. Stringfield (1920–94), who claimed that, on 28 August 1945, the left engine of his C-46 transport plane began to fail, not above Germany, but over Japan. Looking out of the window as the craft 'spluttered oil and lost altitude', he saw 'three unidentifiable blobs of brilliant white light, each about the size of a dime held at arm's length' flying alongside him. They were 'teardrop-shaped' and 'brilliant white, like burning magnesium'.

It was only in post-war civilian life, however, that Stringfield thought to associate these blobs and the 'mysterious force' supposedly generated by them with his engine problem – once he had become a prominent ufologist, and noticed how often UFOs are said to cause vehicle engines to fail. Writing in 1957, Stringfield explained how, prior to 1950, he didn't have much interest in UFOs, but once he encountered a pair of local saucer witnesses, 'all at once' his own wartime experience 'leaped into real significance'. Previously, 'remotest in my mind were spacemen and spaceships', with the terrifying aerial event having been largely 'forgotten along with other distasteful events of the war years'. Yet he now saw that it 'suddenly lent tremendous support to the suggestion that saucers were interplanetary', leading him to swear off using aeroplanes altogether, as his 1945 encounter 'took on a new and ominous meaning' for him.

But was this just because Stringfield wanted it to? Whilst in 1957 he could write of how 'it is my opinion that the objects were propelled devices', he also admitted that 'I have many times since 1950 tried to reconstruct the facts of the incident, hunting for details, trying to remember my reactions' but 'the terrors of the moment, plus the erasure of time, have left me little to go on, save only the starkest high points'. Due to pressing circumstances, Stringfield never submitted an official report on the day, leaving no immediate written record to look back at. Therefore, many details of the encounter 'are hazy', he admitted, as 'I had no reason at that time to rationalise the objects or try to identify them.' And, were it not for 1947 and Kenneth Arnold, maybe he never would have. The C-46 Stringfield flew in was termed a 'Flying Coffin' by US troops due to its propensity for fatal malfunction; indeed, it was whilst out looking for the wreckage of just such an unreliable craft over the Cascade Mountains that Arnold had spied his first ever saucers skipping across the skyline in 1947. The problem was that certain of the C-46's components kept on unpredictably bursting into flames and exploding during flight. Did one really need airborne ETs to make its engine wheeze?

Stringfield's later recollection and reshaping of his 1945 scare certainly influenced the future of foo-ology, though, with researcher Keith Chester, author of the most comprehensive book about foo-fighters to date, *Strange Company*, published in 2007, being inspired to write his text by late-life chats with Stringfield, who by now expressed the view his 1945 Japanese foos were 'extraterrestrial aircraft'. The account of his sighting Stringfield provided for Chester's book makes it sound as if he was 'sure' they were advanced tech-nology directly 'responsible' for the engine failure at the time, when previous accounts of his clearly suggested otherwise. Stringfield's ET interpretation was naturally also then adopted by Chester himself. So, if you go out and buy the best book available on the subject today, this is the line you will find endorsed by its author. In such ways, old memories, remade anew, can echo still down the ages.[24]

* * *

Being harmless, official channels don't seem to have paid foos too much mind. 'Keep a watching brief' was the general idea, polite code for 'do nothing'. They were investigated, as they had to be, but official conclusions tended to cursorily brand them as 'either aberrations [in perception made] under the stress of operation, or misinterpretations of some phenomena or other'.[25] Reasonable enough – but what 'phenomena or other', precisely?

In 1944 and 1945, as reports of foo-fighters increased, the US Navy commissioned medical studies into visual illusions amongst airmen, finding that, with the naked eye, it is surprisingly easy to mistake a stationary star for a moving light like that of another aircraft due to a visual phenomenon known as 'autokinesis' which causes such bodies to appear to swing around in the sky. Whilst such ideas cannot be used to explain away all reported foo sightings – especially those witnessed by several crew members or separate crews simultaneously, and from different angles of sight – doubtless some wartime UFOs were purely illusory. Significantly, the original name given to autokinesis by its initial discoverer, the German naturalist and explorer Alexander von Humboldt (1769–1859), back in 1799 was 'Sternschwanken', or 'Swinging Stars'. To some hardline sceptics, that is all the foo-fighters themselves were: stars, wobbling about in befuddled pilots' eyes.[26]

A 1940 British Air Ministry report, 'Phenomena Connected with Enemy Night Tactics', drew a similar conclusion, talking of how 'The strain upon a member of the crew maintaining a vigilant look-out for long periods of time is intense, and, under such conditions, the stories of shadowing [by aerial lights] are apt to stimulate the very natural tendency to think that any unidentified shape seen, or imagined, in the sky is an enemy aircraft', it being 'interesting to note' that the vast majority of sightings considered came from single crew members, not multiple ones. A 1942 Air Ministry report, 'A Note On Recent Enemy Pyrotechnic Activity Over Germany', blamed high-altitude fireworks, specifically intended to act as optical illusions to induce unease amongst pilots: 'At a distance they are reported to look very similar to aircraft falling in flames and it is thought that they are intended to give crews the [false] impression that a large number of aircraft are being shot down in flames and that the defences are stronger than they really are.'[27]

Another look was taken at the foos towards the war's end by a US scientific intelligence officer, mathematician and physicist named Howard P. Robertson (1903–61), his best guess being that they were some obscure electromagnetic or electrostatic phenomenon, or maybe an illusion caused by light reflecting off airborne ice crystals, but nothing of genuine military significance. In later life, Robertson was asked by the CIA to look again into what were by now being called UFOs as head of a special study called the 'Robertson Panel', reporting back in 1953 that, as regarded the foos, 'If the term "flying saucers" had been popular in 1943–45, these objects would have been so labelled.'[28]

So, whatever they might have been – ball lightning, unusual atmospheric plasmas, stress-induced misperceptions, autokinesis, take your pick – the foo-fighters really were, in some sense, nothing but fire, just like Professor Smokey said they were. Sometimes, where there's feu, there's fire and nothing else, just an accidental perceptual mistranslation from one visual language into another. The trouble was, some people preferred to speculate that 'Where there's foo there's a solid and structured craft' instead, even though there manifestly wasn't.

Chapter Two

Metal Gear Solid: The Schweinfurt Raid and the Post-War Transformation of Foo-Fighters into Full-Blown Flying Saucers

Once Kenneth Arnold's 1947 sighting was made known it was not long before the foos, in danger of being forgotten, were dredged up from the mythology of the war just ended and repurposed anew for the dawning Cold War age. Reports linking saucers back to Nazis and foos, in the sense that they were actually being piloted or remote-flown by German military scientists, were very much in the minority at the time, but they did exist. Italian ufologist Maurizio Verga, a close and reliable student of this whole subject, has determined that the first known print article linking Arnold's post-war discs with the wartime foos appeared in the *Seattle Times* on 28 June 1947, mere days after the pilot's seminal encounter near Mount Rainier.[1]

Others soon followed. On 8 July 1947, under the headline 'Saucers May Be "Foo-Fighters", Flier Suggests', the *New York Times Herald* ran an interview with war veteran Captain Dewey E. Ballard, who argued that, 'Assuming they are not some hoax or hallucination, I think . . . [Arnold's saucers] will turn out to be foo-fighters'. The foos, said Ballard, were designed by the Nazis as 'a psychological weapon', and the saucers of 1947 'could be a similar type of weapon, designed to keep a populace stirred up or excited' by causing mass panic.[2] The *Texas Morning Avalanche* of that same day interviewed another war veteran, Captain Charles Odom, who stated the flying saucers were the very same bauble-like 'crystal balls' once deployed aerially by Germany. According to Odom, these balls were 'electronically operated, and while in mid-air would send back to a radar-screen on the ground the altitude, speed and other data of bombers it approached'. As they were 'apparently magnetised' these spheres would tag alone with bomber formations, providing air defence units with real-time data. Surely, said Odom, the new-fangled discs were just more modern foos?[3]

Without Kenneth Arnold, a 1952 *New York Times* report about 'strange-looking orange globes' tailing aircraft during night flights over Wosnan and Sunchon in the then-ongoing Korean War might have been headlined 'The Foos Are Back' by some desk-based veteran with a long memory. Instead, it was titled 'Discs Seen in Korea' . . . even though the things weren't disc-shaped, but 'hurtling globes'. Nonetheless, they were described by the *New York Times* as being 'the latest version of the five-year-old flying saucers', not the latest version of the decade-old and more similarly globular foo-fighters.[4]

It was not just the media, but the military. When in May 1947 a report of a rather foo-like object, 'spherical in shape, with diameter of approximately 3–4 feet' which 'appeared to be burning' over Budapest was passed to US agents in Hungary, no imaginative connection to Arnold's saucers could yet be made. Come July 1947, however, a US military report concerning 'silver balls, flashing across the sky in daytime' over rural Hungary could now be linked quickly back to 'the current riddle of the similar metallic objects seen over most of the United States'.[5]

Already, foo-fighters were beginning to be reconceptualised as early flying saucers. But in the late 1940s flying saucers themselves were yet to be properly reconceptualised as alien spacecraft, a notion which during ufology's youngest days was limited to a very tiny fringe indeed, mostly made up of obscure mystics in California or planet-gazing sci-fi and rocketry fans. An excited R.L. Farnsworth (1909–98), President of the American Rocket Society, appeared in papers in early July 1947 saying, 'I wouldn't even be surprised if the flying saucers were remote-control electronic eyes from Mars', but most ordinary people would have been.[6]

* * *

In a well-known 14 August 1947 Gallup poll conducted in the wake of Arnold's encounter, the idea his saucers were ET vessels did not even statistically register. The most popular non-dismissive answer was to guess they were secret weapons – but US ones, not Nazi items:

No answer, don't know:	33%
Imagination, optical illusion, mirage, etc:	29%
Hoax:	10%
US secret weapon, part of atomic bomb, etc:	15%
Weather forecasting devices:	3%
Russian secret weapon:	1%
Other explanations:	9%

Amongst 'other explanations', Gallup didn't mention either Hitlerites or Martians – although one religiously inclined lady thought they indicated the end of the world, and another man thought they were flying cars developed by DuPont Motors![7] The very first full-length feature film dealing with the subject, 1950's cheap-and-cheerful b-movie spy thriller *The Flying Saucer*, also featured the clear plot device that such discs were the inventions of terrestrial science, with the entertainment media thus both reflecting and reinforcing the general presumption that saucers were human creations at this stage of affairs, although subsequent alien invasion movies of the 1950s like *Devil Girl From Mars* and *The Day the Earth Stood Still* soon put paid to all that.

Some purported saucer inventors trod a similar path of mental reinterpretation, such as former Brazilian Army Captain Aldencar de Silva Peixoto, who in 1950 used the pages of *Popular Science* to explain how, back in 1939, he had invented a revolutionary new super efficient propeller which operated on a principle called 'aero-rowing'. In 1944 he had shown a prototype to the US Embassy in Brazil, on account of the widespread domestic perception that 'the Brazilian who invents is always a crazy person', but the treacherous Yankees must have then stolen it to power their own 1947-launched saucers, he now thought. 'I have suffered a lot, and it doesn't matter if they kill me' for revealing this betrayal, Captain Peixoto wailed. By 1955, he was back in print, once again bemoaning that his magic propeller had still not been given funding by the Brazilian nation – and yet now Peixoto made no mention of its being used in top-secret USAF UFOs at all. According to Rodolpho Gauthier Cardoso dos Santos, a chronicler of early Brazilian saucer lore, this was because, by this later point in time, 'flying saucers are no longer associated with aircraft from superpowers in the national imagination and became seen as possible interplanetary ships' instead.[8]

Yet, whilst most citizens questioned by Gallup thought the saucers pure hooey, editors had papers to sell, and the minority angle that foreign powers might have caused the 1947 saucer wave was worth more of a shot than saying aliens were flying them at this point. Although 1 per cent of Gallup respondees fingered Russia as the likely culprit, some canny editors still preferred to blame the Nazis. On 12 July, a French-language Canadian newspaper, *La Patrie*, announced, on the basis of a single completely anonymous source, a direct link between Arnold's discs and Nazi foo-fighters. This unknown informant, possibly that indispensible journalistic source known as 'May

Dupp', claimed that during the Ardennes offensive of December 1944, Allied troops had observed explosive 'ultra-radiant globes' at work, which functioned as 'strange bullets'. The Allies secured these globular foos' crashed remains before taking them back to the US and Canada, where, aided by captured German scientists, they had been back-engineered to create the discs Kenneth Arnold had then seen.[9]

Equally fictional were 9 November 1947 reports filed from Geneva by Canadian reporter Lionel Shapiro (1908–58) that the military strongman General Francisco Franco (1892–1975) had been sheltering three escaped German scientists under 'personal sponsorship' in his own continuing dictatorship of fascist Spain, where they had built El Caudillo 'two highly advanced weapons of war'. One was a miniature nuclear warhead possessing 'a startling disintegrating power' and small enough, at only 8.7in long, to be mounted on the tip of an artillery shell, devised by a fiendish Professor Halkmann. Franco's second super weapon was a special long-range 'electromagnetic rocket' with which he had shot down two transport planes under the cover of 'unexplained accidents', before, rather daringly, proceeding to test fly them over the US, leading to that summer's headline-making saucer wave. The missiles, known as KM-2 after the initials of their Nazi inventors, Professors Knoh and Muller, definitely worked, as they had been test-launched off the coast near Malaga, 'while Franco watched from the deck of his yacht'.

Shapiro claimed he had personally 'stumbled upon the story three weeks ago by accidental interception of a document cataloguing the weapons' being circulated by 'the agent of an independent European spy organisation', who intended to sell blueprints for Franco's foos off to the highest bidder. Russian agents seemed the most eager, threatening to kill anyone who got in their way. If that all sounds a bit too Ian Fleming for its own good, you may be right; Shapiro was also a writer of thrillers and spy stories, with a new novel, *The Sealed Verdict*, out to promote in 1947.

The notion of 'Spanish Saucers' is now wholly forgotten, but lingered on vaguely until 1949, by which time it was being suggested a living Hitler was hiding out in Spain too, his new weapons functioning via devious gyroscopic wizardry. Joke stories and letters also appeared in the US media teasing that Hitler was squatting in a Grand Canyon cave and test-firing a new breed of guided V-2 rockets out over the US, or else proposing he had fled Berlin to Mars before sending saucers to contact his remaining disciples, pleading for help in beaming back down again.[10]

Once news of US saucers reached war shattered Europe, a number of desperate German citizens began contacting US authorities claiming to be ex-Nazi space scientists and offering to reveal their secrets in return for safe passage to the well-fed, well-paid capital of the Free World. In July 1947, a German dentist, Dr T. Kelterborn, wrote to the US Civil Governor in Frankfurt, pronouncing grandly that, 'I would like, as the inventor of these apparatuses, to announce myself to the US Administration.' Kelterborn said that, in 1944, he had handed over plans for a flying saucer, including 'rough sketches of the construction site' he had made for them to 'a German Inventors Office' in Berlin, but had 'never received a response'. Evidently the Luftwaffe had stolen his idea, which had in turn then been pilfered by the Russians, who were now invading US airspace. The best solution was to rely upon the dentist to de-fang this new Soviet threat. 'I alone am in the position, under certain circumstances, to reveal my invention,' Kelterborn promised – those 'certain circumstances' surely involving free passage to sunny Florida and a few suitcases full of dollar bills.

Even more implausible, in August 1947 one Guido Bernardy, also of Frankfurt, wrote a five-page letter to US General Lucius D. Clay (1898–1978), the serving Allied Deputy Governor of Germany, confidently announcing two psychics had informed him Hitler was alive and busily test-launching a series of 'disc-bullets' from a secret submarine, hoping to stir up global conflict anew.[11] But foo-fighters had stereotypically been globular in form, not discoid, had they not?

* * *

During the war, vanishingly few combatants reported seeing any flying saucer shaped things at all. Post-1947, this changed, and witnesses began to reassess and readapt their original foo-encounters to fit in with new visual stereotypes about how precisely UFOs should now appear. In 1957, sailor William J. Methorst told of a sighting he had made aboard a Dutch Navy vessel in 1942 in the Timor Sea near New Guinea. It was, he said, a 'huge illuminated disc', specifically described as 'a craft', which circled high above his ship for hours before suddenly flying away at 3–3,5000mph. Would he have seen this specifically as being a 'disc' at the time, though, or was this just an interpretation misleadingly layered over the original experience some time afterwards?[12]

An account of 'a round-shaped thing looking like a discus . . . very slightly luminescent' seen over Normandy in 1944 by a German officer named Heinz Heller illustrates a common problem with such stories. Heller felt unable to report this disc at the time as, there being no such thing as flying saucers yet, he did not know what it was, or how best to describe it, and so feared ridicule. Imagine seeing a motor car, a helicopter or a tank in 1583; how would you explain to others what that was? Hence, suspiciously to some, Heller's alleged wartime UFO experience, like so many others, is only known of from a post-war report.[13]

You can say the same about the post-war account of Allied airman William D. Leet, whose B-17 was 'kept company by a foo-fighter, a small amber disc, all the way from Klagenfurt, Austria, to the Adriatic Sea' in, 'as I recall', November 1944; but what if Leet recalled incorrectly? In a 1979 article, Leet spoke of how 'the object's outline was a perfect circle – too perfect' and its colour 'a luminous orange-yellow – too luminous', which just makes it sound like a bright light, albeit one emitting an 'unbearable' heat, not necessarily 'the weird craft' or 'unknown object that seems to be from out of this world' it had become in his mind, post-war. 'It positively was neither man-made nor a natural occurrence,' he could say by 1979, but 'a companion from another world' which disappeared 'precisely in the way that an electric light goes out when turned off by flipping a switch', the implication being that just such a switch was indeed flipped, probably by aliens. Yet, once again, contemporary proof of the event is lacking as Leet's report 'mysteriously disappeared' from his unit's records.[14] How very unfortunate.

Consider also the following 1958 account culled from the German magazine *Weltraumbote*, in which a witness speaks of a foo hovering over Dresden in March or April 1945:

> It was round, and had neither propeller nor wings . . . hovering noiselessly in the air. Then it suddenly disappeared like a broken soap-bubble. I also recall that the unfamiliar object was silvery-coloured and flat – not round like a balloon. I especially remember the sudden disappearance like something that wanted to avoid my gaze . . . that evening, I spoke to a friend. 'Oh, did you see it too?' he asked. No doubt aircraft pilots also observed it.[15]

Note how eager the witness is to emphasise that the foo was flat and round, not spherical, in shape, something which by 1958 would have been taken to give the report extra credibility. In 1945 itself, the exact reverse may well have been the case. At that point, proto-UFOs were still meant to look like silver Christmas-tree baubles, not items of metallic tableware.

* * *

There is one definite case of wartime flying 'discs' being described in print using that specific Kenneth Arnold-anticipating term, however. It came during the daring 'Schweinfurt Raid' made by Allied B-17 Flying Fortress crews over ball-bearing factories in the small German city of Schweinfurt on 14 October 1943, an account of which first appeared in a non-UFO book, writer Martin Caidin's (1927–97) otherwise straightforward 1960 factual history *Black Thursday*. Here, Caidin spoke of 'one of the most baffling incidents of World War II, and an enigma that to this day defies all explanation', when US bombers of the 384th Group swung into their final bomb run, only to encounter 'a cluster of discs' in their flight path. These discs were 'silver-coloured, about one inch thick and three inches in diameter', and 'gliding down very slowly' towards the B-17s 'in a very uniform cluster'. One B-17 collided directly with these discs – and yet they passed straight through its right wing as if made of thin air, 'with absolutely no effect on engines or plane surface'. Another disc audibly hit a second B-17's tail, yet there was no explosion. Near to the discs, a 'mass of black debris of varying sizes of clusters of three by four feet' was also spotted lingering by the bomber crews.

Given the specific repeated use of the term 'discs' by Caidin, many ufologists drew the obvious conclusion and triumphantly copied out portions of his 1960 text in their own subsequent titles as conclusive proof the wartime foos were real, physical, pre-1947 flying saucers. In later life, Caidin too became a UFO writer, of both fiction and non-fiction, who claimed to possess psychokinetic powers. Given this fact, sceptical researcher Andy Roberts wondered what precisely his account was based on. Caidin cited a specific wartime memorandum about the incident, which should have been easy to look up; but, when Roberts did look it up, it wasn't there. Caidin had said the report was labelled 'SECRET'. Was this just a double-bluff to cover up a blatant lie on his behalf? Or evidence of a wider government cover-up of the deadly truth about killer UFOs?

Neither. It later turned out the memorandum did exist, it had just been filed away under a different reference code. Should you want to look it up yourself, it is now sitting safely in The National Archives bearing the new code AIR 40/464. Read it and you will see that the file does indeed feature repeated use of the magic word 'discs', meaning all this really did happen!

But things are not as they initially seem. Look at the account cited by Caidin again. Whilst evidently real, the silver discs were 'about one inch thick and three inches in diameter'. If they were German-piloted flying saucers, then they can only have contained mini-Nazis, meaning the Third Reich must have secretly developed a shrinking ray during the war, too. Andy Roberts notes the original reference code for the report was FLO/1BW/REP/126, the letters 'FLO' standing for 'Flak Liaison Officer', indicating a more mundane explanation; the Germans were trying out some unusual anti-aircraft flak devices or radar deflection strips, something supported by the rather flak-like 'mass of black debris' also observed nearby. If they were strips of radar deflecting metal, discoid or not, then such gizmos are very thin and flimsy and would no more damage an aeroplane than driving into a wind-blown newspaper would damage a car, thus explaining why it could look as if some had passed like ghosts through wings or aircraft tails.[16]

During another bombing raid over Stuttgart on 6 September 1943, something similar occurred when large clusters of 'silver discs about the size of half-dollars' floated down onto Allied planes. Some fell upon the wing of an unlucky B-17 and 'immediately' started to burn. The scorched B-17 did not return. Ground-based analysts ventured the disc may have been a sticky pellet containing flammable white phosphorous or thermite. Other reports made during this period of explosive 'pie-plate' and 'doughnut-shaped' projectiles make it obvious these were not flying saucers at all, but more prosaic high-altitude arsonists.[17]

When the original Schweinfurt Raid report was submitted, the word 'disc' was not yet a loaded one. It just meant 'disc', a flattened circle, nothing more. By the time Martin Caidin was writing in 1960, the term 'disc' now meant 'UFO', which within a specific Second World War context had itself since come often to mean 'Nazi secret saucer weapon'. Yet again, we have a case of pure conceptual back formation, another verbal pun pulled straight from the madcap frames of Smokey Stover. Had the concept of flying saucers already existed in October 1943, I submit that the authors of the Schweinfurt memorandum would have avoided using the term 'discs' like the plague. Far from supporting the idea of wartime Nazi UFOs existing, therefore, as at first appeared to be the case, the fabled Report FLO/1BW/REP/126 in fact only undermines the whole notion. In the confusing world of ufology, the best evidence can sometimes be the worst.

Chapter Three

Discoid Inferno: The Saucerers' Apprentices Invade the Newspapers

On 21 May 1950, the Austrian weekly news digest *Wochen Echo* ran with a front-page banner headline boasting, in highly Dalek-like terms, about 'DAS WUNDER VON SCHWEINFURT, 1944: DEUTSCHE UNTERTASSEN VERNICHTEN 145 SUPERFESTUNGEN', or 'THE MIRACLE OF SCHWEINFURT, 1944: GERMAN SAUCERS EXTERMINATE 145 SUPER-FORTRESSES'. As no photographs of this event existed, because it never happened, the story came complete with a large comic-book illustration showing a squadron of Nazi UFOs shooting down US B-29s (a mistake, as they were B-17s flown over Schweinfurt – B-29s never saw service in Europe, only in the Pacific region) with lethal laser beams.

The paper carried supporting testimony from a German ex-Luftwaffe pilot, saying mini-saucers really were used against the Allies that day, these being two different types of device, 3 to 4m in diameter, code-named 'Qualle' (generally translated as 'Torment', it actually means 'Jellyfish') and 'Korkus' ('Corkscrew', supposedly, although the actual German term for such a device is 'Korkenzieher'). Note how the report doesn't even get the year right, the particular Schweinfurt Raid (there were actually several) during which miniature flak discs were seen occurring in 1943 not 1944; still, the dating of fairy tales is rarely exact. But was a small fee for his words the *Wochen Echo* informant's only motive in spreading such lies?

Many embittered Nazis never got over losing the war, and for solace a few tried spreading the myth that the Germans, being the Master Race, were indeed responsible for inventing the foos and other subsequent saucers, for who else could have been clever enough to have done so? From the 1950s, a number of revisionists and cranks began approaching the press, who welcomed them with open arms. The history of this sorry episode has been expertly documented by Italian ufologist Maurizio Verga, and if you want a fuller outline, I direct you to his researches online, ideally to be supplemented by those of his equally sceptical British counterpart, Kevin McClure.[1] What follows in this chapter is an account of the most significant, strangest or most amusing of self-styled saucer creators and their inventions, not a comprehensive catalogue. During the Internet age, the litany of different designs has now mushroomed to unmanageable proportions. Knowing your Flügkriesel from your Flügelrad, your Pirna Disc from your Haunebu II, your Vril RFZ-5 from your Vril RFZ-6, or your Omega Diskus from your Turboproietti is an art of sorts, but those who master it stand in relation to real aerospace specialists much as Pokémon obsessives stand towards qualified zoologists – that is, experts in a fictional discipline. If you do want to complete your own personal Nazi UFO Pokédex, though, then I provide a few useful websites in the notes, where you can examine fake photographs and compare detailed technical specifications and construction histories if you really want.[2]

Interestingly, many of the very first putative saucer inventors to surface were from the Anglosphere and South America, not the German-speaking world. In the *Baltimore Sun* for 8 July 1947 a Tennessee watch-maker alleged that in 1943 he had sent the US War Department plans for a flying disc powered purely by a rubber belt, but had received a terse reply calling his proposal 'not feasible'. Obviously they had kept his design and replaced the rubber band engine with an atomic one, meaning the true credit for Arnold's sighting was surely his, the watch-maker complained.

Or possibly it belonged instead to W.H. Ashlin, a Chile-based English engineer, who declared in July 1947 that he had in fact invented flying saucers back in 1939, and sent them off to Britain during the war, where they had since been perfected. Chile, Ashlin said, should be 'proud to have been the birthplace of so brilliant a creation'. It was. So proud that a Chilean architect, Edgar Pinkar, quickly claimed the saucers as products of his own native Chilean genius, not Ashlin's, explaining they were really called the 'Supergiro Model 69-P'.

In August 1947, a Brazilian named Alcides Teixeira Kopp walked into the offices of Porto Alegre-based newspaper *A Fôlha da Tarde* with four small discs under his arm, each containing 'no less than 5,000 electrical wires, all interlaced in code'. He said these devices could fly at 10,000kmph and possessed a special homing function, or 'modern boomerang mechanic', each being an aerial 'warrior' capable of producing 'earthquakes and oil-fires', and 'sawing airplanes' in half. He requested State funds to build more, bragging he had previously invented a form of 'amphibious cars' for use by Wehrmacht troops back in 1929, having been commissioned to do so by 'a German named Kaiser'. Kopp materialised again in 1957 professing to be a 'nuclear researcher and specialist in interplanetary studies' who had invented 'the wheels that spin in space'. Days later he was sitting behind bars. A policeman had seen his photo, and recognised him as being wanted for bigamy.[3]

However, in March 1950 another large UFO wave erupted across Western Europe, reviving continental media interest in flying saucers. Five years after the war's end, the time now seemed ripe for its losers to rewrite the standard version of its history. This curious phenomenon began not in Germany but in her old Axis ally Italy, where on 24 March *Il Giornale d'Italia* ran a front-page story proclaiming that the 'dischi volanti', as flying saucers were known domestically, had been a joint Italo-German invention.

These jingoistic claims were made by an actual member of the pre-war Italian fascist parliament, Giuseppe Belluzzo (1876–1952), Economics Minister from 1925 to 1928 and an acknowledged aerospace engineer who had built the first Italian steam-powered turbine in 1905, the holder of several patents and author of nearly fifty books. The article carried Belluzzo's own byline, and came complete with a basic blueprint for an unmanned circular aircraft some 10m wide which, the former fascist averred, had its origins in a secret Italian project of 1942, later taken over by Nazi scientists operating in Norway, whose unbuilt designs had been captured by the USSR in 1945. The recent post-war waves of sightings meant Russian technicians must have successfully implemented these plans, but readers might conclude this did not alter the cheering patriotic fact the dischi volanti were really Italian.

Belluzzo implied these Soviet saucers could easily by now have been adapted to drop atom bombs, helping his speculations reach the media abroad, his testimony being reported in the *Los Angeles Mirror* under the rather blasé headline 'Flying Discs "Old Story", Says Italian'. Several US papers repeated Belluzzo's comment, 'There is nothing supernatural or Martian about flying discs . . . they are simply rational applications of recent technique'. The governing principle of the saucers, said Belluzzo, was 'very simple' and their construction 'easy', being performed 'with very light metal'. They were unmanned, 'like the wartime German V-2 rockets', and could descend and explode either when their fuel ran out or via 'an automatic-timing device'.

Both Hitler and his ally Benito Mussolini (1883–1945) had shown personal interest in these valuable wonders, with the US press adding that Belluzzo had drawn up plans for one personally, but that these had been taken away by Il Duce and had since 'disappeared'.[4] An ensuing announcement by Brigadier General Ferruccio Ranza (1892–1973) of the Italian Air Force that none of this was in any way true garnered rather fewer breathless column inches worldwide.

* * *

It appears Belluzzo never actually claimed to have helped build and fly the saucers personally, despite what others would later claim on his behalf, but handily he gave no names of those specific wartime Germans and Italians who supposedly had tried to do so, giving chancers ample opportunity to claim it was them. On 30 March 1950, as part of a general discussion about the then-ongoing European UFO wave, the mass-circulation weekly German news magazine *Der Spiegel* repeated Belluzzo's claims, but also introduced a new figure named Rudolf Schriever (1909–53), who was both the true wartime designer of viable flying discs and a full, pure-bred German.

Presenting himself as a qualified aeronautical engineer and former Luftwaffe Flugkapitän, or 'flight captain', it seems that Schriever had actually been a test pilot for the Heinkel aircraft company at their factory-cum-airfield in Eger, in what is now the Czech Republic, but without any specific technical training background. Whilst he could certainly fly a vehicle, he could no more have designed one than Neil Armstrong could have built his own moon rocket, as his totally unworkable sketches showed. Displaying a cut-away cockpit within which a lone pilot *stood up* pulling levers, Schriever's saucer diagram, when later reprinted in English, came complete with such highly sophisticated technical labels as 'FUEL', 'PADDLES' and 'WINDOW'.

For a genius, Schriever had since fallen on hard times, reduced to delivering the US Army newspaper *Stars and Stripes* to bases in Bremerhaven via truck. Yet, during the war, he had successfully designed a circular 'jet-helicopter' with vertical take-off capabilities. Schriever placed a pilot's cockpit at the centre of a large circular bladed turbine, a bit like sticking a giant goldfish bowl in the centre of a massive horizontally oriented electric fan. Beneath this turbine were three jet engines. Initially, Schriever did not say his creation had ever successfully flown. It was almost ready to be properly tested out in Nazi-occupied Prague in April 1945, but the speedy Russian advance put paid to this, forcing him to flee with his blueprints and a scale model, both of which were furtively stolen in 1948. Following German defeat, he met with 'representatives of foreign powers', but these presumable Commies no longer needed him. It was Schriever's opinion his former assistants had been kidnapped away to Russia, where they had since developed the saucers now buzzing the globe, based on his original designs and stolen material.

Schriever's claims arrived in *Der Spiegel* just before 1 April, on which appropriate date the International News Service conducted a telephone interview with 'the forty-year-old graduate of the University of Prague', in which he offered to build the US military a 'workable prototype' of his flying fan 'within six or nine months', if given appropriate facilities. The discs currently invading Western skies, Schriever said, were 'certainly not pipe-dreams or visitors from Mars', and to prove it he provided a detailed description of how his 'flying top' with its 'three co-axially mounted sections . . . able to rotate independently' would work:

> The control-cabin, he said, would be in the upper section of the main gondola section. Beneath the lower gondola would be a rotating cartwheel-like affair forming a hub 14 yards in diameter with three-yard-long paddles in place of spokes. Three starting-jets would be slung beneath this cartwheel to set off the rotation. The hot gases given off by the jets, Schriever added, would give the impression of 'balls of fire' in flight [hence the wartime foos]. He estimated that each gondola of his flying top would weigh about three tonnes and would be nearly 12 feet wide and just under 11 feet in height. Schriever said that the ship would be able to ascend at a little better than 300 feet per second and that the paddles would revolve at a top speed of 2,600 miles an hour.[5]

Schriever then took to writing letters promoting his work to women's magazines like *Heim und Welt* (*Home and World*), German saucers now jostling for space with the latest fashions in hats, make-up and soft furnishings. Details of Schriever's basic story later changed, both in his own telling and that of others, so that, far from being an overgrown paper boy, he was actually smuggling valuables in and out of US bases on behalf of a clandestine post-war Nazi underground cell.

In a 1952 interview, Schriever said his craft had been conceived in 1941 as a vertical take-off solution to a wartime lack of runways, and that by June 1942 a working, non-manned model had successfully been flown. By 1945 in Prague, a full-size manned prototype was fully built and ready to be flown too, with himself as the daring test pilot, details he had omitted back in 1950; accordingly, he provided a heroic photo of himself in aviator's uniform. Furthermore, he now said his plans and model had been stolen in 1945, not 1948. Maybe Schriever had since realised that, as Arnold first saw his presumable back-engineered Commie saucers in 1947, the chronology of his yarn did not fully add up.

In Schriever's wake, the Hamburg weekly journal *Die Strasse* reprised Giuseppe Belluzzo's original claims, adding the detail that German engineers had collaborated with him on the saucer building project even though, in initial Italian press reports, Belluzzo never professed to have constructed any saucers himself at all. One of these men was Kurt Schnittke, a self-styled inventor from Regensburg, who had supposedly created a circular mini jet-helicopter of his own, an unmanned foo-fighter with twin rotors revolving around a central sphere, filled with combustible fuel tanks, landing gear and radio-control apparatus, intended to infiltrate enemy bomber groups and explode (so why the landing gear?). At the end of each rotor was a jet rocket for propulsion, making a metallic sphere by day become 'a luminous disc' at night due to the specific rocket chemicals being burned. Schnittke was very clear that, whilst the initial idea was Italian, the end product could never have been developed without the innate design genius of patriotic German scientists like himself.

* * *

In April 1950, Hans Kosinski, ostensibly a former Luftwaffe officer, wasted further newsprint by claiming that five full-size Nazi saucers had successfully been built and then dismantled and shipped out to Antarctica in 1944 on Hitler's direct orders, away from the Allies' reach. The story of one Professor Scholtz also gained traction in Italy, Scholtz having built a successor to the Nazis' real-life V-1 and V-2 missiles, known as the V-8. Weapons V-3 to V-6 were doubtless bad enough, but the V-7 was even worse, being an actual atom bomb, which Scholtz's remote-controlled V-8 mini-saucer was intended to deliver. By 1944 eight such discs were ready, and successfully flown in front of Hitler. A hundred V-8s were eventually built at a factory in Pomerania, but when Russian troops approached, instead of using them to nuke the Communists, Hitler inexplicably ordered the vessels all be blown up instead.

In June 1952, Paris-based newspaper *FranceSoir* printed twin stories about an arguably entirely invented German engineer and ex-colonel named Dr Richard Miethe, together with images of him in both a white lab jacket and, for some unfathomable reason, a swimming costume. Miethe (or the journalist pretending to be him) called his own wartime German saucer the V-7. Like so many ex-Nazis, Miethe was given asylum by Israel, and was now living in Tel Aviv. Happy to be identified as a Nazi scientist despite being surrounded by angry Jews, Miethe compared his V-7 'exceptional machine' to a giant 'Olympic discus, an immense metal disc of circular form' which, 'at a distance of several thousand metres . . . [could] more-or-less resemble the saucer of a set of table-ware'.

With a diameter of 42m and containing 'extremely complicated . . . gyroscopy', it was powered by twelve jet-powered reaction turbines lining a metal ring which rotated around a pressurised central cabin with space for three crew, the turbines being fuelled by a form of 'compressed gas based on helium' so efficient it allowed the V-7 to break the sound barrier and maintain 20,000km of continuous flight across 16 hours without refuelling. These turbines produced 'neither visible flames nor smoke' because 'the gases from combustion are recovered by an extremely clever compression-system, discovered in 1938 by a British engineer'. It could also 'easily' be used unmanned to deliver bombs, 'guided by radio and radar', and possessed 'the ideal aerodynamic form'.

Eighteen gallant Nazi test pilots had died during early flights, but this amazing 'supersonic helicopter' had since been perfected by the Russians, who had stolen away 'beyond the Urals' three of the six other unnamed engineers who helped build it back in the Reich, the other three anonymous scientists now being expediently dead. Prior to Miethe's escape, copies of his V-7 blueprints had been hidden within the walls of an SS castle, which the Americans tore apart in vain, being too stupid to even discover the valuable silk stockings hidden in the cellar. Miethe concluded thus: 'I therefore assert, that if flying saucers are in the skies, they were built in Germany, as developed under my orders, and probably reproduced by Germans in chains in Soviet captivity.' Miethe's tale was reproduced in other French and Italian papers, alongside truly risible fake photos of the V-7 in supposed flight over the Baltic Sea in 1944.[6]

How real was Dr Miethe? *FranceSoir* had him as recently working for Egypt developing radio-controlled missiles for use against Israel, under the direction of a group of former V-weapon experts headed by Dr Kurt Fuellner, owner of the aerospace firm Physikalische ArbeitsGemeinschaft (PAG). However, the Germans had for unspecified reasons refused to hand over their results to their Egyptian employers, thus being booted out of the country without full payment. The team leaders had gone to Hamburg, but Miethe preferred to try his luck in Israel. Possibly this was because, after the war, rather than surrender to the British or Americans, Miethe had escaped by air to Addis Ababa, then on to Cairo, where he had joined the Arab Legion, where several wanted Nazi war criminals had also sought refuge from Allied death sentences, the implication being that he too was a fugitive unable to return to German soil.

To a degree, this accords with known reality. A Dr Kurt Fuellner did indeed employ German experts to develop rockets for the Egyptian military, who had to leave the country in March 1952; their trials had failed due to lack of resources and the government in Cairo was making unwanted attempts to forcibly nationalise Fuellner's firm. But was Miethe really one of Dr Fuellner's employees? His appearance in *FranceSoir* bears all the hall- marks of reporters trying to make a genuine but slightly dull story about far off Egyptian military affairs into a more reader friendly, paper shifting yarn about saucers, to fit in with yet another major sighting wave then ongoing across the Western world during 1952.

Maybe the hacks made Miethe up wholesale. Maybe he was just a convenient fantasist of the usual German nationalist variety, or a chancer trying to sell dud info about Egyptian rocket research to the Israelis, whose word reporters happily took at face value. We may never know. In the 1990s, a British aviation researcher named Bill Rose (b.1948), who claimed to have seen authentic photos of successful test flights of Nazi UFOs, produced a group snapshot purporting to show Miethe in the company of key members of the V-2 rocket programme. If genuine, this would certainly be significant; yet no documentary evidence of Miethe's association with these men has been found by mainstream historians of German rocketry. Miethe remains as elusive as one of his V-7 foos.[7]

Whatever the truth, the main immediate consequence of Miethe's claims was to flush Rudolf Schriever back out again. To claim official ownership of his brainchild, by November 1952 German newspapers were reporting that

Schriever had gone so far as to file an official patent application for his flying top saucer. However, its description had since changed from his original 1950 outline to become much more like the V-7 of his possibly made-up rival Miethe – thus, a fictional device alters its shape in order to become more like another equally fictional device, thereby to gain more illusory credibility. The circular and parasitic relationship at work in building up the entire Nazi UFO mythos is already embarrassingly evident.

* * *

Then, in 1953, something extraordinary happened: Canadian media revealed the existence of a genuine military aerospace project to create a peculiar, flattened disc-like aircraft to the world. On 11 February, the *Toronto Star* reported that the A.V. Roe aerospace company (also known as AVRO-Canada) was developing an actual working flying saucer at its plant in Ontario, in conjunction with the US and Canadian governments. Aerial photos of just such a craft, later known as the AvroOmega or AvroCar, were taken sitting outside AVRO's hangars, forcing Minister for Defence Production, C.D. Howe (1886–1960), to admit to the Canadian House of Commons that the stories were true. In October 1953 a romanticised painting of the item made the front cover of *FATE* magazine's 'SPECIAL SAUCER ISSUE', together with the unambiguous headline 'CANADA BUILDS FLYING SAUCER'. But had Canada really done so? Yes! . . . And also no.

Designed by expatriate English engineer John Carver Meadows Frost (1915–79), the AvroCar photographed was just a wooden mock-up, but, according to the media, was intended as a wingless, near circular aircraft capable of flying at up to 1,500mph, hovering in mid-air and making 180-degree turns on a sixpence. Supposedly, Canada planned to build an entire fleet of AvroCars to defend neighbouring Alaska because, being able to take off and land vertically like helicopters, they negated the lack of feasible runways in frozen polar type regions.

It later emerged news of Frost's baby had deliberately been leaked to drum up public support and further funding; the Canadian Research Board had already stumped up $379,000, but much more was needed. So well oiled was the operation that British war hero Field Marshal Bernard Montgomery (1887–1976) was even persuaded to drop by the AVRO factory and eulogise the contraption. Sadly, in December 1954, it was announced the project had been scrapped as being too costly for something so 'highly speculative' in nature, but this later turned out to be disinformation.

The PR scam had worked, with further covert funding being provided from the USAF, who were very interested in acquiring a viable vehicle of a 'VTOL', or 'Vertical Take-Off and Landing', nature.

John Frost had first arrived to work for A.V. Roe in that seminal year of 1947, it sometimes being said he was inspired by that summer's decisive Kenneth Arnold sighting. By 1951, Frost was trying to make a small circular metal plate float around using an air hose, submitting a proposal for a 'Turbo-Disc' to upper management in 1952. This would utilise something known as the 'Coandă Effect', discovered around 1910 by the French-Romanian scientist Henri-Marie Coandă (1886–1972), who observed that air flows will change direction to follow the line of suitably curved surfaces, thereby producing a pull in the opposite direction, something Frost hoped could make his craft hover on a cushion-bed of redirected air.

Frost initially envisaged the machine relying on gyroscopes for balance and having two rotating rings on its underside, one spinning clockwise and the other counter-clockwise, lifting the thing up with flows of air produced by jets of a gas-turbine variety, which sounds not entirely unlike some of the media-pushed pseudo-designs of Rudolf Schriever et al. Accordingly, a legend has since arisen that Frost may have been directly inspired by one of these men. Supposedly, a file exists somewhere within Canada's National Archives – for which no reference number is ever given – detailing a trip of Frost to West Germany in 1953, where, in the company of British and Canadian officials, he was allowed to cross-examine a captive German engineer. This unnamed Miethe-like mastermind had allegedly worked on successful Nazi discs near Prague, giving Frost valuable tips.

Maybe the ex-Nazi advised Frost to abandon his initial proposed saucer shape altogether. Establishing his own 'Special Projects Group', Frost got management go-ahead to develop his cherished 'Project Y', and before long the circular saucer was looking more like the digging end of a spade, this being deemed more aerodynamically apt. Following the 1954 injection of funds from the USAF, however, Frost's brainchild became 'Project Y2' and turned more saucer like once again, now being described as 'a supersonic research aircraft having a circular platform'.

The USAF hoped its VTOL capabilities would lessen need for runways, which, with their large static concentrations of grounded aircraft, made tempting targets for Russian long-range bombers or missiles. A VTOL flying saucer would allow a future generation of military UFOs to be parked almost anywhere, making mass destruction of the national air fleet impossible. Much tinkering on 'Project Silverbug', as the scheme became christened due to the vessel's passing resemblance to a giant metal ladybird, continued behind closed doors before, in 1960, a more-or-less fully circular prototype was flown in public. Sadly, the demo revealed the AvroCar was little more than a weedy, unstable, two-seater aerial hovercraft which failed to remain airborne for more than a few minutes at a time, and which barely levitated above the tarmac. Military funding was withdrawn for good and Project Silverbug cancelled in 1961.[8]

* * *

This raises the question of whether the development of a flying saucer is actually aerodynamically possible. If not, this would prove that the Nazis did not build any during the war; not necessarily that they did not *try*, simply that they could not have *succeeded*. In 1939 a German farmer named Arthur Sack won a national competition to design a powered model-plane with an unusual, pancake-like craft of his own creation. Sack's model couldn't actually take off, and had to be launched into the air by virtue of Sack standing there and throwing it by hand, like a child's paper aeroplane, whereupon it managed 100yd of self-powered flight, barely flopping over the finishing line. Nonetheless, the full 360-degree circular winged design, dubbed the Bierdeckel, or 'Beer Tray', by amused Luftwaffe test pilots, was innovative enough to catch the attention of the Reich's Air Ministry, who in 1944 facilitated development of a full-size largely wooden prototype, the Sack AS-6 monoplane.

The AS-6 was a propeller driven craft with wheels, not designed to hover or possess VTOL capabilities like the AvroCar, but it does show the Nazis were willing to experiment. The German aerospace giant Messerschmidt actually offered to take over full development duties from Sack, but he refused. However, the reality of the full-size AS-6 proved disappointing. The plane failed to make it into the air properly during test flights, taking a short hop upwards before tumbling down with collapsed landing gear. This gained it a new test-pilot nickname – the Bussard, or 'Buzzard', so called because it spent most of its time sitting on the ground, scavenging parts from other dead aircraft to gobble up as its own. The AS-6 was strafed by enemy fire one day, never repaired and then dismantled before invading US troops could get their hands on it; quite why they would have wanted to do so is another matter.[9]

In 1950 details of a further pair of twin experimental craft developed by the US Navy between 1942 and 1947 called the 'Flying Flapjack' (or Vought V-173 and Vought XF5U if you want to be technical) were released. First constructed in 1942 by the Chance-Vought Corporation, following 'discoidal' or 'Zimmer Skimmer' designs by engineer Charles H. Zimmerman (1908–96), the Flapjack was an experimental near VTOL combination of primitive helicopter and jet plane, somewhat resembling the Sack AS-6. Broadly semi-circular, like another misshapen pancake, it had twin propellers mounted on small arm-like protuberances at the front and two stabilising fins instead of wings on either side, leading to its other nickname of the 'Navy Flounder', resembling as it did a robotic flatfish. Zimmerman's Flapjack could reputedly hover slowly at 35mph, or reach top speeds of 400–500mph if preferred. The US Navy desired quick and easy take-off from aircraft carriers, so a later model added a ring of jet nozzles around its outer rim. Some sightings of UFOs during the early Kenneth Arnold era may perhaps have been glimpses of one of the Flapjack varieties at work.

If the US Navy could successfully develop such a vehicle during the war, there is no inherent reason why the Nazis could not have done something similar themselves. The problem hinges upon your definition of what 'success' means. As with the AvroCar, the V-173 could indeed fly, but it also tended to Flounder. Indeed, so unstable and excessively vibratory was the Flapjack that photos of the folly were, by some accounts, only released to the public in 1950 as part of an official campaign to reassure them that flying saucers were not real and that they could not present a danger to US airspace even if they were; after all, the US had tried to build one themselves, and it was rubbish. Much better helicopters and jet planes soon came along and consigned the propeller driven Zimmer Skimmers to history. Prototypes of the AvroCar, XF5U and V-173 now sit safely grounded in US aerospace museums, for the edification and amusement of us all.[10]

Away from the world's well-funded militaries there have been any number of lone saucer inventors down the decades since 1947, but none are known to have genuinely succeeded. In 1970, patent number 1310990 was lodged on behalf of British Rail for a '120 foot-long interplanetary saucer', driven by 'a controlled thermonuclear fusion reaction ignited by laser beams'. The patent was automatically registered in British Rail's name because it was the eccentric design, apparently on worktime, of a scientist in its Derby R&D department named Charles Osmond Frederick (b.1936), rather than because they had any genuine plans for an atomic return-ticket service to the moon and back. It seems Frederick's project began as a design for a new kind of lifting platform for trains, but then grew rather out of hand until it ended up being a plan for a full-blown interplanetary space vehicle, optimistically intended to carry ticketed passengers just like an ordinary Earth train. The patent lapsed in 1976, due to non-payment of renewal fees, so technically anyone could now make the BR saucer for themselves, presuming they can manage to solve the minor preliminary problem of creating a fully working laser ignition nuclear fusion engine to power it with first.[11]

In 2005, though, an unanticipated coda was added to the whole story when a British former hovercraft engineer, Geoff Hatton, utilised a £250,000 grant to successfully fly a miniaturised, unmanned AvroCar-like VTOL drone, one-fifth of the original machine's size, called the GSF7 – GSF here standing for 'Geoff's Flying Saucer'. Hatton genuinely did initially create this thing almost alone, in a kind of shed in Cambridgeshire, from 2002 onwards: as one amused 2009 report in *The Engineer* put it, 'The industrial estates of Great Britain hold many secrets . . . Head to a small estate just outside Peterborough, for example, and among the aquarium superstore, the party goods stockist and the brakepad installer, you'll find a company that makes flying saucers.'

Roughly saucer like in form, the GSF7, part-powered by the very same Coandă Effect once exploited by John Frost, actually flew properly, with the US and British governments entering into talks to develop it further as a surveillance drone. In 2007, the inventor won a contract with the US government to do just this. Yet, whilst Hatton's mini-AvroCar did work, it appears that other competing designs proved even more capable, drone-wise, and Hatton's company GSF Projects folded in 2008 due to lack of any further forthcoming military cash. The rights to the design were then bought up by another private company, AESIR Ltd, but they also appear to have since become defunct, and so the drones we now see invading our skies today are, sadly for UFO-lovers, not terribly saucer shaped.[12]

* * *

The overall conclusion would seem to be that, yes, you can build a basic flying saucer of sorts if you really want to, but given that such things are not very good, why bother? Nevertheless, in the early 1950s the limited capability of saucer shaped aircraft was not definitively known, as demonstrated by the fact the AvroCar was still in receipt of military development funding which would eventually reach some $10 million, and the official revelation of the weird vehicle's actual existence suddenly lent surface credibility to the stories of the German UFO-builders. According to *FranceSoir*, following its first interview with him on 7 June 1952, the V-7 inventor Richard Miethe had been offered the chance to go abroad by 'a large American company' and develop his saucers further there. Had other Nazi aerospace geniuses been made similar offers to help develop the AvroCar?

In 1949, US Marines Major turned military aviation journalist Donald E. Keyhoe (1897–1988) was asked to utilise his old contacts and look into the saucer mystery by the popular newsstand men's magazine *True*, which evidently specialised in printing stories that weren't. The resulting piece, appearing in January 1950, was one of the most widely read articles in US print history, being hastily turned into the first full-length book on the subject, *The Flying Saucers Are Real*, which sold over 500,000 copies and introduced the general public to the idea UFOs were nuts-and-bolts alien craft being covered up by the government.

Keyhoe reported other angles too, recalling a phone-call from the pseudonymous former intel officer 'John Steele', who fed him info that flying saucers were British inventions, based on captured Nazi prototypes, back-engineered from spring 1947 onwards. However, said Steele, initial remote-control models had a tendency to develop a mind of their own, and whizz off all over Europe, bringing unwanted attention. Accordingly, development was shifted to remote areas in Australia and Canada. When it later emerged the AvroCar had itself originated within Canada, these claims took on new resonance – at least until it turned out Project Silverbug was hopeless. If John Frost really was inspired to create his AvroCar by the 1947 UFO wave, as has been alleged, then in fact it would seem that Kenneth Arnold's sighting caused the creation of a secret Canadian saucer development programme rather than a secret Canadian saucer development programme causing Kenneth Arnold's sighting, as Keyhoe's informant proposed.[13]

In February 1953, following hot on the heels of the AvroCar's official revelation, German tabloid *Hamburger Morgenpost* printed a fourteen-part series about the many wonderful weapons the Nazis had allegedly invented behind closed doors, but never used. Here, one Georg Klein, supposedly a former chief engineer with the German Munitions Ministry, enters the scene; extensively quoted, he may actually have written the pieces himself. Klein acted to correlate the most important pre-existing stories of the other

German saucer fantasists, iron out most of the inconsistencies between them (at least if you didn't look too closely . . .), and present the whole thing for the first time as one semi-coherent narrative.

Klein claimed he was the real co-ordinating operational mastermind, with Belluzzo, Schriever, Miethe and a new totally imaginary figure named Otto Habermohl all working under him as talented assistants, drawing up plans and tightening the nuts and bolts so he didn't have to get his hands dirty. Rather than attributing the creation of UFOs to lone geniuses, Klein thus established a more pseudo-realistic space for their construction embedded within the structure of the much larger Nazi military-industrial complex. Unlike his predecessors, Klein posed more as a talented bureaucrat than a solo super brain. The flaw was that it was strange indeed that such a large bureaucratic programme generated no apparent paper trail behind it; the solving of one plausibility problem often only leads to another.

According to Klein, Hitler's saucer story began in 1941, when rotund Luftwaffe chief Hermann Goering (1893–1946) demanded the development of a new generation of radical aircraft with 'alternative forms' – such as ones that were wholly circular. The key romantic date of a successful test flight for the first German saucer was also introduced by Klein for the first time here, that of 14 February 1945.

These initial articles provided Klein with a media calling card. An interview in *Welt am Sonntag* for 25 April 1953 opened by placing Klein's claims in the context of the AvroCar's development, to lend them initial credence. Gladly did Klein then reminisce about being present at his saucer's first piloted lift-off in Prague, telling of its special, heat-resistant metal alloys, sophisticated gyroscopic stabilisation devices, potential top speed of 4,000kmph and ability to be 'guided by rays'. He even speculated about their potential for use by civilian airlines, due to their capacity to 'carry thirty-to-forty passengers'.

Klein regurgitated all this in interviews again and again from a first-person perspective, so helping bring the legend to life. As follow-up articles lifted these quotes direct and then presented them as back-up for the claims of other fantasists, the whole narrative structure of the myth became ever more self-supporting. If one liar was supporting the lies of another liar, why would either deny the other was telling the truth? Inconsistencies in the various descriptions given of the discs were cleverly dispelled by Klein claiming there were two separate programmes of Nazi UFO development ongoing, each devoted towards building different types of vehicle:

> One type actually had the shape of a disc, with an interior cabin, and was built by the Miethe factories, which had also built the V-2 rockets. This model was 42 metres in diameter. The other model had the shape of a ring, with raised sides and a spherically shaped pilot's cabin placed on the outside, in the centre of the ring. This was built at the Habermohl and Schriever factories. Both models had the ability to take off vertically and to land in an extremely restricted area, like helicopters.[14]

It seemed the Habermohl-Schriever discs were built at a factory in Prague – later identified as belonging to Škoda, which explains why they soon began breaking down and crashing all over the place like at Roswell – whereas Miethe's saucers were constructed at a plant in Breslau. Before the Soviets could capture the Škoda factory, employees rather stupidly destroyed all the saucers stored there instead of simply flying away in them to safety, whereas the engineers in Breslau did not receive enough advance warning, meaning Miethe's plans and disc engines were captured to serve as the models for subsequent back-engineered Soviet saucers 'in accordance with German technical principles'.

Giuseppe Belluzzo had helpfully died in 1952, meaning he could not contradict Klein's version of events, not even when the German claimed to have been 'corresponding [with Belluzzo] for some time', presumably via Ouija board. Miethe probably did not exist, and neither did Habermohl, so they were unlikely to cause him any problems either. Klein thus felt safe to say that, as the Russians advanced on the Prague saucer factory, Miethe had flown away in a rare Me-163 rocket fighter, which is about as likely as a bank robber getting away in a passing F-1 car, and to present the fictional fellow's supposed design drawings for public education. By drawing a circle on a big sheet of paper before hanging it on his wall and pointing at it in front of photographers, Klein thus tried to appear plausible.

Obligingly, Rudolf Schriever had died in a car accident in Bremen on 16 January 1953, in broad confluence with the AvroCar story breaking, which made eerily perfect timing for Klein, allowing him to hijack the story completely. Barely a month passed between Schriever's death and

Klein's emergence; why had he never come forward beforehand? Possibly because Schriever was the last man standing who could have contradicted his invented narrative with a pre-existing fiction of his own. Admittedly, some later claimed that Schriever did not die in a car accident at all, with sightings of him continuing to be made until 1965, but perhaps this was just his doppelgänger.

In April 1954, German magazine *Die 7 Tage* cheekily produced a new design for Dr Miethe's proposed saucer, with the cockpit placed not in the centre of the disc, but leaning over its outer edge to accommodate a central stabilising gyroscope, an unusual notion it supported with made-up design drawings of its own . . . drawings which Klein then passed off as genuine ones made by Miethe himself in following media appearances. Although they now had proof Klein was lying, how could *Die 7 Tage* expose this imposture without simultaneously exposing its own? When a French toy manufacturer then spotted this new rather wonky saucer design now being attributed to Miethe and produced a tatty tin flying saucer based upon it (albeit with a Soviet-style red star on top and labelled as a full interplanetary spaceship), it gave yet further superficial credence to the idea such vessels might really have existed.

In 1954, perhaps the largest wave of UFO sightings ever known hit Western Europe, so Klein made his rounds of the press once again, now downgrading Belluzzo's impact on events. Belluzzo was a non-German, you see – although actually, as he had claimed no practical personal construction role at all in the original 1950 *Il Giornale d'Italia* reports, Klein was inadvertently expanding the Italian's part at the same time as talking it down. By now, Klein was in Switzerland, providing interesting opinions about the AvroCar and seeking funding to create a workable electric-powered prototype of Miethe's designs, capable of holding two or three pilots. Exploiting post-Roswell rumours of UFO crashes, he also implied such downed craft were related to the earlier, less developed, prototypes of his underlings. Weirdly, Germany's leading aircraft design magnate, Ernst Heinkel (1888–1958), actively believed Klein's stories – or so the papers said – enhancing his standing further.

Wisely, most of the purported saucer inventors had spoken of utilising jet engines and rocket engines to power their craft, these being genuinely innovative technologies which really had been developed and deployed in limited numbers by Germany towards the war's end. It thus seemed logical to think a successful saucer might have had a circle of downwards-facing jet engines located around its lower rim. In 1947, US sci-fi magazine *Fantastic Adventures* had printed a speculative back-cover blueprint guessing how one of Kenneth Arnold's saucers might have flown – in a similar fashion to Schriever's or Miethe's craft, with a jet ring. Klein's oft-shown V-7 blueprints were basically just another version of the *Fantastic Adventures* designs, only passed off as being real. The precise gap between fact and fiction in the still young and growing Nazi UFO story was already becoming rather confusing. It was about to grow even more so.

Chapter Four

V for Vengeance, F for Fake: The Magic Bullets of the Wunderwaffen

In 1956 an interesting book was published on the continent, *German Secret Weapons of the Second World War*, written by Major Rudolf Lusar (b.1896), ostensibly a former German intelligence officer for the Luftwaffe, at least according to the potted author biography he provided to accompany his text. It has since proven difficult to establish precisely what Lusar actually did during the war, although he himself claimed to have been a qualified engineer employed by the Reich Patent Office in Berlin. However, an apparent 1962 interrogation of Lusar as a witness in a war crimes tribunal relating to the infamous Oradour-sur-Glane massacre, in which an entire French village of 632 men, women and children was wiped out by the Waffen-SS in 1944, has recently come to light in which Lusar tells prosecutors that, whilst indeed an engineer, he actually served as an anti-aircraft artillery officer in Western France during the conflict, not as a Patent Office official in Berlin, with his true rank being Captain, not Major – unless he was later promoted and transferred.[1]

Whatever the truth of his military career may have been, Lusar's advertised role on the dust jacket certainly made him seem like the ideal person to write a book dealing with the subject of Wunderwaffen, or 'Miracle Weapons'. Also known as Geheimwaffen, or 'Secret Weapons', the term described a series of projects, like the V-1 and V-2 rocket bombs, which were intended to win the war via advanced technological means once Axis troops became badly outnumbered as the US and Russia entered the field of combat from 1941 onwards.

The V-1 and V-2 undeniably stood as being great technological achievements on behalf of German science and engineering, although even these two most famous of Hitler's Wunderwaffen had their defects. The V-1, colloquially known to beleaguered Londoners as the 'Doodlebug' or 'Buzz-Bomb', was a kind of pilotless, jet-powered glider loaded with high-explosive materials, a strange cross between aircraft and missile, a rocket with wings. Guided by gyroscope and compass, it could be programmed to attack certain co-ordinates, then launched direct from bases in France to fly across the Channel to rain down death upon key targets within England's capital – in theory, anyway.

In practice, it was only possible to programme a V-1 to hit the London area in general. The focused targeting of specific individual sites was far beyond the semi-robotic missile's capabilities, making it much more useful as a 'terror weapon' designed to induce mass civilian panic than as a means of destroying important facilities in pin-point raids. Even then, only 20 per cent of V-1s launched actually managed to hit the English capital, with thousands crashing not long after take-off. Intrepid Nazi aviatrix Hanna Reitsch (1912–79) volunteered to solve such problems by strapping her glamorous blonde self to a V-1 and guiding it down towards a precise goal manually, like some unholy cross between an Aryan kamikaze pilot and a vengeful Wagnerian Valkyrie, but such a noble sacrifice was not to be, with Hitler sadly turning down her offer.

The subsequent V-2 rocket was the world's first ICBM, or Inter-Continental Ballistic Missile, a supersonic device which at its best flew at around five times the speed of sound, having a potential attack range of some 225 miles or so. Importantly, the V-2 was the first man-made object to achieve a state of sub-orbital space flight – thus meaning that the Space Age, which we tend to think of as beginning during the 1950s Cold War rivalry between the US and USSR, was arguably actually initiated by Nazi Germany in the mid-1940s.

The project to build the V-2 was such an insanely ambitious one that it took a barely credible 65,000 separate design modifications before the missile – or, if you really insist, 'space rocket' – and its fatal on-board warhead could finally go into full production and enter mass deployment against London from September 1944 onwards. But, just as with the V-1, there were problems with the rocket's internal guidance system, meaning it could only be fired against generic targets like a large city, not at explicit ones like a munitions factory, thus making it no true substitute for precision-bombing raids. V-2s could also be unreliable during launch, and not infrequently veered off course completely or exploded in mid-air like faulty fireworks.

So, once again, this particular Wunderwaffe could not win the war alone, no matter how incredibly advanced a piece of kit it was. The V-1 and V-2 did kill and maim thousands of innocent civilians and reduce their homes to rubble, however, thus meaning that, in their other desired function as simple 'Vengeance Weapons', or Vergeltungswaffen, they in fact worked quite perfectly. But the main aim of warfare should be to actually win the war in question, not merely to slake a desire for revenge against the enemy, thus making it a matter of debate as to whether all the valuable time and resources spent developing these V-weapons might not have been better expended by Hitler elsewhere.

Although Whitehall initially tried to cover up V-1 and V-2 attacks as being mere 'gas explosions' to avoid a collapse in civilian morale, at least some Nazi Wunderwaffen projects were undoubtedly real, as all those Cockney corpses and smoking buildings conclusively showed. As such, chronicling their history should have given Rudolf Lusar plenty of potential material to discuss without needing to resort to any dubious mention of flying saucers.

Amongst the other genuine wonders produced or planned by Hitler's military-industrial complex as the war neared its end were the V-3 super cannon, given the false name of Hochdruckpumpe, or 'high-pressure pump', to disguise its true nature and purpose – that of being the largest artillery gun array ever built, consisting of fifty huge cannon lying protected inside a fortified underground hill complex near Calais, intended to pound London into submission with a constant rain of high-explosive shells. Whilst in practice the V-3 did not actually have the desired range to hit England's capital from across the Channel, and even had trouble firing off its projectiles properly without its gun tubes malfunctioning, its innate potential as a weapon of mass destruction was so alarming to Britain's high command that the RAF felt compelled to destroy it nonetheless, unlike with non-existent Nazi UFO bases. On 6 July 1944, 35 tons of bunker busting Tallboy bombs were rained down onto the V-3 complex during a raid by a group of Lancaster bombers from 617 Squadron, better known as 'The Dambusters', successfully rendering the site unusable.

Then there was the Landkreuzer P-1000 Ratte, or 'Landcruiser Rat', a planned giant tank so massive it would need to be equipped not with an ordinary tank turret, but a full-scale naval artillery gun of the kind normally used on battleships. Sadly, as the Ratte, encased within its intended 10in of solid Krupp steel, would have weighed around 1,000 tons, it would have been unable to fit through tunnels, use roads without ploughing their surfaces up, or cross bridges without making them collapse, causing the landcruiser to fall into the water below and become a sort of battleship after all – or, more likely, a submarine, given that it would immediately then sink.

Other Nazi Wunderwaffen, however, such as jet- and rocket-powered aircraft, worked very well indeed, but simply could not be manufactured in great enough numbers to help turn the tide of war, as we shall later see. Yet this failure of mass-production capacity did not alter the fact that, like the equally innovative and world-leading V-1 and V-2, many of these war machines were brilliant achievements in the realm of applied scientific research. The Luftwaffe was a particular beneficiary of such expertise. If you believe some accounts, German fighter pilots may even have been the first men to break the sound barrier in their craft, and there is no doubt that the nation's most prominent and celebrated aeronautical innovators like Alexander Lippisch (1894–1976) and Willy Messerschmidt (1898–1978) were inventors of great ability and ingenuity.[2]

So, Herr Lusar should have had no trouble whatsoever filling his pages with genuine German technological achievements and theories, about which, it must be said, the Major appeared inordinately proud. Indeed, clear eyed readers might be able to notice that his book was rather revanchist, even somewhat pro-fascist, in its subtext, but this did not prevent it from becoming something of a standard text on the topic of Wunderwaffen for a while – which was unfortunate, as certain elements of it appear to have been less than reliable.

According to Lusar, after the war Allied troops had turned up at his Patent Office workplace and carried off thirty trucks' worth of files, the entire contents of which, fortunately, he was able to fully remember. As these files now allegedly lay classified and inaccessible within US military archives, this gave Lusar ample opportunity to make certain things up and slip them in amongst pages of genuine technical information about V-1s and V-2s to sell more copies – namely, a completely unnecessary two-page section on Nazi flying saucers, a truly incredible class of Wunderwaffe which surely made up for the embarrassing fact that other projects like the unsuccessful V-3 super cannon and Landcruiser Rat never really made it off the drawing board.

It is self-evident Lusar simply gathered together 1950s newspaper stories about the topic, before adding in a few new extra details of his own for good measure. This can be seen by the way he misspells 'Belluzzo' as 'Bellonzo', a common typing error that had crept into press reporting of the legend. Lusar's intention to celebrate the innate German genius for engineering can easily be detected in his purple prose:

> Flying saucers have been whirling around the world since 1947, suddenly turning up here and there, soaring in and darting off again at unprecedented speed with flames encircling the rim of the saucer's disc. They have been located by radar, pursued by fighters and yet nobody has so far . . . managed to ram or shoot one down. The public, even the experts, are perplexed by an ostensible mystery or a technical miracle. But slowly the truth is coming out that even during the war German research workers and scientists made the first moves in the direction of these flying saucers. They built and tested such near miraculous contraptions. Experts and collaborators in this work confirm that the first projects, called flying discs, were undertaken in 1941. The designs for these flying discs were drawn up by the German experts Schriever, Habermohl and Miethe, and the Italian Bellonzo . . . Schriever and Habermohl, who worked in Prague, took off with the first flying disc on 14 February 1945. Within three minutes they climbed to an altitude of 12,400m and reached a speed of 2,000kmph in horizontal flight! . . . Schriever escaped from Prague in time; Habermohl, however, is probably in the Soviet Union, as nothing is known of his fate. The former designer Miethe is in the United States and, as far as is known, is building flying saucers for the United States and Canada at the A.V. Roe works. Years ago, the US Air Force received orders not to fire at flying saucers. This is an indication of the existence of [back-engineered] American flying saucers which must not be endangered . . . There also seems some hesitation to recognise that these novel flying saucers are far superior to conventional aircraft – including modern turbo-jet machines – that they surpass their flying performance, load-capacity and manoeuvrability and thereby make them obsolete.[3]

Lusar implies it would be psychologically difficult for the victorious Allies to admit that, in certain respects, their Nazi enemies were simply better than them – and so they never did, the whole thing was covered up. Notice how, by this time, Schriever had definitely personally tested out his own saucer in Prague (later versions even have him crashing it and dying then, not in a subsequent car accident, totally ignoring his apparently Lazarus-like 1950s media appearances) whilst Miethe, in light of the revelations about the AvroCar, had now gone to work for A.V. Roe.

Lusar's exciting passage, as intended, made news stateside, so much so that in March 1957 an official denial of its contents was made by the US war hero and military aviation trendsetter General James H. Doolittle (1896–1993), by then Chairman of the National Advisory Committee for Aeronautics (NACA), who said 'it just ain't so' that Germany had secretly developed both flying saucers and a long-range bomber capable of crossing the Atlantic to blast US cities without refuelling, as Lusar's text had also said. NACA called Lusar's claims merely 'an advertisement for a book', adding that, in the auto-biography of the engineer whom Lusar wrote had perfected the successful long-range bomber, there was no mention of him successfully having done so: as with so many Wunderwaffen, there were aspirations for such a thing, but no operational Amerika Bomber end product.

This was reported under headlines like 'No Flying Saucer Built by Hitler' which, whilst sceptical, may inadvertently just have given the book further free PR and thus helped it find an English-language publisher. Meanwhile, a follow-up US intelligence report of 29 March 1957 confirms no evidence of Dr Richard Miethe's existence could anywhere be found, A.V. Roe having 'no knowledge' of such a non-person ever having worked for them. Tellingly, when Lusar's book did appear in translation in the US in 1959, it was pub-lished not by a military history press, as may have been expected, but by the New York-based Philosophical Library, which normally specialised in more esoteric subject matter like philosophy, religion and spirituality.[4]

* * *

As the war progressed, many Nazis from Hitler downwards placed emphasis on 'quality over quantity' when developing new armaments, recognising the Reich's increasing disadvantages in manpower and resources. A nuclear bomb would have been handy, but the Jewish scientists helping perfect one for the US had already been expelled, so other avenues had to be explored, once inevitable defeat approached. As early as October 1943, by which point the invasion of Russia had obviously failed, a propaganda speech was given alluding to 'a collective secret of which the whole German people are already aware' – namely, that Hitler had some new arsenal of unbeatable

Wunderwaffen in reserve, just waiting to be unleashed, once the opposing Allied armies had walked right into the scientists' trap by stepping upon sacred German soil. Desperation and hope being close twins, excited talk about what Hitler's favourite architect and Nazi Armaments Minister Albert Speer (1905–81) contemptuously called 'the Air Magic being put together by Uncle Heinrich' became widespread.

The highly avuncular figure in question was Heinrich Himmler (1900–45), the head of the SS, an organisation that had increasingly insinuated itself into military production and research as the war progressed. This was unfortunate, as the mystically inclined Himmler believed it might be possible to recreate scientifically the lightning weapons of the ancient Norse gods like Thor, whose magical hammer Mjöllnir could spew out lightning bolts. In 1944, engineering firm Elemag-Hildesheim proposed the highly speculative plan of drawing electricity straight from the atmosphere before redirecting it towards enemy targets. Himmler loved the idea, not because he really understood its workings, but because he believed the Norse gods were the original ancestors of the white Aryan race, who had possessed 'paranormal powers and extraordinary weapons', since misremembered under labels like Thor's Hammer.

To Himmler, this was not a literal hammer with which the thunder god caused storms, but a 'highly developed tool' which used 'not natural thunder and lightning' but an artificial form, with his clever sky god ancestors possessing 'an extraordinary knowledge of electricity' which allowed them to tap into cosmic forces inherent within the universe. Ancient statues of such deities hurling thunderbolts might contain coded clues to their weaponry's principles; he asked this be looked into by his special SS archaeology and racial research division, the Ahnenerbe, or 'Ancestral Heritage Unit'.

Archaeologists don't normally design weapons, but Himmler despised the modern trend towards subject specialisation, preferring a more holistic world view in which anything an expert on Stonehenge had to say on physics was as legitimate as anything a physicist had to say on Stonehenge. Wherever a god was depicted 'holding an axe and appearing in a flash of lightning', whether 'in pictures, sculptures, writing or legend', this was proof lightning cannons were a better bet than atom bombs. As 'the Aryans did not evolve from apes like the rest of humanity' but were born from within 'living kernels' of cosmic ice within outer space, Himmler commissioned a feasibility study into the idea. It concluded the idea was not feasible.[5]

According to the debatable testimony of the French-Tunisian writer Philippe Aziz (1935–2001) in his 1978 book *Secret Nazi Societies*, Himmler once had pamphlets airdropped over German troops informing them about the visions of an old Swedish shepherd who had enjoyed future apparitions of unmanned, round aircraft launching fire against the Reich's enemies to reassure them that salvation via saucer was on the way.[6] You can see why Aziz thought he would be believed in this claim. Considering Himmler's own on-record enthusiasm for abysmal drivel like prehistoric lightning guns, it does seem plausible enough that, had the idea of flying saucers actually existed prior to 1947, he would have been only too happy to have commissioned the SS to try building one.

In certain areas of R&D actual technical experts were sidelined in favour of fascist fanatics, and the Nazi war machine thus wasted money and effort pursuing illusions. If to Himmler nuclear bombs represented unacceptable 'Jewish Physics' in action, then Thor's Hammer seemed like 'Aryan Physics' fighting back against it. But even the real Wunderwaffen did not prove enough in the end, as shown by the 1943 Battle of Kursk, when (at least according to the standard narrative, now somewhat disputed) smaller bands of technologically far superior German Panzer tanks had been overwhelmed by endless waves of cheap and cheerful Soviet T-34s like lions eaten alive by thousands of tiny lice.

Albert Speer warned that making the German public so many false promises would only end in tears; ramping up production of ordinary weapons may have worked better. Given his job, if anyone would have had knowledge about hidden fleets of Luftwaffe flying saucers equipped with special lightning cannons, or engine-scrambling spherical foo-fighter drones, it would have been Albert Speer. Yet, in December 1944 Speer convened a meeting of experts, concluding that 'You have certainly seen that we do not have, and never will have, a Miracle Weapon!' Disappointingly, 'miracles . . . are not possible', he admitted, perhaps thinking of debacles like the Landkreuzer Ratte. Unlike Himmler, Speer did not believe in the existence of Thor's Hammer (although confusingly this was actually the chosen code-name for a proposed much larger and longer range V-2 variant, also known as the A-9 or Amerikaracket, which it was hoped would one day strike New York).

Repeatedly, Speer urged abandoning the whole Wunderwaffen narrative, but was overruled in favour of mad propaganda schemes like mailing out anonymous letters containing supernatural 'prophecies' that V-weapon-powered victory was imminent. Speer could have explained that the military effectiveness of even the genuine V-weapons was actually rather limited, not only due to their frequent unreliability, but also on account of the restricted production capacity for such mechanically complex items caused by the relentless Allied saturation bombing of German component factories, but few wanted to hear him.[7] Germany did have those V-2 rockets, though, and some speculated that perhaps they possessed certain geheim, even more wunderbar, properties than had publicly been revealed. Following Hitler's suicide on 30 April 1945, rumours spread that he had in fact sneaked away towards the nearest rocket-launching site, to flee abroad upon a V-2. He would have needed to hold on very tight; V-2s had no capacity whatsoever for carrying passengers and exploded directly upon contact with the ground. Maybe he had just been spending too much time speaking to the similarly suicidal Hanna Reitsch?[8]

By the 1950s, this scenario had mutated into only slightly less ludicrous whispers that Hitler had actually escaped justice in a saucer; Austria's *Wiener Echo* published survey data on 10 October 1954 demonstrating many of its readers really did believe this. On 3 October, the paper had deliberately prompted such credulity by printing the silly claims of the 'French researcher' Georges Grondeau, who asserted Hitler's chosen destination was the South Pole, his Wunderwaffe saucer kept airborne in the absence of any fuel by the Earth's magnetic fields alone. That must have been how Thor flew his spaceship too.[9]

* * *

Why did the idea of V-weapon German saucers appear so plausible to some? For one thing, the Nazi Propaganda Minister Joseph Goebbels (1897–1945), who promoted the whole Wunderwaffen narrative to the public in the first place, was very good at his job. Discovering development of the V-1 and V-2 at Peenemünde, a wooded island in the Baltic, the RAF bombed it heavily. Accordingly, impenetrable underground factories and research centres were subsequently hewn out of rocks and mountains by concentration-camp slave labourers, where British bombs could not reach. Goebbels developed this basic fact into the rather less truthful notion of the Alpenfestung, or 'Alpine Redoubt', a supposedly impregnable network of underground cave fortresses in the Tyrolean Alps, from where top Nazis would resist the Allied invaders, before launching a successful Wunderwaffen-powered counter-attack.

However, the Alpenfestung did not truly exist as anything other than a vague plan, which Goebbels wildly inflated as part of a misinformation campaign to wastefully redirect enemy troops into the mountains, away from actual German positions. Yet it also boosted domestic morale, and some citizens believed in it. You would guess the Alpenfestung myth fed into later absurd post-war legends about Nazis supposedly hiding away from justice inside the Hollow Earth, but it fed into Wunderwaffen mythology too; who knew what wonders lay buried beneath Germany's mountains, far away from Allied spies?[10]

Apparently, some UFOs were stored down below, at least if we accept the 1995 report of a purported concentration-camp survivor forced to labour at Peenemünde himself, helping remove a long-range Wunderwaffe cannon to safety. Here, the Russian POW purportedly saw a 'strange-looking craft . . . like an upside-down washing-basin', being rolled out from a cavern complex on wheels one day, before launching and toppling over in a gust of wind. Very forgivingly, the POW ran to help the downed Nazi pilot, but it was too late, the bath-tub was 'swallowed in flames'.[11] One man who genuinely worked at Peenemünde was the SS' Wernher von Braun (1912–77), a rocket scientist of genius, not only one of the main fathers of the V-1 and V-2 missiles, but also of the later US space programme, helping put men on the moon for NASA. At the end of the war, the US extracted over 700 Nazi rocket engineers and other scientists like Braun from all over the Reich, spiriting them away to work for them across the Atlantic.

In August 1945, US President Harry S. Truman (1884–1972) authorised 'Operation Paperclip', apparently named after the paperclips which held these captured Nazi scientists' intelligence files together, on condition those 'Paperclipped' off to the US were not dyed-in-the-wool Hitler lovers. Many were, though. Braun himself was initially described as a 'security risk', complicit in the hanging of prisoners. As 20,000 slave labourers had been worked to death or executed at Nordhausen, the late-war centre of Nazi rocket production, it was impossible that many of the Paperclipped engineers would be entirely innocent. Nordhausen boasted a special underground V-2 factory named 'Mittelwerk', staffed by concentration-camp inmates who were forced to live and work on-site 24 hours a day in truly abysmal conditions. Mittelwerk proved so deadly that, come the war's end, more people had actually died making V-2s than had died after being hit by them.

So, the Paperclipped rocket men's records were whitewashed and their crimes covered up by the US military and, later, by NASA. Yet their creations proved exceedingly useful to their new masters in Washington: today's cruise missile is based on the V-1, and night-vision goggles came from the Vampir infrared gunsight, for instance. Hubertus Strughold (1898–1986), the former head of aero-medical research for the Luftwaffe, was later praised as being 'the father of space-medicine' and designed valuable life-support systems for NASA astronauts – yet the source of some of Strughold's knowledge had been horrific experiments conducted at Dachau on live human prisoners, who had been locked inside deadly low-pressure chambers and murdered in order to simulate the potential effects of high-altitude conditions on less easily expendable German pilots.

Conveniently for both UFO fans and Uncle Sam, meanwhile, some Paperclipped Nazis had even been developing a Silbervogel (or 'Silver-Bird') sub-orbital space plane, intended for use as an intercontinental 'rocket bomber' able to fly to New York and back in under 2 hours. It never made it across the Atlantic to blast the Big Apple, but German designs did serve as the post-war basis for the US' own later sub-orbital space-plane idea, known as the Dynosaur, as well as Russia's own similar craft, the T-44. The Silbervogel was in truth the nearest the Nazis ever came to making a fully functioning spaceship, but even this relatively low-altitude space plane, a more limited proposition by far than an actual interstellar anti-gravity flying saucer, did not work properly, with its designers being unable to solve key problems like the overheating of its rocket-boosters.

Because of the common failure of these innovative, high-risk weapons to function properly, as clearly seen in the fatal flaws of the Silbervogel and its kin, the term Wunderwaffe is now used colloquially in modern day German to mean 'pipe dream'. However, the existence and occasional effectiveness of such things was obviously not entirely fictional, as shown by the V-1 and V-2, merely much exaggerated; and, given the necessary secrecy and obfuscation which surrounded the Paperclipped war criminals, it was easy for gossip to spring up about what Braun and company were really up to inside their labs at NASA, once news of their recruitment spilled out.

Operation Paperclip provided the basic historical framework within which the saucer related folklore of men like Richard Miethe and his alleged employment by AVRO-Canada could later flourish. Indeed, some 1950s newspaper stories about UFOs specifically blamed Braun for such miracles' construction, which is hardly surprising. Who better to blame than the man who had built the earlier authentic miracles of V-weapons 1 and 2?[12]

Accordingly, a literal comic-book version of the Wunderwaffen semi-legend has since emerged – you can see it in the contemporary French sci-fi comic series *Wunderwaffen*, a 'uchronique', or alternative-history story, in which various incredible Nazi aircraft are deployed from 1946 onwards following the in-strip failure of the D-Day landings. Of the series, it has been said that, 'The plot is incidental, the characters merely cardboard; the beauty is in the beasts of the Nazi war-machine.' It sounds like Nazi ufology in a nutshell.

Indeed, to a certain degree Nazi rocket research actually grew directly out from the field of science fiction in the shape of the famous Verein für Raumschiffahrt, or 'Society for Spaceship Travel', formed in Breslau in 1927 as an organisation for amateur rocket researchers, of whom a 17-year-old Wernher von Braun was the most notable young lion. Some of the Verein's founding members were intimately involved with the making of director Fritz Lang's (1890–1976) classic German sci-fi movie *Frau im Mond* (*Woman in the Moon*), which used highly evocative V-2-like rocket models based on the Verein's own visual designs, and whose script involved the first ever '5-4-3-2-1-blast-off!' sequence at their explicit suggestion.

Thus, Braun's eventual V-2 literally resembled the most prominent and influential imaginary rocket ship in German celluloid history, as both flying objects were essentially versions of the same basic thing. As such, you can certainly see why some people might become puzzled about where it was that fact ended and fiction began. In 1936, the Gestapo, fearing the movie might reveal forbidden secrets of Nazi rocket research to outsiders, withdrew the film from availability and confiscated the prop department's model spaceships, as they were deemed too realistic for comfort. When the real V-2 eventually entered service, to boost morale engineers even painted images of a semi-naked woman wearing nothing but stockings and high heels on their side, sitting suggestively astride both the rather phallic missile itself and a crescent moon – this shameless rocket rider being 'Frau Luna', a lucky mascot directly inspired by Fritz Lang's *Woman in the Moon*.

Originally, the Verein had cannily used the hit movie as an advertising launch pad for their own projects, asking Lang to fund the launch of an actual rocket as part of the film's PR campaign, which would only have confused matters even further. This did not come off, but both the movie and the rocket club fed off one another's publicity to mutual benefit, and in 1930 the Verein contacted the German military, successfully seeking more research funding – the first steps towards the later V-2. But several Verein members possessed bizarre occult-type ideas and became involved in madcap schemes such as a plan to fire a rocket downwards into the ground from the city of Magdeburg in an attempt to penetrate the Earth's crust and thus prove our planet was really hollow, an idea not without its fans in the Nazi Party. If their theory was correct, the upside-down rocketeers hoped, then the device would pop straight back out again from the sea near New Zealand. The Verein's media profile could thus easily be abused (albeit somewhat unfairly) to make them sound like a bunch of prototype Bond villains and mad Nazi scientists, of a kind now familiar to us from many a cheap 1950s b-movie horror flick.[13]

* * *

A key text in spreading the idea of such comic-book Nazi Frankensteins further was a May 1947 article in the US pulp mag *Astounding Science Fiction* by the German rocket scientist and wartime exile Willy Ley (1906–69), a former Verein member and major contributor to the production design of Fritz Lang's landmark film himself, but one who, unlike so many of his former colleagues, had refused to serve Hitler's subsequent plans for Aryan domination of the solar system, fleeing first to England and then on to America in 1935. *Pseudoscience in Naziland*'s lead-in explains how Nazism 'did accomplish a remarkable series of scientific advances', using an approach 'strictly on the shotgun technique: if you shoot enough holes in the unknown, something's apt to drop in your lap. And the Nazis tried everything – anything, no matter how wild!'

Ley doesn't mention flying saucers – annoyingly, they were not due to be invented by Kenneth Arnold until the next month – so preferred to focus on Nazi programmes for finding Allied shipping by dangling pendulums over sea charts, and Verein-echoing attempts to exploit the false idea we lived inside a Hollow Earth to spy on the British fleet from a great distance via cunning exploitation of the consequent fact that the horizon wasn't actually curved. The closest Ley came to UFOs was his tale of an old German occult group who promoted a magical substance called 'Vril', which had allegedly once been kept 'as a State secret' by Britain to maintain her Empire, the same thing being done by the Romans who hid their Vril 'enclosed in small metal balls which guarded their homes' disguised as household gods; a few weeks later, Ley would surely have linked these back to the similarly spherical and metallic foo-fighters.

The article came complete with appealing cartoons of sinister monocle-wearing German admirals waving pendulums over maps, and diagrams of a black and star filled 'PHANTOM UNIVERSE' which orbited within the Hollow Earth, tricking us into thinking it was outer space. Ley didn't believe in any of this insanity himself, he just said many of his old countrymen were loony enough to do so. You don't have to be mad to work for the R&D wing of the German military, then – but it helps:

> When things get so tough that there seems to be no way out, the Russian embraces the vodka bottle, the Frenchman a woman and the American the Bible. The German tends to resort to magic, to some nonsensical belief which he tries to validate by way of hysterics and physical force . . . It was the willingness of a noticeable proportion of the Germans to rate rhetoric above research, and intuition above knowledge, that brought to power a political party which was frankly and loudly anti-intellectual . . . Small wonder the pseudoscientists experienced a heyday under such a regime – but it would be a mistake to believe that these pseudosciences which I am going to describe originated with the Nazis. They existed, and to some extent even flourished, before Hitler. But then they were hemmed in by the authority of the scientists – after Hitler had become Führer, it was almost the other way around.[14]

There was some truth to Ley's words: Pendulforschung, or 'pendulum-dowsing', really was experimented with by the German Navy. U-boat captain and amateur dowser Hans Roeder (1888–1985), misunderstanding how the British were using sonar to locate German submarines, guessed the enemy must be using pendulums themselves, so gained permission to perform dowsing trials as a military counter-measure, although eventually his unit of psychics was disbanded as the technique simply didn't work. Meanwhile, Himmler decreed every SS geological unit must include a dowser, and ordered attempts to divine gold reserves in the River Rhine, inspired by old Wagnerian-tinged legends of Rhine Maidens and dwarfs guarding 'fabulous treasure' there.[15]

One strain of Nazi knowledge was termed Grenzwissenschaft, or 'Border Science', partly intended to push back against the disenchantment of Nature revealed by modern 'Jewish Physics', as promoted by various leading Jewish scientists whose researches into the subatomic world drew official disapproval from the fascist German State. The term was promoted by the leading para-psychologist and poltergeist hunter Hans Bender (1907–91), who hoped that, by cloaking superstition with a technical-sounding 'epistemology of science', he could win funds and favour. The psychic-friendly Bender preferred hunches to logical thinking, with Hitler himself often conducting public policy in a similar fashion. 'Thinking is an indication of the decay of the brain,' Bender said; 'a panther is too clever to think'. Thus, if Himmler felt in his bones an idea might work, even though there was little actual evidence, it might get the go-ahead.[16]

If Grenzwissenschaft could be combined with Wunderwaffen, all the better; there was a Strahlengeräte, or 'ray device', promoted by a Luftwaffe officer named Schröder-Stranz, which he hoped could blast enemy planes from the sky. When it couldn't, the gadget was simply re-promoted as a means to beam out health rays to German troops, or else locate hidden oil reserves. Actually, like New Age crystal amulets, it did nothing whatsoever, but Himmler still liked it anyway.[17] Yet it is easy to over magnify such comic-strip adventures. Most real German scientists held Grenzwissenschaft ideas in contempt and, as things like death rays didn't really exist, it followed that nor could any real-life Wunderwaffen based on them.

But such comic books have been mistaken for reality, even by serious mainstream researchers. Most notoriously, in 1982 David Masters' book *German Jet Genesis* appeared, dealing with the history of German aviation, printed by Janes, the world's leading publisher of defence-analysis material, whose journals are subscribed to by militaries globally. Yet, amidst profuse details of real technology, Masters' book still provided two pages detailing the non-existent creations of Schriever, Miethe and Habermohl, accompanied by rather comical drawings. Details on German disc design were 'tenuous' and 'very sketchy', Masters admitted, so much so that he, too, misspells Belluzzo as 'Bellonzo', indicating he probably got most of this from Rudolf Lusar. Amongst the equipment on board such Wunderwaffen saucers were 'a laser system, radar, computers and electromagnetic turbines', apparently. The rest of his book is reliable, but by accidentally presenting the saucers as real, Masters helped lend the fairy tale further credibility.[18]

A more recent example is *Hitler's Monsters* by US History Professor Eric Kurlander (b.1973), published by the prestigious Yale University Press in 2017. This comes laden with over a hundred pages of notes, references and bibliography, yet has been criticised for being a 'myth with footnotes', a mere 'simulation of a scholarly work' or a 'simulacrum not only of scholarship, but of the Third Reich itself', which tries to make out the Nazis were far more occult-obsessed than they really were, thereby 'validating popular belief' in this regard. Kurlander does use some fringe books as sources, and certain of his references and quotes have been accused of being misleading. At one point, he apparently uses a fictional role-playing game guidebook, *The Nazi Occult*, as evidence of esoteric Nazi activities in Tibet. One critic taunted the book may even have been a 'practical joke to test the US academic publishing system'.[19]

I think this a little harsh, as the book appears generally reliable, just popularised a bit for the wider public, and I have used parts of it as a source myself. My information about Himmler's desire for lightning-based Border Science Wunderwaffen given above comes from Kurlander, for example. Unable to read his cited German-language sources first-hand, I just have to take it on trust his account is accurate; but maybe it is not, entirely. However, reading *Hitler's Monsters*, I was surprised to find Kurlander fell for some of the post-war saucer builders' yarns, giving seeming credence to a hoax account of a Nazi time-travel craft called 'The Bell' which used special mirrors to see into the past, rumours described as 'impossible to verify' rather than 'completely invented'. He also presents the designs of Rudolf Schriever as being potential solutions to the foo-fighter mystery.[20]

It is hard not to use fringe sources for books like these, but that even a tenured academic published by a high-status press can swallow such Wunderwaffen lies shows how confusing the field has now become. And, when general readers come across Nazi UFOs in otherwise high-quality books like Kurlander's and Masters', many will naturally conclude they are indeed worthy of belief. For me, it is a case of *caveat lector* even when reading my own book!

* * *

To approach the Wunderwaffen narrative in a more sober fashion, you could ignore Grenzwissenschaft entirely and explain instead how Germany had been growing into a genuine scientific superpower since the late nineteenth century. The Verwissenschaftlichung, or 'scientification' of the country, gathered pace from the 1880s, with developments in fields like industrial chemistry feeding into a booming military-industrial complex. Artificial fertilisers, for example, made Germany's citizens and soldiers better fed, made profits for farmers, contributed to the tax base and made Germany more self-sufficient during the First World War. Giant industrial concerns like IG Farben flourished, and by 1930, Germany was spending 1 per cent of GDP on scientific research, compared to only 0.4 per cent in its greatest European rival Great Britain. Scientific establishments known as Kaiser Wilhelm Institutes were established nationally, to ensure resource independence in as many fields as possible. The Nazis later inherited this vast infrastructure, and it was perfectly reasonable to fear they may try and direct it towards creating new Wunderwaffen.[21]

Under the terms of the Treaty of Versailles, the Allied victors of the First World War had forbidden Germany the right to build up their military or even to have an airforce (although a convenient loophole meant that research into rocketry was not explicitly banned, thereby giving a handy opening to the Verein of Braun to insert themselves into the nascent national aerial war machine). Thus, illicit Nazi developments in such legally verboten areas initially had to occur in secret, giving much scope for rumour and urban legend to develop.[22]

During the 1930s there were extensive scares centring upon sightings of uncatchable aeroplanes over Scandinavia, particularly Sweden. Many thought the 'phantom fliers' were Russian, but the panic began in 1933, the very year of Hitler's election, and it was speculated 'Flier X' represented Germany eyeing up Sweden's valuable reserves of iron ore. Actually, German aircraft lacked the capabilities to perform the flights reported at the time, and the whole thing was probably a case of mass hysteria. Had the idea of saucers existed back then, 'Flier X' may have come piloting one of those.[23] Non-existent German pilots had earlier buzzed South Africa during the First World War; villagers fled imaginary bombs, cursed Red Barons for burning their sugar crops and retrospectively reinterpreted simple stars as being advanced German air technology.[24]

In 1946, during the brief interregnum between foos and saucers, Swedish airspace was breached once again, this time by showers of non-existent V-2s known as 'ghost rockets'. These 'wingless planes' were occasionally said to be fugitive Nazis exchanging secret letters by the most inefficient means possible, but most blamed Paperclipped German scientists working for the Russians, launching V-2s over Sweden prior to nuclear war. Unusual meteorological phenomena sparked the scare off, and local earth tremors quickly became Soviet atom-bomb tests, with ghost rockets fingered for demolishing barns, starting fires, killing cows and dropping leaf-munching caterpillars onto crops. A child's blown soap bubbles were somehow mistaken for missile emissions, whilst the military initially investigated supposed crash sites, fanning flames further. By 1947 reason prevailed and the ghost rockets were no more. Instead, the Swedes were now seeing back-engineered Nazi saucers, not back-engineered Nazi V-2s.[25]

Earlier in the century, following promising German innovations in zeppelin design, Britain had suffered similarly. In 1909, when an aeroplane first crossed the English Channel, it was warned that 'England is no longer an island!', and sci-fi novels like *The War in the Air*, about cities being levelled by zeppelin bombs, by H.G. Wells (1866–1946), fuelled paranoia that Britain's naval supremacy may become outranked by German air superiority. In 1909, a kind of proto-UFO wave hit Britain, with phantom German 'scareships' being sighted, even though the Kaiser's pre-war Wunderwaffen lacked the capacity to perform the reported sorties. One dirigible even allegedly landed in Wales, whilst its obviously foreign-looking pilots 'jabbered furiously to each other' in the enemy tongue.

In 1912, a scareship sighting over a naval base at Sheerness led to future wartime Prime Minister Winston Churchill (1874–1966), then employed as First Sea Lord, being quizzed in the Commons. Leading airship inventor Count Ferdinand von Zeppelin (1838–1917), the Wernher von Braun of his day, contacted the *Daily Mail* to deny it was him, having already dismissed the 1909 panic by scoffing, 'I don't believe in ghosts.' German craft were easily the most advanced of the day, but the panic was baseless. Absurd stories about one landing in London and its occupant (who 'looked like a German') giving onlookers an Austrian smoking pipe, or Teutonic zeppelin debris dropped on the beach at Clacton later being sought by German spies, closely anticipate future yarns about FBI agents bothering UFO witnesses, or abductees retrieving ET relics from inside spaceships.[26]

It seems people were imaginatively primed to 'see' German-built UFOs even before UFOs existed, just not in discoid form. If there was anywhere on Earth advanced aerial craft were going to have their home in the first half of the 1900s, it was Germany. Militaristic minded Deutschland was the original home of so-called 'Big Science', the interplay between university labs, industrial R&D units, independent innovators and government funding being more developed there than anywhere else.

The country became a heartland of aeronautical research, with Ludwig Prandtl (1875–1953), 'the father of aerodynamics', properly formulating what certain aspects of air turbulence were in 1904. Prandtl's ideas had potential applications in many fields, but political pressure and control of funding pushed Prandtl into military research. Aeronautics was placed on the curriculum of universities and schools and institutes were founded to apply Prandtl's ideas. Post-war limitations placed on German air research were side-stepped and in 1924–5, Prandtl established the Kaiser Wilhelm Institute for Hydrodynamics in Göttingen, which became the Mecca and model for other such establishments worldwide, pioneering the use of wind tunnels.

Aeronautical research became a totemic issue for the public, who increasingly resented the limitations placed on it by the Versailles Treaty, much as sanctions-busting nuclear research is a rallying point for many Iranians today. But the Great Depression led to budget cuts, and for a time it seemed Germany may fall behind her rivals. So when Hitler entered power in 1933, overall aerospace opinion was overwhelmingly positive, as he made boastful promises to boost grants massively. Various new high-tech wind tunnels and cold tunnels were speedily approved, one of which was so huge it needed the entire annual Portuguese national cork harvest to provide its insulation. With this came a generous increase in staffing levels, with opportunities often taken to impose committed Nazis as project managers.

By 1935, when German air sovereignty was formally declared, Berlin finally stopped pretending it didn't have an air force, with Luftwaffe head Hermann Goering now able to divert funding more easily. Later, the captured research institutes of France and elsewhere were forcibly incorporated into the Nazis' own. The State initially sought to control the aims and admin of the aerospace industry, but not necessarily the specific scientific processes of investigation, giving engineers free reign to achieve what Goering wanted however they personally saw fit. Increasingly colossal pieces of dedicated manufacturing and research apparatus were built, the very essence of 'Big Science', these impressive facilities then being publicised by the Nazis for propaganda.

But once war was declared and it was realised the German rate of aircraft production was relatively low, scientists were told to concentrate on developing a few key fields, not hundreds of tiny innovations or pieces of 'pure science', with long-term breakthroughs sidelined for short-term priorities. Thus, if a lone genius really had designed a saucer, he may have been more likely to get funds to build it before the war, not during it.

And yet, many German scientists were able to fudge the paperwork and pursue their own pet projects anyway. Goering wanted a linear path of 'scientific discovery – technical development – mass production', but aircraft development is a delicate dance between all three. Obsessive secrecy and deliberately stoked Darwinian competition between rival firms led to disorder, waste and unnecessary duplication of research; by playing top Nazis off against one another, scientists discovered they could win patronage for their own favoured ideas anyway. Realising their error, the Nazis gave their scientists looser leash once more. Amidst all the 'Big Science' there was again some room for 'Small Science' too.[27]

Thus, the somewhat schizophrenic nature of the industry means you can argue whatever you like about it. The fact that Big Science Nazis made V-2s indicates they may have been able to make saucers if they put their mind to it, a believer could argue; a sceptic could protest that V-2 Big Science left behind masses of workshops, plans, working models and dead slave labourers in its wake, not to mention the V-2s themselves. A believer may therefore prefer to say Small Science actually developed the UFOs after all, then, thus accounting for the lack of such evidence; a sceptic may ask how Small Science managed to build something even more technologically complex than the V-2 in someone's back shed.

* * *

So what does the actual production history of a real-life Wunderwaffe look like? Let us examine the impressive Me-262 jet-fighter, which could fly a massive 100mph faster than any rival Allied plane. The Heinkel He-178, the world's first jet plane, took her maiden flight in 1939, but was abandoned due to technical problems. The Me-262 itself entered full service in mid-1944, but took a long time to get there. In 1938, commissioned work on a new German jet plane began, with some engine-design tasks being given to Junckers, who subcontracted more engine work out to BMW, with Messerschmidt asked to design an air frame to carry them. Mindful of the unsuccessful He-178, which had a single centrally mounted engine in the rear fuselage, it was decided to use two separate jet engines, one in either wing.

The air frame design was produced, together with a wooden model, by Messerschmidt in June 1939, with a contract awarded to build three full-size air frames for testing in March 1940. But these needed BMW's engines to fly, which were repeatedly delayed. They were too underpowered to actually lift the plane until 1943, and even then proved too heavy to be mounted within the wings, so nacelles had to be developed to carry them beneath instead. Eventually, Messerschmidt went with Junckers engines. On 22 April 1943, Adolf Galland (1912–96), operational head of the Luftwaffe, flew his own personal Me-262 test flight, declaring it felt 'as if an angel were pushing me', and convinced the Air Ministry to put in a full order for more – but the USAF bombed the Messerschmidt factory at Regensburg, destroying the necessary tooling.

Hitler then caused further delay by personally demanding the plane be repurposed into a fighter bomber, obsessed as he now was with bombing England as revenge: 'In this aircraft, which you tell me is a fighter, I see the Blitzbomber', he airily informed its designers in typically delusional fashion, in spite of the craft's inherent unsuitability for such a role. In 1944, production was split into two versions, the Schwalbe ('Swallow') fighter plane and Sturmvogel ('Storm Petrel') fighter bomber. Even after this, fine-tuning of final production models had to begin, followed by pilot training programmes. On 8 August 1944, Lieutenant Joachim Weber scored the Me-262's first kill, taking down a British Mosquito; total kills are known to be at least 735. Overall, 1,430 Me-262s were built, in 7 separate main versions, around one-third of which actually saw service. Over 100 were lost. It is estimated that, without BMW's delays, US bombing and Hitler's meddling, the plane may have entered service six months earlier, perhaps allowing the war to be prolonged for another half a year – just enough time for Berlin to have been nuked like Hiroshima and Nagasaki.[28]

Compare this actual tangled Wunderwaffe production history to that of, say, Rudolf Schriever, which essentially amounts to a man approaching a newspaper with a childish drawing of a flying saucer and saying, 'Look at me, I did that', without any plausible accompanying documentary evidence whatsoever. The Me-262 is totally different. Real, named individuals like Adolf Hitler and Galland are on actual record as being involved. There is an extensive paper trail in German archives. There are official manufacturing contracts, invoices and receipts. There are necessary redesigns, rivalries, production problems and known combat records. There are dead pilots. There was a successful USAF assault on production facilities. There are photographs, proper blueprints and remaining physical examples of the plane, in multiple different versions. The V-7 saucer and its derivatives have none of this. Some Wunderwaffen just didn't exist.

* * *

Once a few decades had passed, and an entire generation had been raised with no direct personal memory of the Second World War, the time was ripe for the Wunderwaffen motif to be exploited anew. The German-born Canadian resident Ernst Zündel (1939–2017) was a prominent neo-Nazi who owned his own underground press, named Samisdat, which specialised in raising money to fund his prominent Holocaust denial activities by pumping out a stream of cheerfully ridiculous books about the Nazi UFO legend, in which he did not actually himself personally believe.

Nonetheless, by attracting the attention of naïve UFO fans by saying Hitler may have helped invent flying saucers, Zündel hoped to make them question the standard narrative of history and become fascists themselves. Failing that, he at least got some more handy cash from book sales to help pay for his lawyers the next time he ended up in court for saying the death camps weren't real. By implying the Nazis were a race of scientific and engineering geniuses, he sought to paint them as a genuine Master Race to the gullible.

Accordingly, Zündel's 1975 underground publishing hit *UFOs: Nazi Secret Weapon?* contained not just copious information about Nazi saucers but various other imaginary Wunderwaffen, like 'flying bombs with built-in computer controlled TV cameras', amazing levitating Himmelsturmer jet-pack troops and a unique 'Pandora's Box' miracle-explosion weapon used to put down the disgraceful rebellion of Jews against their guards in the Warsaw Ghetto. It even turns out the Nazis invented the jumbo jet. So foolproof were German air defence Wunderwaffen that, had only the war lasted a single month longer, 'many experts' felt that 'not a single Allied plane' would have been able to 'penetrate the borders of the German Reich'. Major Rudolf Lusar's book told the truth about all this, but had been 'suppressed' in English; Zündel had been forced to beg his own copy direct from the author. So censored was knowledge about the Wunderwaffen that, in some places, Zündel was obliged to cite his own other fiction-filled books, written under different false names, as his sources of factual info.[29]

Other sources seemed equally unusual, such as 'Dr Philips', who provided diagrams of a curiously penis-shaped solar powered rocket ship he had built Hitler in the 1930s, and which had been successfully flown to the moon. Having known Hitler from their shared time in the trenches, Dr Philips had been gifted a 'special pass' by Hitler, giving him 'sweeping authority', which currently lay locked away in a bank vault. Astronomers' sightings of 'several colourful spots' on the moon matched up with timetables for penis-rocket activities which the doctor mailed out to Zündel.[30]

Another informant was Dr Friedrich Kuhfuss, who fled to Franco's Spain after his family was killed in a US air raid, vowing never to be Paperclipped by 'those barbarians from across the seas or those peachy-complexioned hypocrites along the River Thames'. Kuhfuss revealed the existence of 'Base X', a clandestine research centre located in a haunted SS castle 'somewhere in one of the many hilly areas of Germany'. The ghosts were supposed to keep the locals away, but Himmler's Black Order grew careless. SS scientists habitually went to the village inn with briefcases containing secret documents handcuffed to their wrists before one day they requested all the plates from the kitchen and recklessly stood outside playing Frisbee with them, so demonstrating the basic principles behind UFO propulsion.[31] Conclusive proof that Heinrich Himmler was directly behind the foo-fighters came in the strange fact they were nicknamed 'Himmler's baby', and his surname is derived from Himmel, meaning 'sky/heavens', the very same place where foos were usually seen.[32]

Most atypically for a UFO book, Zündel's title opens with a full-length reprint of the Nazi Party manifesto. This may seem irrelevant, but it 'would be stupid' to discuss UFOs without first discussing the policies of Adolf Hitler himself, as German saucers were a direct expression of the Führer's unique world view, or Weltanschauung. The 'non-German world' had a 'rather sketchy and fragmentary picture' of Hitler's amazing mega-brain, with 'this extraordinary man' being traduced in standard history books, most of which are 'more-or-less fictional accounts', unlike Zündel's own record of saucers pointlessly leaving behind swastika-shaped landing-marks on the ground.

'Many publishers' were offered his thesis, said Zündel, but 'none dared publish it', although 'all thought the material had merit'. Nonetheless, 'against threats and persecution' Zündel and his 'courageous group' of co-researchers 'of diverse ethnic backgrounds' (German *and* Austrian, no doubt!) had 'stood firm' and self-published with Samisdat. Mainstream presses didn't want you to know that Hitler 'was above all else an intuitive, artistic human being', who reshaped German society in his adorable image.

The Reich was governed according to the Führerprinzip, or 'leadership principle', being 'literally run by one man'. What Adolf said went – and when he said to his underlings 'build me some flying saucers', he expected them to do so. For Hitler, two words did not exist – unmoglich and niemals – 'impossible' and 'never'. Nazism was the direct embodiment of Hitler's belief in 'mind over matter', a magnificent, noble movement which would literally make the impossible possible. It was Hitler's 'scornful' response to being told saucers could not be built which ensured that they *could* be built.

So, to read about Wunderwaffen was to educate yourself about the positive nature of National Socialism, meaning 'the unprejudiced individual' will 'never again look at the world with the same eyes', Zündel's book serving as 'a catalyst to study and re-examine many events from a new perspective'. To read the Nazi Party manifesto was thus surprisingly 'necessary to solve the UFO riddle'; likewise, it was essential to comprehend Hitler's hatred of the Jews as 'a very important aspect of the whole UFO story' as, without this motive, Hitler would never have ordered saucers be built to defend the white race from Jewish domination in the first place.[33] Anyway, Hitler was not a 'narrow-minded, racist bigot', nor even a 'moustachioed dictator', but 'a prophet, with a global vision'.[34]

The attentive reader might also realise the victorious Allies, being controlled from behind the scenes by an all-encompassing Jewish world conspiracy, were evil. German defeat by mass-produced ordinary ordnance represented 'quantity winning over quality', leading to 'mass [having] overwhelmed spirit' in typical Jewish fashion – but only, Zündel promised, 'for a space of time'. The V-1 and V-2 had been 'payment against England's treason' and revenge for 'the aimless and merciless killing of German civilians' by 'the US Air Terrorists'. The victors were the true criminals, and their own weapons more wicked than wonderful. Winston Churchill even planned to unleash deadly biological warfare against Germany, and 'it was only a lack of germs' which stopped him.[35]

The hidden reason the Allies declared war on Germany was so they could Paperclip all their Wunderwaffen scientists away. Besides bombing 'their troublesome competitor' German industry out of existence, the Allies 'committed the greatest hijacking crime in all recorded history' when they stole the thirty trucks' worth of patents from Rudolf Lusar's Reich Patents Office, for which 'not a cent was ever paid'. The stingy Yanks only gave their genius prisoners slave-labour wages of $2.20 per day, whilst the cruel Russkies worked them 'around the clock' for three bowls of soup and a single slice of 'dark bread'. On one black night alone, the Soviets kidnapped away 275,000 German technicians, their wives and children. Once they had built the victors their own Wunderwaffen, these scientists then remained 'in quarantine' for years with 'no pencils' until they eventually forgot how to make any more. These Allied 'devils in human form', Zündel complained, were 'the same men who had wailed . . . about the Germans using forced labour in concentration-camps. What hypocrites.'[36]

Many German wartime scientific discoveries were not even offensive in nature, but benevolent, such as a new industrial process which somehow transformed coal into butter; Zündel had forgotten Hermann Goering's famous 1936 speech arguing that, if forced to choose between guns and butter, the German people had best choose guns. 'Butter merely makes us fat!' Goering had said, no doubt thinking of himself, but for Zündel the Nazis had made Germany both well-fed and well-armed: 'for the first time in centuries no German ever experienced want and hunger . . . until the Allies burnt or robbed all the huge warehouses of their contents in 1945 and after'. To prove this, Zündel reproduces several (apparent) photos of starving Aryan toddlers rummaging for scraps in bins, arguing rations given out to conquered civilians were only 850 calories per day, whereas well-fed prisoners in Nazi concentration camps got 'more than double' that daily, in spite of all the 'bony corpses you are still seeing daily on TV'.[37]

But do not despair, o ye fascist faithful. The in fact somewhat retarded Wernher von Braun and his 'conventional' Paperclipped NASA Nazis may have been double agents who were only giving away mere 'wasteful firecracker rocketry' to the naïve, moon-struck Americans to distract from how the genuinely advanced Wunderwaffen scientists had escaped Europe in their UFOs, something overlooked during the Allied orgy of 'booty-hunting, rape and conquest' at the end of the war. Whilst Zündel admitted this may 'read like a story out of a sensational publication (the type usually dealing with crime and sex)', Hitler himself had surely fled on one of these saucers himself too, rather than entering Valhalla, as Goebbels had cunningly lied in 1945.

Following the war's end, an eccentric lawyer named William J. Brock had sent President Truman $5,000 to establish a 'Capture Hitler Fund', believing the surviving Führer's venal followers would soon turn him over out of 'selfishness, greed and avarice' if offered an appropriate reward. But why would Brock have wasted so much cash if Hitler was not still alive, and sleeping in a UFO?[38] This explained why saucers rarely landed, the pro-Nazi author argued: the 'aliens' aboard were humans anyway so already 'know what Earth is all about'. Thanks to the escape of the Aryan ufonauts and the Führer, 'The final outcome of WWII is yet to be declared' promised Zündel. One day, the Nazis would re-emerge and 'take revenge . . . With UFO power!'[39] We're still waiting.

* * *

The leading writer of English-language Wunderwaffen books today is self-declared American 'Saucer Kraut' Henry Stevens, author of *Hitler's Flying Saucers: A Guide to German Flying Discs of the Second World War* and *Hitler's Suppressed and Still-Secret Weapons, Science and Technology*, both published, in 2002 and 2007 respectively, by US firm Adventures Unlimited, who specialise in texts about aliens, conspiracies, free energy, ancient civilisations, fringe science, Atlantis and alternative history, Nazi or otherwise. Stevens used to run a California-based organisation called the German Research Project, distributing videos, books and pamphlets on Nazi UFOs. Able to read German, Stevens has corresponded with some of the old-time German saucer creators, and helped uncover the truth about Himmler's desired Thor's Hammer electricity gun, which it transpired was no such thing.

Stevens provides original copies of letters between SS bureaucrats and the Elemag-Hildesheim engineering firm, plus an English translation. Elemag's basic idea was to emit 'ultra-short electronic oscillations' to force the atmosphere in the vicinity of an enemy plane to become ionised in such a way it would disrupt their engines' insulation, causing failure. Elemag wanted funding to see if this was possible in principle, not to build such a foo-fighter drone immediately. Himmler appeared interested, but a report from Dr Werner Osenberg (1900–74), of the Reich Research Council, to Himmler's Personal Administrative Officer – and dedicated collector of dead Jews' skeletons – Rudolf Brandt (1909–48) made it clear he would not recommend going ahead with the proposal as it would 'take decades' to successfully build the Wunderwaffe in question.

A further assessment, by a Dr A. Meissner, complained Elemag's proposal was 'not for the technical person decidedly important', being 'meant for the lay-person' – presumably being intended to catch the eye of the total layman Heinrich Himmler, not any actual scientists. During the First World War, complained Dr Meissner, a similar con-trick had been perpetrated upon the German High Command, who became convinced that a 'death ray' could be built, wasting resources upon this unworkable panacea 'in spite of severe protests' from experts.[40] Stevens still thinks such an electronic engine-killer may have been invented anyway and christened the Motorstoppmittel – a version was used to make Mrs Mussolini's car break down on a motorway one day to impress her dictator husband, leading the Pope to call it 'the work of the Devil' – but at least he doesn't try and say Himmler had access to Thor's Hammer.[41]

However, being literate in a foreign tongue also means Stevens can read the untranslated writings of various German-language fantasists and introduce their own doubtful Wunderwaffen to the English-speaking world too. One such apparatus was 'The Electromagnetic Vampire', a special cage laced with an energy field used to defend high-security areas. If you enter it, your body 'encounters an almost null-point of energy' able to 'suck the life out of intruders' which was 'as a rule, for the worst'. Two East German divers entered one flooded Nazi basement seeking treasures, but returned bearing 'horrible grimaces' with a 'terribly distorted expression' which proved permanent, both ageing by fifteen years in only a few minutes. Their memories of what they had seen were also completely wiped, making the Vampire the perfect 'home-security system'.[42]

This is a fantastic story. But who is its source? A man named Axel Stoll (1948–2014), who is totally unknown in the US and Britain, but famous in Germany . . . for being mentally ill. Stoll is a popular online German meme, thanks to YouTube videos of his lectures being mined for comic utterances such as 'The velociraptors had their own language', 'What are the pyramids – who knows?', 'The woman's hair, you have to understand, is magnetic', 'Magic is physics by wanting' and 'Television is an electronic Jew'. A qualified geologist, he nevertheless believed that the 'prison-planet' Earth was hollow and full of flowers (and Germans), that Jews caused earthquakes, that AIDS was a hoax, that the sun may be cold and that NASA never colonised the moon because Hitler had got there first.

Stoll belonged to the Neuschwabenlandtreffen, a fringe group who argued for the existence of secret Nazi polar bases and distributed literature explaining Jesus of Nazareth was a fascist. Instead of an abbreviation of 'National Socialist', it turns out the word 'Nazi' is actually derived from 'Nazareth', with Jesus the 'Nazirite' really being 'the first Nazi', not the King of the Jews. All Christians were thus Hitlerites. 'You should be happy if someone calls you a Nazi,' one member explained, 'because Nazi means a sanctified person' like Christ. 'In my first book, *High Technology in the Third Reich*,

I eviscerated the Allies' lies against the German Empire,' Stoll once boasted. Accordingly, he had to seek the protection of the Knights Templar.[43]

Stoll hardly sounds like a reliable informant, and Stevens' 2007 Wunderwaffen book in particular is a strange blurring between genuine Nazi innovations and total fantasy, making the reader question consensus history itself. Amongst the more interesting Wunderwaffen discussed are 'endothermic bombs' to freeze opponents, 'icing gas' which, released over planes by 'robot aircraft', would frost their wings, knocking them from the sky, the Hexenkessel ('Witch's Cauldron') fuel-air bomb, a 'vortex cannon' powered by coal dust and Nipolit self-explosive concrete, which allowed you to build a bridge then blow it up when being crossed by invading soldiers. Medical advances like synthetic blood plasma and '3065', an ultra-cheap non-antibiotic alternative to penicillin, were also manufactured for military use, but have since been covered up by Big Pharma to maintain their high profit margins at the expense of the sick and dying.[44]

Some captured Nazi tech was so advanced it could only be introduced into the Allied supply chain by the US staging fake UFO crashes, then telling scientists who were handed their contents to back-engineer that night-vision goggles and transistors came from outer space, not Germany; to admit post-war US military might was based on Hitler's genius would have been politically unacceptable. The fact a key component in the manufacturing of the early, pre-silicon transistors of the 1940s–1960s was the aptly named met-alloid chemical element *germanium*, however, was most suggestive! Stevens isn't certain this is what happened, he says, he merely leaves readers to reas-sess the standard history books for themselves.[45] Nonetheless, the back-cover blurb, discussing 'the scientific flowering in Germany' under fascism, makes it all sound very exciting:

SUPER-METALS, LASER-WEAPONS AND COLD BOMBS – IN 1944?

Now we know what spooked the Allies in the closing months of WWII and why they were in such a panic to win quickly – they had assembled mind-blowing intelligence reports of Nazi development of supermetals, electric guns and ray-weapons that could stop the engines of Allied aircraft – in addition to highly feared X-ray and laser weaponry . . . There is even a probability that the SS black

alchemists of the Third Reich were experimenting with red mercury [a fictional liquid nuclear fuel] bomb technology. Very exotic
technologies are also discussed including German experiments in
time, sustained fusion reactions, zero-point energy and travel in
deep space.

All of which would have been news to Albert Speer – but he was just 'an
architect who got lucky', with the real inventors working behind closed
doors, out of Speer's loop.[46] Stevens correctly points out that, by the end
of the war, the SS had seized control of much military production, arguing they became an unaccountable Black Order black-ops organisation,
who 'never even bothered to notify the German Patent Office' about their
creations, thus leaving even Rudolf Lusar ignorant of the existence of the
Electromagnetic Vampire.[47] Stevens cites the unlikely testimony of someone shown into the underground Alpenfestung lab of a fiendish German
metallurgist. Here, the scientist had invented a new 'harder than diamonds'
wonder metal, 'IMPERVIUM', subsequently exploited by the Luftwaffe.
One day he was summoned to meet Hitler, who demanded IMPERVIUM
be incorporated into his saucer fleet too. It may also have been used as
armour for the Dosthra, a bizarre aircraft which 'resembled a giant insect',
mentioned in an obscure neo-Nazi novel of 1971.

But whatever happened to IMPERVIUM? Stevens found a website on
which a US company sold knives made with a trademarked alloy of the same
name. Clearly, yet more Nazi Wunderwaffen tech had been surreptitiously
introduced into US industry. Next time you carve your Thanksgiving tur-
key, best thank Heinrich Himmler. Had Stevens searched even more closely
online, however, he may also have discovered that, besides being used for
making high-quality kitchenware, IMPERVIUM was also what the Imperial
starships were coated with as anti-laser space armour in the *Star Wars* series,
and that mentions of this very same super hard metallic substance were
common in generic pulp space-opera stories from the 1930s onwards, being
a kind of sci-fi equivalent of the ubiquitous ACME products in old Warner
Bros cartoons. In other words, IMPERVIUM is clearly not real, is it?[48]

* * *

What are Stevens' motives? Some have viewed them negatively, theorising
his alleged 'eulogies of the SS, references to the Dark Power (Jews), the New
World Order and the sham of democracy indicate a sympathy for the Third

Reich'. Due to alleged online posts under the handle 'fivepercenter', Stevens has also been labelled a Holocaust-denier by some critics, although it seems more accurate to say that 'fivepercenter' (if he really is Stevens) merely disputes specifically that 6 million Jews died at Nazi hands, thinking the original source of this supposedly inflated figure, which was 'pulled out of thin air', to be 'the World Jewish Council, hardly an impartial body'. Prior to this, alleged 'Hollywood Jews' like the actor and bald liar Yul Brynner 'and pukes of his ilk' had 'floated a figure' of 2 million, but this already large number, once only 'whispered in interviews', had since been arbitrarily tripled.

The term five-percenter itself would seem likely to be taken from a bizarre Nation of Islam-spawned US black nationalist cult, the Five-Percent Nation, founded in 1964 by a New York resident calling himself Allah the Father to his followers, but whose birth certificate curiously bears the slightly less grand title of Clarence Edward Smith (1928–69). Simply put, the Five-Percenters think 85 per cent of the global population are kept in total ignorance of the true way the world works by a wicked 10 per cent who seek to hide this knowledge forever from them, and so keep their duped, sheep-like slaves under their control. The remaining 5 per cent of people, being more independent of mind, reject the ignorance of the mutton-headed masses and know full well what the nefarious 10 per cent, dubbed 'The Blood-Suckers of the Poor' by Mr Smith/Allah, are really up to, and do their best to try and wake up the hypnotised 85 per cent from their foolish life-long coma.[49]

So who are this blood-sucking 10 per cent? Whoever they are, they appear to control most of the world's newspapers, websites, film studios, publishing houses and TV stations. As a result, says Stevens, 'the overwhelming spectre of the mass media' still has most of us in its hypnotic grip – presumably, a full 85 per cent of us. Stevens would therefore perhaps like his readers to take a red pill, a term derived from *The Matrix* series of Hollywood sci-fi movies, in which the magic pill in question wakes sleepers up from the unreal computer generated fantasy world they slumber in. He specifically compares our fake media landscape to those laudably consciousness-raising films, whose appearance in cinemas would appear to be somewhat counter-intuitive, given that Hollywood is meant to be run by the evil Ten-Percenters in order to ensure the 85 per cent's eternal ignorance.

The Ten-Percenters must run our places of education too. 'Remember Galileo?' Stevens asks. Well, the Nazis were just like him, discovering scientific wonders then being forced to recant; not by the Vatican this time, but by someone else, someone who pumps false history into children's heads in school, as 'anybody with half a brain' knows. But who, specifically, is to blame for this all-encompassing global plot? 'The conspirators can be found at the nexus of military, industrial, political, financial and media circles', but their 'exact nature' is 'really beyond the scope of this book', so pop a red pill and work it out yourself.[50]

Occasionally elements of the truth slip through, as in the academic Joscelyn Godwin's (b.1945) excellent debunking of the myth of saucer Nazis at the South Pole, *Arktos*, which 'cites and uses the work of known Nazis'. In order to be able to do so, though, such authors must treat fascists' testimonies sceptically and 'mumble an anti-Nazi formula as penitence' to bypass the censors, complains Stevens (*Arktos* is currently published by Adventures Unlimited, just like Stevens' books, so they must be part of the world-spanning media conspiracy, too . . .).[51] There is a cover-up, it seems, aimed at denying people the knowledge that many of their most useful consumer goods were actually invented by Nazis, not by democrats, as with certain brands of luxury kitchen knife. As it is with knives, is it also so with stainless steel saucers? Maybe so. Stevens' conclusion is that, 'The final history of World War Two has not yet been written.'[52]

This is seen more clearly in Stevens' *Hitler's Flying Saucers*, where we are told that 'Technically speaking, we are still living off the corpse of the Third Reich.'[53] However, 'Thanks to the American media and what passes for history' today, not a lot of people know that.[54] Unbelievably, Americans were now so historically illiterate they were genuinely more willing to accept that aliens invented modern life than that Nazis did, although Nazis exist and aliens don't. Government agents had even infiltrated national UFO clubs to spread the lie saucers were extraterrestrial, not German.[55] But maybe being dim enough to agree was not the citizenry's fault:

> What major New York publisher has ever published on German flying discs as opposed to the libraries of books pushing the Extra-Terrestrial Hypothesis – a hypothesis totally lacking in proof? Let me pose the specific question: would Simon & Schuster [a Jewish-founded publishing company] ever publish a book on the German origins of flying discs . . .? If not, why?[56]

Maybe it was because the lines between media and government were now so 'blurred' that 'they can be considered as one'. To tell the truth 'is not the goal' of this corrupt and corrupting system, warned Stevens. Hollywood had become the conspirators' 'propaganda machine', parroting the 'simplistic mantra' that 'all the ideas of the Nazis were meritless, if not dangerous' and that 'the Nazis never had a good idea'. As such, the media had 'boxed themselves in a corner', as if they ever admitted the SS had made the first UFOs, not ETs, 'the question might arise as to if there is another good [Nazi] idea' out there too, causing 'a reappraisal' of certain other issues the Establishment thought they had 'succeeded in putting to bed'.

By labelling any query of the standard narrative 'revisionism', the authorities used Orwellian 'Newspeak' to doom anyone who spoke the truth to 'commit professional suicide'. Hence, 'no politically correct publisher' would touch a book like those of his German sources, 'at least in English'. Historians 'refused to give credit where credit is due' and anyone seeking to write about Wunderwaffen saucers 'runs the real risk of being branded a neo-Nazi', which Stevens would presumably therefore deny being himself.

This has all 'had a chilling effect on real UFO enquiry for over fifty years', during which endless ET garbage has been peddled. Why are they even called 'Nazi UFOs' when 'technology usually does not adopt a political name'? The atom bombs used on Japan were not called 'Democrat bombs' just because the US President who dropped them belonged to that particular party, points out Stevens. This was pure anti-German prejudice. Some in the bigoted, anti-Teutonic media acted as if the war had never ended. As Ernst Zündel also argued, 'The German watchword of those times was "nothing is impossible" and it was clear that in the Reich scientists took this saying to heart.'[57] But the US could never be allowed to know:

> Perhaps we can crystallise this nightmare for the power-elite in an image. Suppose that tomorrow a highly technically advanced flying saucer landed on the White House steps in front of full, live, media coverage. Their nightmare would not be a little grey alien emerging from the saucer, saying 'Take me to your leader.' Their nightmare would be a former SS scientist emerging from the flying saucer saying 'I have an appointment.'[58]

Bemoaning that 'the victors wrote history', Stevens consolingly promises that, due to cowardly academics staying well away from the subject, 'there is plenty of room in this field' for enthusiastic amateurs. 'The most important ingredient in this field is interest', not knowledge, as your previous knowledge about it all will be wrong anyway, thanks to years of your being fed fake Establishment propaganda. There are 'mountains of government files which remain unexplored', so why not scale them yourself? The 'censors did not edit out everything', they 'made mistakes', leaving tantalising hints unblanked. Stevens' book was only 'designed to get you started'. What are you afraid you might discover? That the Nazis were not monsters at all, but ordinary human beings like ourselves who 'got up in the morning and put their pants on just like the rest of us'? As they invented so much of our modern world, 'In fact, [the Nazis] are us', says Stevens.[59]

Are you a Nazi too? Maybe you just don't realise it yet, but will, once you've examined the true nature of Wunderwaffen ufology more fully. And, if the Nazis accidentally created our contemporary society whilst trying to win the war, perhaps they could help solve our contemporary problems as well? How about global warming, for instance? It turns out Nazi UFOs (if I may be permitted to continue using such a blatantly racist term) are environmentally friendly too, as we shall now see.

Chapter Five

Little Green Germans: Epp and Fleissner's Super Suction Saucers and Viktor Schauberger's Exotic Emissionless Engines

Throughout the 1950s Germanic geniuses just kept on coming forwards with their UFO blueprints, although as the humiliation of total defeat slowly faded into memory, their motivations became more financial than nationalistic. The prime example was Joseph Andreas Epp (1914–97), who on 24 April 1958 gained publicity after filing a patent for a 'terrestrial disc', supposedly the culmination of sixteen years' work. In 1953, Epp had already made headlines for inventing a triangular aeroplane; now it was the circular one's turn.

Over the next four decades, Epp repeatedly merged all the other fake saucer inventors' previous stories into his own until he became the ultimate mastermind behind the entire programme. Examining his various interviews and pamphlets, culminating in *The Reality of the Flying Discs* (1994), it becomes obvious he altered his story as and when he liked, leading to any number of contradictions in his overall narrative. As such, the version I give below may not be Epp's full story . . . because there isn't one.

The future inventor showed aeronautical promise even as a small and no doubt immensely annoying child living in Hamburg, where he was constantly bothering adults by asking 'How do flies fly?' and closely observing birds, seeking to steal their secrets. Whilst plane-spotting at Hamburg airport he met General Ernst Udet (1896–1941), a First World War fighter ace and, from 1938 onwards, Generalluftzeugmeister in the German Air Ministry, in charge of aircraft design and production for the Luftwaffe; it was Udet who had first been taken with the novel design of Arthur Sack's circular winged AS-6, unlocking resources to develop it. This was a convenient friend for Epp to have made for two key reasons. First, when he later had his idea

A 1901 French illustration of ball lightning; were foo-fighters simply some similar luminous meteorological phenomenon, encountered by bomber crews and fighter pilots at high altitude? (*Lantzy, Binadot and Bhumiya*)

The ultimately aborted joint US–Canadian AV AvroCar provides proof positive that you can indeed build an actual flying saucer if you really want to – just so long as you don't mind it being an absolutely useless piece of barely controllable junk. (*Avro Canada VZ9 AvroCar*)

The original vision of the military applications of the AV AvroCar later proved to be slightly over optimistic. (*Avro Canada VZ9 AvroCar*)

The US Navy had their own, ship-launched, flying saucer-like plane, nicknamed the 'Navy Flounder' or 'Flying Flapjack'. It did work, after a fashion, but was very awkward to control, later being completely superseded by much more functional helicopters. (*San Diego Air & Space Museum*)

Some Wunderwaffen and their genius-level inventors, such as the V-2 rocket and its proud father, Wernher von Braun (once of the SS, later of NASA) were clearly real, lending superficial plausibility to the idea the Nazis might also have been able to create secret spaceships. (*Cygni_18, BY-SA 2.0*)

Dr Wernher von Braun and his Saturn IB rocket, his dream having become a reality. (*Marshall Space Flight Center of the United States National Aeronautics and Space Administration (NASA) under Photo ID: GPN-2000-000045*)

Leading German engineer Ludwig Prandtl, formulator of the notion of the key aeronautical concept of the 'boundary layer', conducts another interesting experiment. His ideas were later abused by the supposed inventors of a specific sub-class of Nazi UFO, the 'Suction Saucers', which could purportedly fly without using any fuel, and therefore stood as being environmentally friendly. (*Attribution: By Aus dem Nachlass von Prandtl an der Universität Göttingen, Public Domain, https://commons.wikimedia.org/w/index.php?curid=50696*)

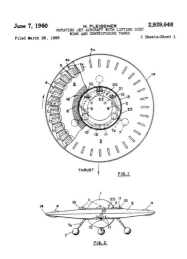

Heinrich Fleissner's 1960 US patent application for a 'Suction Saucer'. It must be borne in mind that ever busy patent clerks don't actually test out such designs to see if they really work, of course . . . (*Google Patents – US Patent 2,939,648 ISC June 7, 1960*)

The reason this exhibit in the UFO Museum at Roswell has a '?' at the end of its label is because the answer to this question is 'no'. This is in fact a model of a Haunebu, a completely different class of non-existent Nazi UFO altogether. How very careless of the curators. (*mr_t_77 from WV, USA*)

Was the object that crashed at Roswell really just a high-altitude military weather balloon? (*US Navy*)

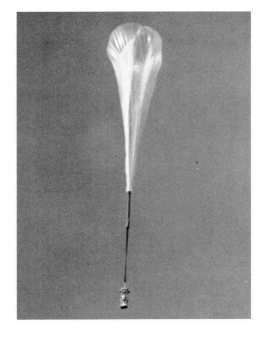

Dr Josef Mengele, the evil Nazi genius behind the Roswell saucer crash, in the opinion of one top US journalist. All those dead 'aliens' aboard were really just stolen infants disfigured by Mengele's surgical knife to look like ETs to spread panic across the US, apparently. (*https://commons.wikimedia. org/wiki/Category:Josef_Mengele#/ media/File:Josef_Mengele,_Auschwitz._ Album_Höcker_(cropped).jpg*)

Acclaimed South American post-modernist author and leading accidental Nazi ufologist Jorge Luis Borges. (*annemarieheinrich.com/ sitio/galeria.php?id=4*)

NAZI BELL

An artist's impression of the possible appearance of the Nazi 'Bell' time-travel craft, and a public monument to the 'Kecksburg Acorn', a Roswell-style UFO which allegedly crashed in the US town of that same name two decades after the war's end, in 1965. As they are very similar in appearance – note the alien symbols/Nazi runes on each craft's bottom rim – it has been theorised by some that both were in fact one and the same infernal machine. Was Nazi war criminal Hans Kammler inside it when it came down in the Kecksburg woods? If so, where is he now? And, just as importantly, how old is he? (*Left – Zusurs – own work; Right – own work, by uploader CC BY-SA 3.0*)

Polish author Igor Witkowski, for whom The Bell tolls. (*Danuta Anna Sharma – Igor Witkowski na I Konferencji Projektu Ziemia w Warszawie (ca. 15:00), CC BY 3.0*)

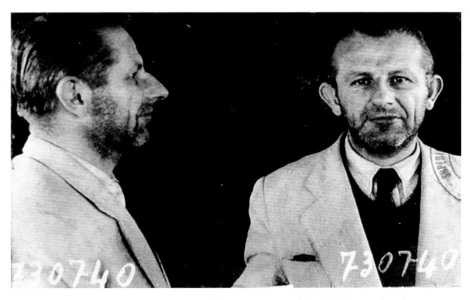

Police mugshots of the comically inept Nazi Abwehr spy Josef Jacob Johannes Starziczny, who tried to trick his way out of a Brazilian prison cell by promising to build his captors' government a free, combat-ready flying saucer, based on alleged top-secret wartime German designs. All he asked for in return was his freedom. (*Medical record 51.156 from the DEOPS-SP collection Department of Political and Social Order – State Police of Sao Paulo.* Electronic Annals of the 14th National Seminar on the History of Science and Technology, *Rodolpho Gauthier Cardoso dos Santos, 'Flying Saucer Inventors in Brazil – Science and Imaginary at the Beginning of the Cold War (1947–1958)'*)

for a flying saucer, Udet proved an excellent high-up contact to ensure it got made. Secondly, Udet shot himself in 1941, thus making him unable to contradict any of this story.

Leaving school, Epp became both a shipbuilding apprentice and a member of the Hitler Youth, but when his pacifist father found out, he burned his son's uniform. Shipbuilding being too easy, in January 1936 Epp began a technical training course at the aircraft engine-manufacturing firm Klöckner Humbold-Deutz, before transferring his immense skillset to the Luftwaffe that September.

Inspired by national heroine and wannabe one-woman V-1 suicide-bomb Hanna Reitsch's successful 1938 test flight of the world's first true proto-helicopter, the Focke-Achgelis Fa-61, in 1940 Epp made either the first workable mini-disc, or else plans for one, and showed these off to his childhood mentor Ernst Udet. The inventor was then rewarded by Rudolf Schriever and Otto Habermohl being ordered to turn Epp's breakthrough into full-size reality at the Škoda factory (or the BMW factory in some versions) in Prague. Following the loss of the Battle of Britain, Hermann Goering personally tried to interest Hitler in Epp's saucer as a means to drop an atom bomb on England, but the Führer wasn't interested, probably because Germany didn't have any atom bombs. Epp's saucer programme was initially managed by the Luftwaffe, then taken over by Georg Klein, who acted as an intermediary for Albert Speer, before eventually the SS took charge.

Schriever unnecessarily fiddled with the length of the turbine blades, making his prototype saucer unstable, but Habermohl sensibly followed Epp's original measurements, meaning his own model flew properly. In Dresden and Breslau, meanwhile, Richard Miethe and Giuseppe 'Bellonzo' (here, Epp inadvertently revealed he had just copied all this from the newspapers by repeating the frequent media misprinting of Belluzzo's real name) made their own attempts at scaling up Epp's original prototype, with Epp himself becoming rather sidelined.

The chief engineers named above all convened in Prague on 14 February 1945 when their combined efforts led to the first successful launch of a flying saucer. To mark the occasion, Epp took photographs, which look remarkably like someone has cut a rough saucer shape out of paper and then glued it to a window. Sometimes Epp carelessly claimed to have taken the saucer's photo in 1944, before it had even been built. As further proof, Epp also produced a personal letter from one of the saucer's test pilots,

Otto Lange, in which Lange confirmed Herr Epp deserved main credit for inventing the discs. Oddly enough, Lange's letter was produced in Epp's own handwriting.

Why did none of the other famous saucer inventors ever mention Epp's central role during their own prior 1950s media appearances? Maybe they just didn't want to be associated with such a shamelessly inconsistent figure. An alternative narrative has it that Epp had made his first prototype disc in 1939, or maybe 1936, in full-size form, crewed by two men and capable of flying at 2,000kph – or, sometimes, he had merely planned it. This prototype was called the 'Helioplane', with illustrations showing a disc with a miniature helicopter rotor on top, a bit like a novelty beanie hat.

However, Epp had problems sourcing appropriate turbo jets to initiate blast-off, and when he became aware of the work of the other key German saucer creators, Epp visited Prague to see what they were up to – rather different from handing his design over to Schriever et al. and inspiring *them*, as Epp at other times said. Stimulated by what he saw, by 1943 or 1944 Epp had already rendered his Helioplane obsolete with a second, larger, eight-engine, eight-to-ten-crew model named the 'Omega Diskus', which possessed full multi-directional flight capabilities at speeds of up to 3,800kph – although alternative dates and technical details are of course available. In 1958 Epp produced a 1:10 scale model to be photographed by journalists.

After Hitler's defeat, Epp had problems finding another job as a UFO inventor, so trawled bombed out cities scavenging scrap with which to create more saucer models, trading cigarettes and food for components on the black market. In 1948 Epp was in Barcelona, working until 1951 as a technical designer in a fridge factory. Back in Germany, he resumed toil in shipyards, before his 1953 unveiling of a triangular aeroplane won funds from duped investors, enabling him to start work on a larger Omega Diskus model to display to other potential backers. Epp then moved to East Germany, successfully helping the Communists build a full, working saucer, but the Russians were unwilling to allow their proxies to develop their own super weapon, and the project was abandoned – quite why Moscow didn't just scoop it up as their own, Epp didn't say.

East German secret agents also suspected the ex-Hitler-Jugend Epp of holding unacceptable political views, so he fled to Bremerhaven in West Germany to work anew on his disc in safety. However, Western spies now suspected Epp of being a Communist, and stole his blueprints.

It was not until 1958, when he made headlines for filing his saucer patent, that Epp was finally able to start large-scale disc designing once again. Now the East German spies showed back up, this time wanting to buy his prototype. In panic, Epp sought refuge abroad. In 1956, Epp had already legally patented his proposed propulsion system for the craft in the US, offering manufacturing rights to the USAF, only to be turned down. Apparently, the Americans were already secretly building his rival Richard Miethe's own saucer designs with AVRO in Canada, so didn't need any Omega Diskus.

This, at least, was the approximate new version of his life story which Epp spun to potential backers from 1959 onwards, when he travelled to France and Italy armed with his 1958 patent, seeking foolish investors to fund the enlargement of his Airfix UFO into a real one. As the space race heated up during the 1960s he then began promoting it as a potential solution to the quest to land a man on the moon; his circular helicopter thing had now morphed into a full-blown spaceship. Epp could not keep track of his own falsehoods. In one 1965 interview, he spoke of Schriever and 'Bellonzo' as still being alive, when both had been dead for over a decade; as he didn't know Belluzzo's real name, it was understandable Epp had missed his obituary appearing in the papers. (So ingrained had the myth become, by the way, that Belluzzo's obituary in the *New York Times* actually led with a recap of the noted Italian politician's 'invention' of UFOs!)[1]

In the 1990s Epp entered into correspondence with none other than Wunderwaffen-worshipping Henry Stevens; unconvincing twin photos of finished Nazi discs sourced from one of Epp's letters sit proudly on the cover of his 2002 book *Hitler's Flying Saucers*. Stevens, to his credit, noticed inconsistencies in Epp's story too. Less creditable were the explanations he then advanced to account for them. Based on their correspondence, Stevens reports there may have been fifteen different prototypes of Epp's ship built in Prague, and that the 14 February date given for its launch was simply that of the official test flight of one particular version, thereby accounting for some contradictory dates later given by Epp for when he took his photos of the Omega Diskus in flight. As for the apparently forged letter from the saucer's test pilot Otto Lange, Stevens proposes Epp had a 'chance meeting' with Lange one day, drafted out a note confirming his achievements on the spot by hand, then gave it over to Lange to sign.[2]

But there was another, rather greater, inconsistency. The photos of a completed saucer sent to Stevens by Epp did not appear to be of his own Omega Diskus at all, but of another Nazi craft entirely . . .

* * *

By the 1960s, as the notion of alien invasion took increasing stranglehold over ufology, the golden era of the fake German saucer builders was coming to an end – but not completely. The last significant ex-Nazi inventor appeared in newspapers as late as May 1980 in the shape of the 76-year-old Heinrich Fleissner, who had quietly filed his own US patent application back in 1955 for a manned discoid craft with a central fixed control dome surrounded by a rotating jet-propelled ring, powered by twin fuel tanks of hydrogen and oxygen.

So far, so Rudolf Schriever. To the paper reading public, Fleissner's only real contribution to the legend was to add new minor data about landing gear. Nazi UFOs now possessed special extendable legs, equipped with 'inflatable cushions' on the end to act as 'feet', allowing them to safely touch down on bodies of water, like certain aquatic insects. Unlike most of his earlier rivals, Fleissner also said his own long-limbed saucers could fly outside the Earth's atmosphere as well as within it; indeed, their top speeds were better in outer space, at 10,000kmph compared with 3,000kmph.[3]

To the expert eye of Henry Stevens, Fleissner's claims could be used to explain the anomalous photos Epp had sent him, which were actually images of a class of craft now known by true aficionados as 'suction saucers'. Stevens located a copy of Fleissner's 1955 US patent, which does genuinely exist – it bears Patent Number 2,939,648, coming complete with detailed labelled technical diagrams. It is important to note, however, that a patent doesn't actually have to work to be successfully registered – officials don't sit there and build their own spaceships to check they can really fly when someone submits an idea for one.

Stevens links Fleissner's patented craft back to Ludwig Prandtl, the German aerospace genius we met briefly earlier, experimenting with giant wind tunnels. Prandtl's chief discovery was that of the 'boundary layer', which related to the thin but powerful flow of air over the wing of a flying aircraft that slows it down due to turbulence, friction and drag. If it was possible to reduce or eliminate the boundary layer, by inducing a smooth process of air passage known as 'laminar flow', you would increase the speed and efficiency of your plane.

The Germans tried several ways to do so, including, as with the abortive Sack AS-6, designing somewhat circular wings. Less radically, but more successfully, simpler swept-back wings could also help do the job to a certain degree, as exploited by several innovative craft like the Me-262. Another brainwave was that of 'suction wings'; slots were cut into planes' wings and auxiliary engines utilised to suck the boundary layer of air in through the wing itself, redirecting it back out towards the rear fuselage. Yet this solution proved impractical, as it turned out multiple engines and slots would be needed on each wing.

Stevens' conclusion is that the Nazis therefore secretly combined their plans for suction and circular wings into one single, convenient form. If you imagine the circular saucer as a giant circular wing enveloping a central cockpit, it eliminates the need for any rear fuselage whatsoever, thus destroying a major source of drag. Fleissner was supposedly a fluidics engineer, fluidics being the specific sub-field of aerodynamics dealing with the boundary layer. Examining Fleissner's patent diagrams and the saucer images posted out by Epp, Stevens noticed both possessed 'slots running around the periphery of the saucer into which air was scooped'. Did this mean the saucer snaps actually showed Fleissner's craft, not Epp's, and that he had successfully developed previous German research into suction wings into a fully working UFO?

For Stevens, Fleissner's saucer could have taken off using ordinary fuel, then, after reaching a certain altitude, slowly allowed the liquid hydrogen and oxygen stored in its twin circular fuel tanks to bleed into its jet engines. At this point, after closing over its air slots, 'there is no reason this saucer could not become a spaceship', able to operate in the airless regions outside Earth's atmosphere, as Fleissner had promised.

But what if the slots on the circular wing also sucked in boundary layer air from the atmosphere, transformed it into liquid air using 'special equipment', and then burnt it within an internal combustion chamber? The hot air and steam could be used to turn a turbine – Italian disc designer Giuseppe Belluzzo's chief speciality, remember – which would then generate enough power to run an electric engine. Once the saucer had used conventional fuel for take-off, it could thenceforth draw all further energy from the atmosphere, thus allowing it to keep aloft forever; an aircraft powered by the sky itself!

If it ever needed an additional nitro burst, it could burn one of its conventional fuel reserves up briefly to escape pursuers, whilst aerodynamic forces generated by its circular shape would suck it through the air automatically, aiding flight further. The machines would become more like birds, which also need no refuelling, surfing along upon air flows. In Fleissner's suction saucers, 'turns would be made by turning the [otherwise fixed central] cabin as a whole, thus turning the rudder just as the prehistoric flying reptile the pterodactyl turned its flight direction using a rudder [i.e. crest] located on top of its head'.[4] The subtext is that the Nazis successfully developed a non-polluting, clean source of free energy which has since been suppressed. Stevens notes that, whilst Fleissner's US patent was filed on 28 March 1955, it was not actually granted until 7 June 1960. Perhaps AVRO exploited this lengthy delay to incorporate suction-wing technology in their AvroCar whilst avoiding infringing copyright laws and having to pay Fleissner royalties?[5]

One sub-genre of contemporary UFO lore posits that benign aliens worry intensely about our dying planet's health, and wish to help wean us off fossil fuels, but are being blocked. Perhaps the most surprising such theorist was Paul Hellyer (1923–2021), Canada's Defence Minister between 1964 and 1967. Once no longer involved in front-line electoral politics, in the years prior to his death in 2021 Hellyer became ever more free to speak his mind – and what a mind it was. A proponent of monetary reform and opponent of globalisation who warned Canada it may one day be annexed by the USA, Hellyer spent years penning works like *Jobs for All: Capitalism on Trial*, *Goodbye Canada*, *The Evil Empire: Globalisation's Darker Side* and *The Money Mafia*.

Whilst still Defence Minister, in 1967 the strange statesman unveiled a 130-tonne concrete UFO landing pad in Alberta, as 'a symbol of our faith that mankind will maintain the outer universe free from national wars and strife'. A UFO witness himself, Hellyer claimed saucers' engines were long ago back-engineered by (non-Nazi) human scientists, unlocking the secret of free, clean, infinitely renewable energy for all.

Yet, because global banks and the US Federal Reserve had conspired together since 1910 to control the world economy, news of this could not be allowed to leak out, as it would destroy the oil industry. 'The world financial system is a total fraud,' Hellyer argued in 2011, designed to make the rich get richer whilst the poor get poorer and the planet is raped to death with oil drills. Green alien kit could 'help preserve [the planet] as a happy habitat for Earthlings', yet vested financial interests did not care. Hellyer suggested an escape from the current economic impasse: 'In the unlikely event that these [power] sources are not yet commercially viable, all we would have to do is ask one of the friendly [ET] species to help us.' Rather than global militaries 'treating them as enemy aliens and doing our best to shoot them down', maybe we should 'adopt an acceptable level of intergalactic civility' towards our future off-planet economic partners instead?

There were 'about eighty' non-native eco-friendly humanoid races of 'star-visitors' on Earth, revealed Hellyer, some of whom, like the 'Nordics' and 'Tall Whites', could easily pass as 'being from Denmark'; one group of Scandi-Aliens with high levels of disposable income liked to dress as nuns and go secret-shopping in LA. If only government warmongers would reverse their policy of 'shoot first and ask questions later' towards their spacecraft, Hellyer promised, the aliens may one day gift us so much more.[6]

Paul Hellyer was not an anti-Semite, and when he talked of 'big banks', this was not code-word for 'Jews'. But it would be very easy to subvert Hellyer's basic argument. When delusional US saucer nut Major Wayne Aho (1916–2006) – known as 'Major A-Hole' to his many detractors, who said he had completely invented his military rank – began promoting investment in a fake 'Ultron Electrical Accumulator' powered saucer called the OTC-X1 in 1959 and was consequently committed to a mental ward, members of the extremely right-wing John Birch Society put it about that the true reason for his incarceration was that an International Jewish Banking Conspiracy simply wished to cover up his revolutionary discoveries.[7]

Claiming that greedy, fossil fuel-loving Jews run our world as puppet masters and are concealing the amazing perpetual motion engines of German suction saucers allows the Nazis to become the surprising, Green-friendly good guys, able and willing to save mankind from environmental apocalypse. However, the idea of 'Green Nazis' does actually possess a certain grain of truth to it. The term Blut und Boden, or 'Blood and Soil', was promoted by Nazi agriculture chief Richard-Walther Darré (1895–1953) in books like *A New Nobility Based On Blood and Soil* and *Peasantry as the Life-Source of the Nordic Race*, in which he suggested an innate connection between the superior Aryan race and their superior Aryan soil; ironically, Darré himself had been born on foreign soil, in Argentina.

In Nazi propaganda, rural life was contrasted positively with the negative 'asphalt culture' of the dirty, corrupting city, filled with literal smoky pollutants and more metaphorical ones in the shape of the Jews. Accordingly, the State Hereditary Farm Law of 1933 limited the privilege of being farmers only to 'those of German blood'. The Hitler Youth had to perform a year of land service and yokels were praised for having higher birth rates than their urban counterparts, whilst the desire for ever more soil within which the German volk could plant their roots was cited as justification for invading eastern lands like Ukraine, intended to act as the Reich's future 'breadbasket'. To Darré, 'To remove the German from the natural landscape is to kill him.' Some Germans considered their race the Native Indians of Europe, forcibly removed from their natural way of life by invading Roman and Christian colonisers who had increasingly forced them to live in cities and become that most despicable of things, 'civilised'.

Darré was also a supporter of something called 'biodynamic agriculture', a discipline derived from the ideas of the Austrian-born mystic Rudolf Steiner (1861–1925), who conceived of the soil of a farm as enjoying mystical communion with the heavens, with the growth of its crops directly influenced by the rays of the stars, a kind of agricultural astrology. Several high-ranking Nazis were sympathetic to Steiner's ideas, including Heinrich Himmler, a one-time chicken-rearing country boy himself. As biodynamic farms were supposed to be self-sufficient, they could potentially make Germany less dependent on artificial fertilisers, and thus have less need to import chemicals from abroad, which would not only be environmentally friendly, but also handy in times of war.

SS food bureaucrat Hans Merkel (1902–93), hating the way 'soulless' modern farms had 'become a factory', promoted biodynamic farming as a great way to create a 'new peasantry', connected to the soil of their forefathers and their collective ancestral spirit, dubbed the volksgeist. Biodynamically grown grass was used on athletics fields during the 1936 Berlin Olympics to much propaganda fanfare, whilst there were even experiments made in this area within concentration camps. The Green Nazis also passed various animal protection laws, whilst several prominent Party members professed to be vegetarians, a claim often also made for the pet-loving Adolf Hitler himself, albeit somewhat debatably.[8]

Yet from the 1960s onwards the post-war global environmentalist movement has grown apace, so some neo-fascists have tried to claim that the Green Nazis invented various Green Wunderwaffen as well as all those nasty CO_2-producing ones which went around exploding and belching out smoke all over the place like the V-1 and V-2. According to our old friend Ernst Zündel, for example, Hitler was always 'steering his scientists towards using Nature, not opposing it'.

Rather than firing unclean explosive shells at enemies, Zündel had the tree-hugging Green Nazis in his books utilise a Wunderwaffe Sound Cannon instead, which emitted non-polluting sonic booms and shock waves. Tested out on stampeding dogs and pigs, standing in for sub-human Russian infantry, the beasts ended up either 'frozen to the ground' or 'paralysed for hours'. There seems little historical evidence for this particular Wunderwaffe's existence, but that is only because it sounded like thunder when fired. When people during the war heard thunderclaps, how do we know it wasn't a Nazi Sound Cannon being used instead?

Similar was that other 'New Age weapon' the Aeolus Bag, 'used to fight off the seemingly endless hordes of Mongolians that were spewed forth from Asia's vast steppes', whose sound waves were so severe all opponents and their vehicles began 'disintegrating' on the spot. Again, this explains the lack of evidence for this particular Wunderwaffe's use in terms of corpses and wrecked tanks; they had all disintegrated.

The Sun Cannon was a solar powered Green wonder weapon, meanwhile, used by those pollutant-hating Nazis who were 'well-versed in Greek mythology', and imitated old tales of the sun's rays supposedly being concentrated on the ships of Athens' enemies through a lens, setting them aflame. Huge mirrors were placed on trucks and rotated up into the eyes of enemy pilots, blinding them, Zündel said. Germany itself wasn't sunny enough for this to work in domestic combat, but the Afrika Korps had used it to great effect in North Africa's desert sands.[9]

Oddly, Zündel doesn't mention it, but after the war there were also numerous newspaper stories that the Nazis, inspired by a 1929 proposal by the fascist-friendly German space scientist and rocket engineer Hermann Oberth (1894–1989), had planned one day to build a giant pre-fabricated sodium mirror in space, redirecting solar rays onto the Earth to incinerate cities or boil away entire oceans, in what, ironically for such an emissionless Wunderwaffe, amounted to militarily directed acts of hyper concentrated global warming. With such a 'sun-gun', the *New York Times* reported, the Nazis hoped to 'demolish nations at will and rule the world'. Drawings of this proposed device look amazingly like a huge, disc-shaped UFO beaming gigantic tractor beams down onto our planet.[10] Surely the flying saucer itself could now be repositioned as just another such Green Wunderwaffe?

* * *

The other key figure in our eco-friendly suction saucer legend is Austria's Viktor Schauberger (1885–1958). Rather than a 'propeller', Schauberger boasted of creating an 'impeller' which drew water inwards on a torpedo or boat, thus 'sucking' its way through the water rather than 'pushing' its way through, as with a traditional propeller, a method which was allegedly nine times as powerful and efficient. By applying similar principles to aircraft, he sought to build a machine which would suck itself through the clouds in fuel-less fashion.[11]

Of our main saucer building protagonists Schauberger alone actually has something to his story, enjoying a certain cachet amongst non-Nazi environmentalists even today. The introduction to one modern day account of his life was provided by David Bellamy (1933–2019), once British TV's favourite child-friendly bearded naturalist and promoter of wildlife conservation, whilst another biography contains a preface by Swedish conservationist Kai Curry-Lindhal (1917–90), of the UN Environment Programme – but both essays praise Schauberger for his ideas about sustainable forestry and water management, not UFO propulsion systems. In 1951, Schauberger set up The Green Front in Austria, one of post-war Europe's first conservationist movements, so he was a man of genuine planet-saving credentials. Like many Green Nazis, he also had leanings towards biodynamic agriculture, designing special ploughs in supposed line with its tenets.[12]

However, several writers have since spun Schauberger's story to argue the Nazis could have reversed global warming and other such ecological horrors, as seen in the output of the small Ruhr-based publishers Teut-Verlag, or 'Teutonic Publishing', run by Richard Schepmann, son of the former Brownshirt storm-trooper Wilhelm Schepmann (1894–1970). Schepmann gained a six-month suspended sentence for inciting racial hatred in 1983, and energetically pushed a line of texts linking Nazism with UFOs and New Age issues during the 1980s, such as D.H. Haarmann's three-volume *Secret Wunderwaffen*.

Haarmann taught there was an all-encompassing post-war Jewish conspiracy involving Big Government, Big Banks and Big Oil, aimed at suppressing knowledge of how Nazi UFOs worked – namely, by using Schauberger's free-energy 'implosive' technology sourced from the planet's innate electromagnetic fields, rather than the dirty 'explosive' energy of fossil fuels. Possibly, proposed Haarmann, this Nazi free-energy panacea was a literal Holy Grail – SS Ahnenerbe archaeologists may have used the Sangraal's mystical power in their implosion engines to enable marvellous, gravity defying manoeuvres.[13]

In 1934, in his capacity as an inventor, Viktor Schauberger somehow gained an official meeting with Adolf Hitler, but there are several versions of this conference now floating around within the conspirasphere. In one, Schauberger had requested it take place between him and Adolf alone, but a hostile scientific rival attended nonetheless. Schauberger was 'allowed to speak without interruption for one hour' by Hitler which, if true, is indeed remarkable, with Viktor describing how he could provide all the Reich's energy needs from water and thin air alone. Hitler then pushed a button and in walked a secretary, who was told to 'Give this Austrian, who has ideas that interest me, all he needs to prove that he is right.' As Schauberger left, however, his rival accused him of putting 'idiotic ideas' into Hitler's head, which so offended Schauberger that he refused to attend a second summons from the Führer, just to be 'abused by that underling'.[14]

A different version says the great quantum physicist Max Planck (1858–1947) was present instead, dismissing Schauberger's ideas with the jibe 'Science has nothing to do with Nature!' before flouncing out. Worse, Schauberger now had the audacity to warn Hitler that his proposed Thousand-Year Reich would be so eco-unfriendly he would be lucky if it lasted ten. Surprisingly, he was not then immediately marched straight outside, shot and made to begin pushing up daisies.[15] Such discrepancies make the meeting sound fictional, but it did actually occur. Letters in the German Federal Archives prove that, in July 1934, Nazi economist Albert Pietzsch (1874–1957) did indeed engineer a seminar between the two men, but show Hitler was sceptical of Schauberger's ideas and annoyed by his haughty attitude and refusal to reveal specifics about his magical methods; he had been courting Mussolini too, hoping for a bidding war. Schauberger soon felt he had overplayed his hand and wrote off to both Hitler and Himmler saying that, as a proud Austro-German, he now wished to offer his ideas exclusively to the Nazis. Yet Chief of the Reich Chancery Hans Lammers (1879–1962) thought he was a fantasist, a pure 'autodidact' who should be kept away from Hitler lest he manage to con him like a fake alchemist promising to turn lead into gold.[16]

Quite what happened next is a matter for debate, as Viktor's story has developed into something of a fable. Schauberger's initially rejected ideas were remembered by some Nazis, and in 1938 fanatical anti-Semitic propagandist Julius Streicher (1885–1946) was supposedly tasked with funding his attempts to extract electricity direct from flowing water (that is, not by driving a turbine or wheel, but straight from the liquid itself). Allegedly, he got 50,000 volts from some apparatus or other, which led to a physicist being dispatched to investigate. Angrily, he demanded to know where the inventor had hidden the electrical wires in his machine – but there were none. Sadly, Schauberger could find no practical applications for his discovery, but if his electricity extractor really worked, you may have thought it would have had innumerable practical applications![17]

Part of the problem with Schauberger's narrative is that he generally operated alone and didn't like to release full details of his designs, making notes in a cryptic shorthand code lest 'the capitalists, socialists and Communists' pervert his findings for use against Nature. Plus, as most of his devices, from water purifiers to submarine turbines, all operated on similar principles, he confusingly tended to use labels for each interchangeably. The flying saucer he allegedly later built is often called a 'repulsine' craft, for example, but Schauberger might also use this term for a water distillation instrument, or randomly call them 'repulsators' instead. Also, when he began working for the Nazis, the Gestapo ordered his investigations must take place in secret, meaning there are no direct records of some – which, sceptics might say, is simply proof they never took place at all.[18]

The most popular version of Schauberger's story has it that, in 1941, upon Himmler's direct orders, an SS-Standartenführer named Zeireis gave Viktor the choice of developing free-energy engines, 'atom-smashing' devices and anti-gravity flying saucers, or else be summarily hanged, and his family punished. Taken to Mauthausen concentration camp, he was made to pick the best engineers from the inmates and set about his work, during which hundreds of camp labourers died. In spring 1945, just before the war's end, Schauberger's repulsine saucer achieved blast-off, smashing up through the ceiling of his engineering shed, trailing an eerie silver-blue-green glow after it.[19]

This is exaggerated, but apparently based upon a certain core of truth. In 2001, military aviation journalist Nick Cook published *The Hunt for Zero Point*, detailing his search for secret anti-gravity technology. The text was much criticised as Cook was duped by several false claims, as we shall see in a future chapter, but during his researches Cook travelled to the Schauberger Institute in Austria, where his family continue their ancestor's ecological work. Here, archive documents showed that, in 1941, Schauberger had commissioned Vienna's Kertl engineering company to build him a prototype repulsine engine following his own specific design instructions, a suction-type device consisting of two linked metal plates with whorl-shaped gaps inbetween.

Triggered by an initial ignition motor, this would then be switched off and the machine become self-powering; air was supposed to be sucked into the whorls between the plates, spinning a turbine and generating a vacuum of great power, which would then suck more air into the thing, and so ad infinitum. Then, it could either levitate indefinitely, held aloft by the air flow, or be connected to a gear shaft, creating a perpetual motion fuel-less electricity generator. Did it work? Not as designed, but it did something. When turned on one day in the great man's absence by one of his colleagues, Aloys Kokaly, it spun around and generated so much lift it smashed into the ceiling and was ruined, an event which, if it really did happen, thus happened here and not in a concentration camp right before the war's end. Unable to source appropriate replacement parts, Kertl then abandoned further development.

Schauberger's papers show he now became convinced Professor Ernst Heinkel, the leading German aircraft designer, had illegally seen his patent for this repulsine device and stolen it for use in his own planes. Heinkel persuaded the Reich Patent Office to give Schauberger a patent on the repulsine only for use in water purification and distillation, scribbled Viktor, which shows just how amorphous his inventions were. Heinkel couldn't make the stolen design work, however, so approached Viktor for help through an intermediary. Schauberger easily saw what Heinkel's mistake had been, but went to work for the rival aircraft company Messerschmidt in 1942 instead. Here, his repulsine device failed again, reaching 'meltdown' when switched on due to the use of sub-standard materials and manufacturing techniques. Schauberger now wondered if his work was being deliberately sabotaged.[20]

Viktor does seem to have been engaged in genuine prototype work during this period, but Cook was unable to discover any mention of Schauberger in Heinkel's own files. Whether this is because Heinkel was unwilling to put his chicanery down in writing, or because this was a paranoid fantasy on the inventor's behalf, is debatable.

During the war, Schauberger spent a brief spell inside a mental hospital. Attending a regular physical examination to check up on old wounds sustained during the First World War, he was instead taken to the psychiatric ward and interviewed – maybe he unwisely started chatting to the doctor about having invented a perpetual motion machine. Accounts differ, but his son Walter said he was trussed up in a straightjacket within a metal cage. As mental patients were often given a lethal injection under Hitler as being a waste of the State's precious time and resources, Schauberger interpreted this as an effort by his enemies to get him out of the way, so he stayed calm and answered questions rationally. Being pronounced sane by doctors, he was soon released, but does appear to have had something of a persecution complex.[21]

More certain is that, in April 1944, Schauberger was compulsorily drafted into the Waffen-SS, the organisation's combat wing, ostensibly to command a parachute company – highly unusual for a man then aged 59 with old war wounds. This appears a cover story for him being forcibly transported away to work on five separate devices for the SS: a water purifier, an electricity generator, a means of developing hydrogen fuel from water, a machine for creating intense heat and cold and a fliegende scheibe or 'flying disc' (Nick Cook anachronistically translates this specifically as 'flying saucer'), another levitating repulsine plate.

As aides, Schauberger was given a choice of twenty-five hand-picked qualified prisoners from Mauthausen concentration camp, and access to labs and resources, although as materials grew ever scarcer he had to make do and mend, salvaging scrap from an old tank. Schauberger insisted his men be released into workshops and fed and clothed properly if they were to be able to work productively, which was agreed to. All this is confirmed in Viktor's contemporary diaries, presuming they are accurately dated. Design drawings alleged to be from Schauberger's Mauthausen era were reproduced by Nick Cook in his book, and do indeed resemble what we now think of as UFOs, as do photos of prototype repulsine devices made after the war.

On 28 February 1945, Viktor's operations were moved to the Austrian village of Leonstein to avoid enemy bombing. Here, on 5 April, work on the first full fliegende scheibe prototype began; on 6 May, it was due for its first test flight. Waking up that morning, though, Schauberger found his SS guards had all fled in the face of the Allied advance. On 7 May, Germany surrendered to the US and Britain in the West, and on 9 May to the Russians in the East. Viktor was now taken into US custody and placed under house arrest for nine months, under the apparent misapprehension he was involved in creating some manner of atomic energy appliances, with his old flat in Vienna being searched then blown up by the Russians.

Years later, when he read Rudolf Schriever's jumble of falsehoods in the newspapers, Schauberger concluded other SS scientists had secretly been developing his repulsine machines themselves too. In February 1956, Schauberger wrote a letter to the West German Defence Minister explicitly claiming to have once invented a 'flying saucer', but he would never have been able to tell his SS masters that at the time.[22]

Initially this seems remarkable proof that, as Nick Cook put it, 'the Nazis had been deeply involved – no question – in what can only be described as flying saucer technology'.[23] But this is not so. Technical drawings of Schauberger's repulsines do look like UFOs, but only until you consider they were about 1.5m in size and were not crewed vessels. If we trust Schauberger's accounts, they did generate some kind of propulsional lift, as shown by one flying into a factory roof, but this propulsion does not seem to have been directionally controllable. In any case, they were intended as prototype *engines*, not *aircraft*; the vessels such things would then have been placed inside as power units need not themselves have been discoid, any more than ordinary jet planes are themselves shaped like giant jet engines.

Thus, what we have here amounts to a strange kind of toy. It may have spun around and lifted off the ground by very unusual means, and have been worth investigation as of potential interest to science, but it was not a flying saucer at all, in spite of Schauberger's pre-1947 use of the close-but-no-cigar term fliegende scheibe. Viktor Schauberger did not invent flying saucers. But he did help invent a fairy tale.

* * *

Schauberger's life story is as fascinating as it is bizarre. Acclaimed by one biographer as 'the legendary water-magician from Linz' (Adolf Hitler's childhood home, possibly explaining why the Führer had heard of him and was once willing to grant him an audience), he came from a long line of forest wardens whose family motto was 'Fidus in silvis silentibus' ('Faithful to the quiet forests'), which young Viktor certainly was, going for long solo childhood walks through the local woods, where Nature quickly became his consuming obsession, particularly water.

His father taught Viktor to eschew book learning for the evidence of his own eyes, a principle which had allowed the Schauberger family to recognise 'the inner healing power of water' for many centuries now. This principle sometimes allowed the Schaubergers to see some very strange things, like logs floating upstream, disobeying the laws of Newton. As Viktor's guiding principle was 'First understand Nature, then copy it', it is no wonder he later tried to make anti-gravity devices.

One observation made by Schauberger Sr was that water was 'lazy' by day, but much more energetic by night, as it 'curls up and sleeps' in the relaxing sunlight, something his son found to be true when he met a spring which had once been vigorous and lively when its source had been shaded by a stone hut. The hut being pulled down, the sun-bathing stream soon grew indolent and dried up. The hut being reconstructed, the shaded spring once more returned. Water was 'the Earth's blood', concluded Viktor, and veins in the human body were not straight, so it made sense rivers were not straight either, with their winding curves intended to accumulate deposits and build them up banks littered by sun-obscuring trees and bushes which would act as leafy sun shades, stopping the water slipping into a coma.

Once he grew into an adult and became a forester himself, Viktor's other first-hand observations of Mother Nature's secret ways were equally as odd. Sometimes, he would see large egg-shaped river stones begin to 'dance', moving about for no apparent reason, before floating impossibly to the surface and creating circles of ice around themselves as if expelling cold energy.

Another time, staking out a waterfall to catch 'a dangerous fish-poacher', he witnessed a trout leaping up the waterfall, as in many a Nature documentary – yet this particular trout had a unique method of negotiating the vertical water path. Instead of jumping up and swimming energetically against the tide, it began spinning around wildly until such a point as it just suddenly floated up the waterfall in an anti-gravity fashion, much as Viktor's spinning repulsine plates later worked. Examining waterfalls more closely, he became convinced he could see energy forces lurking within them in the form of a shimmering 'channel of light', which the clever trout would exploit by spinning into before then being 'sucked upwards as in a whirlwind'. The conclusion was obvious – there were unknown energetic forces hidden within Nature which, if only they could be tapped, could make stones swim and fish fly.[24]

Theorising that, when a river wound its curvy path, it built up certain vortex-related forces within its waters, Schauberger entered a design contest organised by the landowner Prince Adolf von Schaumberg-Lippe (1859–1916), who had plenty of valuable timber in his forests, but no viable means of transporting it to market, so needed a new network of log flumes building. Viktor's entry was so abnormal it was initially treated as a joke, due to its 'idiotic shape'.

Most flume designs followed the same basic principle as a canal, being as straight-lined as was practical, so as to get wood to market in the shortest possible distance, but Schauberger's zig-zagged all over the place to create artificial liquid energy vortexes and featured various inlets into which fresh cool water from shaded areas could flow, to re-energise the lazy warm water which had been sedated by the sun. He was partially inspired by a snake which crept into his trousers one day, which he threw into the river and watched swim away. The correspondence between the snake's s-shaped body, its s-shaped swimming motion and the s-shaped river path and current made him realise that, in a successful log flume, form and motion must each be as one.

Unexpectedly, when tested out Viktor's snaky log flume worked the best, and the Prince made him Head Warden of his entire forest estates as reward. When word reached the Austrian government, they appointed him State Consultant for Timber Flotations, a role considered so economically important he was paid in actual gold. Yet jealous academics, who noted Schauberger had no educational qualifications and could not actually explain how his log flumes worked, ultimately played politics to force him out of the job. Whenever he personally built his flumes, they did well, but whenever others tried to copy them, they did not, a peculiar quirk which also affected his later repulsine devices, and a constant theme in the annals of free-energy and anti-gravity research.[25]

A State Commission was thereafter formed to investigate Schauberger's findings, headed by a leading hydraulic engineer named Professor Philipp Forchheimer (1852–1933), of Graz University of Technology, who, despite possessing deep initial scepticism, found to his shock that Viktor was quite correct in what he was saying, even though his achievements appeared inexplicable. Schauberger now tried arguing water was an actual living organism, fed by plant life, and that widespread deforestation after the First World War had killed off Austria's rivers more completely even than too much sleep-inducing sunlight did.

Forchheimer organised a scholarly conference to discuss all this, but when Schauberger himself tried to explain his discoveries by asking assembled delegates whether or not they had ever seen a boar taking a piss, because the spiral motion of its urine was precisely that created by a non-lazy river during its own spiralling path, they thought Viktor was taking the piss himself. Forchheimer calmed them down by trying to translate his colleague's earthy language into more academically acceptable equations on a blackboard, talking not of animal urine but 'cycloid spiral curves', but the situation well illustrated how Schauberger's status as an autodidact with little formal education stymied his career.

Disturbed by the filthy state of the River Rhine, for example, Viktor proposed installing 'energy bodies' within its bed, simple flute-shaped devices which would have made the water spiral more in its path, thus de-silting and re-energising it. Unfortunately, he then implied the river's stones had once danced around as if alive within its formerly clean and energy filled waters, bumping against one another and giving off bright sparks, leading to ancient legends of dwarfs living on the riverbed making shining golden jewellery, talk hardly calculated to win the proposal official bureaucratic approval.

As for why his findings could not easily be reproduced in labs, Schauberger had two suggestions. Maybe there was a big conspiracy, with industrialists covering up the potential free-energy applications of water vortexes and the life-giving capacity of non-lazy water to grow crops even in desert areas, which would ruin the profits of energy companies, fuel distributors and farm-machinery manufacturers. 'Maintaining the mystery of water maintains the value of capital,' he complained. Alternatively, as rivers were living beings, small extracts from them brought into laboratories were by definition already dead, with any such 'water corpse' being unable to perform the wonders of an actual river; you couldn't extract blood from a fish then still expect the stuff to swim in a tank.[26]

However, once Hitler annexed Austria, Schauberger's conception of living water being like blood fitted in well with the 'Blood and Soil' doctrine of the Green Nazis. Schauberger once saw some lake water developing into a sudden vortex-like whirlpool, sucking down floating tree trunks into its maw, before abruptly becoming a huge water spout 'of at least the height of a house', gushing up a fountain in a 'turning, cup-like pillar' as the lake bed rumbled loudly 'like thunder'. There appeared no stimulus for this procedure – unless what he had initially witnessed was old water dying, and then new water being reborn from its corpse.

If water in a river was alive, Viktor supposed it had to die and be born too, like all living creatures. And, if new water could be born from old water, then water could literally expand in volume, much as a human female 'expanded' in volume when pregnant – imagine a puddle giving birth to a litter of smaller baby puddles, and you get the general idea. But if rivers were flowing channels of the planet's living blood, then its blood could become infected or tainted by pollution, much like a good German's blood could become ruined by unnecessary race-mixing.

Forests were the clear and nourishing base for the natural life force of water, as nutrients from trees fed into the blood rivers, providing sustenance. Yet water from rivers also then feeds into plant life, which is then eaten by animals, which are then eaten by humans. Destroy a forest, and you destroy the food chain; human blood itself degrades by cutting down trees, with deforestation ultimately causing cancer and a general decline of the volk.

Modern industrial 'civilisation' was a contradiction in terms, an artificial, inorganic creation designed to promote profit, not spiritual or physical health. Not being a paid-up Nazi himself, Schauberger doesn't specifically deride it as 'Jewish', but others would have done. There was a vicious circle at work here. Decline in our environment led to spiritual and physical decline in man, which made him industrialise further, causing more environmental decline, making our mentalities even worse, leading us to build ever more factories and cities.[27] This was tragic, as a nation's ancestral memory could be carried in its blood, and if clouded this could lead to racial memory loss:

> Even matter is inert energy. This also applies to blood, which is a materialised power-flow that carries energy from past generations through present to future generations. This flow is not broken with the person's death, but is carried further to his successors. However, this energy can be degenerated, for example by negative technology, so that the thoughts and outlook which have accumulated within a person's being [from their forefathers] over thousands of years, is lost.[28]

Yet for certain special people whose veins still ran clear and pure as an unpolluted river, it was still possible to 'summon up from his blood all this reservoir of knowledge', and to 'choose between knowledge and science', the former being true wisdom, the latter false. Naturally, Viktor himself, belonging to a family of foresters, who had long ago once been blue-blooded Austrian aristocrats to boot, possessed the power of blood knowledge, something which allowed him to see things others couldn't, like levitating fish, and build things nobody else could, like repulsines. His inventions were thus attempts to materialise his blood visions, to recover ancient lost knowledge like an Ahnenerbe man, not to create new things per se. If city educated academics couldn't see their value, then that was because their own blood had been rotted by civilisation and its discontents. Good blood made good thoughts accumulate. Bad blood produced only bad ideas.

The universe itself must have had an inherently spiral structure like that of water vortexes, Schauberger perceived, as seen in the spiral structure of galaxies. Nature abhors not a vacuum, but a straight line. Left to themselves, particles will orbit in circular motions, like moons and planets, not be forced into passing down straight wires or pipes like in our modern day electric machines and combustion engines. The image of a canal replacing a river, you might say, was an emblem of all contemporary social evil. By replacing curves with straight lines, mankind thoughtlessly removed his inherent connection to the spiral galaxy.[29]

After the war, Schauberger invented a new brand of water pipe, using not straight tubes, but imitating the twisted horns of a Kudu antelope. When water ran through such curly wurly pipes, the rates of friction against the sides were much lower and a 'strange light phenomenon' was said to have been emitted, though whether an ordinary plumber of unclean blood would have been able to detect it is unknown.[30]

* * *

If ours was a spiral universe then, like water, it too must have been alive. Probably, it possessed 'attractive' properties, as when women attracted men towards them like living sexual magnets. Attraction was good: it drew things inwards, joining them together, being 'implosive', like an inwards-swirling centripetal vortex. Repulsion was bad: it spat things outwards, splitting them asunder, being 'explosive', like an outwards-swirling centrifugal vortex. Both forces were cosmically necessary, as with death and birth, but in modern industrialised society, explosive technologies disastrously over dominated, with steam engines often being only 50 per cent efficient, as well as inherently destructive. Over reliance on them meant ours was becoming a literally dead world, with increasing environmental degradation.

Explosive engines, or 'fire technology', broke things down via heat or combustion, as with fossil fuels, making all such pollutants inherently bad; even hydroelectricity was bad, as water's passage through turbines killed it with straight lines and steel. Unlike explosions, 'Everything that is natural is silent, simple and cheap,' Viktor would say. The proposed splitting of the atom was the ultimate explosive 'offence against Nature'. What was needed was the reverse-atomic equivalent of 'implosive' engines instead, which would run on inexhaustible supplies of free energy and cause the levitation of objects. If only we knew it, the 'empty' air around us was not empty at all, but filled with invisible 'trace elements' and 'chromosomes' of once-living creatures, broken down by Nature's centrifugal disintegrating forces into 'atomic decomposing energy' which was now just sitting there, 'merely waiting an impulse to be revitalised' by catalysing it to spin within a constructive, centripetal fashion, as Viktor's repulsines aimed to do.[31.]

Therefore, by spinning water properly in a special centripetal device, it may be possible to transform it into a 'highly potent' fuel, so abolishing petrol. Combustion engines, too, could be scrapped for more natural means of propulsion, like those employed by flying trout. Indeed, the type of engine used in his repulsine discs was dubbed a 'trout turbine' by Schauberger, being based ultimately upon yet more gravity defying piscine antics he had observed down by the river. 'Birds do not fly, they are flown, and fish do not swim, they are swum,' he liked to say, indicating how both animal types were borne along by currents of air and water, not by laboriously physically propelling themselves forwards with exhausting motions of arms and legs like a stupid human swimmer.

How could trout sometimes stay still in a fast-flowing river, whilst the water all around them sped ever onwards, or even manage to rush against the prevailing force of the stream like the anti-gravity upstream-floating logs of Viktor's forefathers? Schauberger noticed a trout sucks in water through its mouth, then expels it back out through its gills. But, when it re-emerged, certain microscopic curves on the gills caused this water to spiral about in a positive, centripetal fashion, something which, when combined with 'certain trace elements' inside the trout, changed the water being expelled into a new type of liquid termed 'juvenile water', which possessed far different qualities to ordinary water. This baby water then flowed along the fish's body, creating 'a secondary system of water circulation' which surrounded it like a force-field-cum-propulsion system. By regulating centripetal water output from its gills in the desired fashion, a fish could stand still in the river, go with the flow, or swim against the current as desired. When it came to a waterfall, by spinning around, it could then manipulate this ability to fly vertically up the mountainside.

In theory, the same principles applied to air as well as water. If you sucked air in then spat it back out again in such a way as to create centripetal vortexes, then you made things levitate, potentially non-stop, once the initial air sucking impulse had been triggered with a starter motor – this is basically the same principle Epp and Fleissner later used in their own suction saucer designs, which must surely have been 'inspired' by Viktor's. Schauberger called his contraptions 'bio-technical', meaning that, whilst ostensibly mechanical, they were really based upon examples drawn from living Nature, like his beloved trout. Considered so, Schauberger's repulsine disc takes on an entirely new form – he was trying to build a sort of circular flying fish to swim through the air! So, flying saucers are really flying fish.[32]

Schauberger's unsupported first-person accounts of dancing stones and levitating trout do sound rather unlikely. His post-war Swedish disciple Olof Alexandersson's counter-suggestion is that perhaps such phenomena really did once occur in the remote forested areas of his hero's youth, but that centrifugal forces have since raped the planet's rivers so hard they have now vanished, like dodos.[33] Or possibly it just wasn't possible for anyone other than the pure-heritaged Austro-German Herr Schauberger to see such marvels, as they were essentially imaginary blood visions rather than literal perceptions of physical reality. After all, another source of invaluable information about water's true physical properties came to Viktor one day when, whilst sitting quietly by a forest stream, he found his consciousness leaving his body and entering into the water, where 'an intelligence' like a pagan river god literally spoke to him, telling him all about what kind of movements it needed to pursue in order to remain healthy, and why.[34]

Other sources of inspiration were equally as esoteric. Like many an alchemist and astrologer, Schauberger believed in the old hermetic dictum 'as above, so below', with the spirals of all healthy, natural things down here on Earth reflecting those of galaxies above us in the heavens, including the spirals within human beings. It has been pointed out the German term for the spinal column, Wirbelsaule, really means 'spiral column', indicating the German people may traditionally have viewed the body less as a physical machine based on rigid bones and pathways, but 'more as an energy path'. Whether true or not, it is certainly how Schauberger himself saw matters.[35]

Perhaps the greatest German genius of all time, Johann Wolfgang von Goethe (1749–1832), equal parts poet and scientist, held the view that Nature itself was 'God's living garment', an 'active and living' thing, constantly 'struggling from the whole into parts' through a process of evolution, and this was a view Schauberger shared, thinking God a 'Divine Weaver' of Creation after this same fashion.[36] Like Goethe, who would get nowhere near having a paper accepted in *Science* or *Nature* today, Schauberger's view of reality was basically a Romantic one, not a coldy logical perspective, and sometimes he perhaps let his imagination run away with him.

Yet, as hard-headed independent witnesses of academic qualification, many of whom were initially total sceptics, have provided statements that some of his repulsine devices did indeed sometimes do rather strange things, there is at least some possibility Schauberger might have been onto something but that, having no meaningful scientific education, his explanations for how his inventions worked were simply loopy and excessively fish-based, thus ensuring their quick automatic rejection by the mainstream. Referring to his dire predictions of Earth's impending ecological collapse, the huge-bearded Old Testament prophet and ex-mental ward inmate once fulminated angrily that, 'They call me deranged. The hope is they are right.'[37] But were they?

* * *

To one of Schauberger's modern biographers, Alick Bartholomew (1930–2015), his repulsines worked on the following highly technical-sounding principles:

> As the velocities produced by the centripulsing process increase, the air molecules become cooler and more condensed through the interaction of both centripetal and centrifugal forces. The reduction in volume may reach 1/816, when air is converted into water, and produces a powerful vacuum inside that rapidly draws in larger amounts of air, creating a secondary vacuum above the saucer. The extreme centripulsion and densation not only produce an anti-gravity effect, but also raise the energy level beyond the physical, so that the electrons and protons are compressed back into their fourth-dimensional origins. All of these actions contribute to the levitational effect, enhancing the principal upwards force provided by the densely compressed atoms passing through the aerofoil slits of the turbine blades before being thrust out between the outer cowl and the inner cowl with explosive force, hurtling the saucer into the semi-vacuum above it.[38]

Whether that actually means anything or just sounds like it does, I shall leave you to decide. According to Nick Cook in *The Hunt for Zero Point*, Schauberger's inventions were not just based upon unknown vortex-based energy magic, but the somewhat scientifically respectable (by comparison) notion of Zero-Point Energy, which holds that empty space is no true void, but filled with background radiation from some unidentified source, 'a seething mass of energy' of a virtually limitless nature, if only it could be tapped into.

It appears that the Zero-Point Energy Field was experimentally proven to exist in 1997, though it is debatable how much energy is in it: some say there is enough in an empty coffee cup to boil the world's oceans, others that there's not enough energy in the Earth's empty atmosphere to boil a cup of coffee. But, if you could tap this field, and it turned out to be big enough, you would have free clean energy forever; and if you perturbed the Zero-Point Energy Field around any given object, it would theoretically take off and levitate.[39] Did this explain Schauberger's repulsines? It might help explain his sad fate after the war.

Ernst Zündel was an early promoter of Schauberger's 'electromagnetically powered flying hats' as the solution to the UFO mystery, obtaining photos of his saucer like repulsine generator models and prototypes, then using his skills as a professional graphic designer to paste German military insignia on the side of them in his books. Zündel's father had once been a lumberjack and his son Pierre became a Professor of Forestry, possibly explaining how he knew of Schauberger. Then again, he also used the fringe author Michael X. Barton's (1937–2003) 1960 book *The German Saucer Story* as a source, which claimed Hitler was alive and well in Argentina and building saucers based on Viktor's principles. He could also have read the Austrian occultist and New Age thinker Leopold Brandstätter's (1915–68) 1956 text *Implosion Instead of Explosion?* which argued Schauberger had discovered a quasi-supernatural alternative to nuclear energy.

Wherever Zündel heard Schauberger's story, he obviously didn't know how it ended, so just invented a conclusion himself. Living in the US after the war, Viktor was 'well-financed and supported by a group of mysterious, but obviously wealthy people', presumably code for Jews, for whom he was designing UFOs, said Zündel. As always happens to those greedy enough to take the Semitic shekel, however, Schauberger came a cropper as 'one day in Chicago he just vanished'. His 'battered body' was later found, but it was never discovered who did it; maybe it was gangsters, who 'tried to beat his revolutionising [*sic*] secrets out of him and accidentally killed him'.[40]

This assassination was a complete invention on Zündel's behalf, but Schauberger really was exploited in the US of the 1950s. Schauberger's papers show that, in 1958, by then 72 years old and in poor health, he had been approached by a German-American with connections to US intelligence agencies named Karl Gerchsheimer, acting on behalf of steelworks millionaire Robert Donner, who wanted Schauberger to move to Texas, where an entire research establishment and millions of dollars awaited him. Schauberger agreed to go to Texas for only three months to set up a repulsine lab, then leave his son Walter in charge, believing Gerchsheimer and Donner were working on behalf of the US government, who would put his free-energy devices to work for the benefit of mankind. But progress proved slow and Schauberger was effectively prevented from returning home until, through fatigue, he ended up signing a document which hadn't been translated properly, accidentally giving away the rights to all his ideas and committing him to silence about what had gone on. On 25 September, a mere five days after finally returning home to Linz, Viktor died a broken man.[41]

The conspiracy theory thus arose that, thanks to his discoveries about the Zero-Point Field, Schauberger was exploited and ruined by the Americans, who stole his anti-gravity tech to make UFOs, and suppressed his free-energy teachings to ensure their gigantic fossil fuel companies could stay in profit. 'They took everything from me, everything,' he justifiably complained. 'I don't even own myself.'[42] But who were 'they'? Might they have been . . . the Jews?

Once, when Schauberger was using a repulsine device to somehow transform sewage water into crystal clear pure drinking water, he was approached by 'some senior and highly educated Austrian Jews' who asked him where he had obtained such knowledge. The Jews, he said, admitted they had possessed this same secret wisdom 'since ancient times', but that it had been 'lost long ago'.[43] But was it really lost, or were the Jews just covering their information up?

How could ancient Jews have known about the Zero-Point Energy Field? Maybe what they had actually known about was something called the Black Sun. The precise meaning of this concept is complex but, briefly put, the symbol is used as an alternative swastika by neo-Nazis today in lands like Germany where display of the real thing is generally illegal. But it is also supposed to be a physically extant invisible twin to our more visible normal sun, whose black light suffuses the entire universe, bathing the Aryan race with special spiritual energies of some kind. Maybe it is also the inexhaustible Green free-energy source which lies behind the Zero-Point Energy Field, and this is what Viktor Schauberger had been tapping into when making his eco-friendly anti-gravity suction saucers for Himmler?

Enter Henry Stevens again, who praises Schauberger for inventing a class of UFOs dubbed 'field-propulsion saucers', but proposes that the propulsive energy field in question shone out from this Schwarze Sonne, to give the dark celestial body its original German name. Schwarze Sonne, of course, has the initials 'SS', an organisation Stevens appears keen to rehabilitate, calling them 'Hitler's myrmidons', and bemoaning the 'negative caricature' of them promoted by our PC modern media, which induces a lamentable 'knee-jerk type of condemnation' every time they are mentioned. Yet actually they were 'initiated individuals', whose concept of the Black Sun 'bordered upon the religious', with the swastika itself, contrary to all standard historical knowledge, being a symbol of it. But then, mainstream historians deliberately covered all kinds of things up, even lying that 'SS' actually stood for SchutzStaffel, or 'Elite Guard/Defence Echelon', as the body had its pre-war origins in Hitler's personal bodyguard unit, rather than Schwarze Sonne.

Stevens' Black Sun sits at the centre of our galaxy, with everything else rotating around it, being a spiralling 'cold, collapsing implosive vortex' like those imagined by Schauberger, a 'vast machine, using all the matter and energy contained therein', sucking matter into it. The Black Sun's existence is admitted by modern science, says Stevens, but under the false name of 'black hole'. The spinning Nazi swastika symbolises it, but there may be other Black Sun vortexes which spin the other way and so provide 'a doorway into another dimension', from which matter and free energy 'spew forth like a fountain', a form of 'creative, living energy' which those unjustly maligned men from the SS were planning to use to create an entire 'new science' to power their eco-friendly saucers. 'We are all part of this machine whirling through space,' says Stevens, so to try and power our civilisation with anything other than Black Sun power would be to rebel against Nature. Only the Green Nazis had been wise enough to see all this.[44]

The cover of Stevens' 2007 book *Hitler's Suppressed and Still-Secret Weapons, Science and Technology* features a Nazi eagle clutching a Black Sun symbol within its claws, with the book containing much speculation about German free-energy research. Apparently, a man named Hans Coler tried creating perpetual motion free-energy U-boats for the German Navy, exploiting 'space electrons' which were drawn into 'attracting spaces' in an electrical circuit, something 'still unrecognised by accepted science' – probably because accepted science, unlike that of the Nazis, is inherently unnatural.[45]

The Germans also conducted intensive research into creating synthetic fuels, managing to extract 'gasoline, diesel fuel, lubricating oils and greases' from coal, all of which is actually perfectly possible, using methods known as the Bergius and Fischer processes. Germany was short on natural resources like oil, but sought a state of 'autarky', or economic and industrial independence in terms of such materials nonetheless under Nazi rule, meaning the Third Reich put a lot of effort into research in this field, which did yield genuine results. By 1944, it is estimated German chemists were producing 124,000 barrels of synthetic fuel per day to power Hitler's war machine.

However, during the post-war oil crises caused by OPEC flexing their muscles in the Middle East, these amazing industrial processes, which the victorious Allies knew all about, never resurfaced to save the day. Why? Because, revealed Stevens, initially it would cost more to set up the specialist plants needed to convert coal into petrol, Nazi-style, than it would to import oil and fuel from abroad, as US industrial experiments had conclusively shown. In the long term, it may help avoid periodic fuel-price spikes, but perhaps Big Oil cartels and vested stock-market interests would prefer the public not to know this.[46]

Yet all this paled into insignificance compared with suppression of Nazi scientific knowledge about the Black Sun. The problem is that the Nazis' concept of what science itself is may have been totally different to that of the Allies, who simply would not have understood Nazi physics when they saw it, ignorantly 'relegating these paradigms to the world of the occult' and dismissing them as mumbo-jumbo. Therefore, 'Nazi culture itself' contained something inherently worthwhile which we decadent democrats dismissed at our peril. Stevens quotes another fringe theorist to the effect that, when the Allies stumbled across relevant Nazi records, they 'couldn't handle' this 'mutant strain of non-linear physics' as it was simply 'beyond their cultural frames of reference'. That was why they had to Paperclip so many Wunderwaffen scientists; US and British engineers couldn't comprehend such miracles any more than an Elizabethan would understand a Game Boy.

However, when the Anglo-Americans Paperclipped all this science back home, 'they found out too late that it came infected with a virus. You take the science on, you take on aspects of the ideology as well.' Obviously, the victors could not admit their new best tech was based not simply upon their enemies' superior technological capability but, even more damningly, upon their superior conception of the very universe itself, so as usual everything had been hidden. What the Nazi saucer scientists created was really a form of 'technological magic' based upon the old occult notion of 'as above, so below', as espoused by Viktor Schauberger, which linked mankind directly back to the cosmos, as with the connecting effect upon us of the stars in astrology.

Interestingly, influenced by the likes of the inventor of biodynamic farming Rudolf Steiner, Schauberger himself explicitly believed in the existence of a second, much larger but invisible hidden sun whose rays and solar winds warmed the entire solar system, touching even our very souls themselves, an idea which certainly sounds compatible with that of the Black Sun. As repulsine-type engines tapped directly into the Black Sun by imitating its spiralling, vortex-like motions, argues Stevens, they thus 'function as miniature versions of our universe', becoming, in effect, tiny black holes, as secretly symbolised by the swastika. To develop Stevens' argument, you might say that flying saucers were actually thus powered by swastikas – something the brainwashed anti-Nazi masses could never be allowed to discover.[47]

The disturbing thing is, Henry Stevens does have a certain point. The Nazis did, to some extent, possess a different concept of physics to their enemies – at least superficially. In the opinion of Adolf Hitler, 'There is very likely a Nordic science, and a National Socialist science, which are bound to be opposed to the Liberal-Jewish science', a dogma which led to around one in four German university physics professors being removed, accused of being Marxists or Jews, and of teaching the 'wrong' kind of physics accordingly. Pleasingly, many sacked academics then travelled to the US and helped build the first atom bomb, something the Nordic scientists who stayed behind singularly failed to do (although some conspiracy theorists prefer to maintain otherwise, rather raising the question of why Germany failed to win the war).

'From now on the question for you is not to determine whether something is true, but to determine whether it is in the spirit of the National Socialist revolution', a Nazi official once told a gathering of academics. But as Hitler expressed hyperbolic sentiments to the effect that 'A new era of the magical explanation of the world is rising, an explanation based on will rather than knowledge' and 'There is no truth, either in the moral or the scientific sense', it could sometimes seem the official Nazi view of science was indeed a borderline branch of occultism.

The Nobel laureates Philipp Lenard (1862–1947) and Johannes Stark (1874–1957) hated the new direction physics had taken since the discoveries of the regrettably Jewish genius Albert Einstein (1879–1955), whose theory of relativity Lenard did not understand, thinking its growing acceptance evidence of a worldwide Jewish conspiracy. For Lenard, 'Jewish Science' was abstract mysticism, whose conclusions could not be proven directly with your own eyes, a disturbed fantasy which contravened all common sense by substituting an imaginary sub-atomic realm for the everyday physical one we actually lived in – Viktor Schauberger, who had seen fish flying and stones dancing with his own eyes, even if sceptical Jew-brained academics could not explain mathematically how such things happened, would have agreed with him. Nordic Germans, thinking Nature sacred, preferred to observe it practically, worshipping it by unveiling its mysteries, whereas Jews wished to overthrow Nature and enslave men to dead, spiritless formulae and technology.

In 1934 Stark coined the term 'German Physics', saying only pure, white Aryans could make genuine scientific discoveries, delusionally reinterpreting portraits of famous dead scientists as displaying 'Nordic-Germanic' features, even if they had none. Aryans' superior physiques naturally allowed them to perform experiments more easily than puny Jews, who probably couldn't even lift a test tube. The Nazi scientist's well-toned body 'does not shrink from the effort which the investigation of Nature demands of him', Stark declared, winning Hitler's admiration.

And yet, such ideas were largely rhetorical. If a Jew's ideas had to be exploited to make a new kind of plane fly, they would still be used. The ideas of 'Jewish Physics' could always be arbitrarily twisted, like Stark's portraits of foreign scientists, to imply they were actually indicative of 'German Physics' at work. Nazi military planners wanted weapons that worked, how they did so was immaterial to them. That the SS proved open to listening to ideas about repulsine engines doesn't mean they were all mystics secretly in touch with the Black Sun, it just means they considered many fantastic sounding notions with possible military potential. Remember Himmler's lightning gun?[48]

* * *

It isn't hard to find other Nazis with weird pseudo-scientific ideas about free energy. The most notable was Ronald Richter (1909–91), who managed to convince the pro-German Argentinian dictator Juan Perón (1895–1974) to effectively place him in charge of the nation's nuclear research facilities from 1948 to 1951, culminating in a bizarre media conference in which Perón, convinced his protégé had succeeded in creating limitless electricity from controlled thermonuclear fusion, promised he would soon provide cheap nuclear energy for domestic consumption to be 'sold in half-litre bottles, like milk', or even given away for free, something Perón deemed 'transcendental for the future life' of our planet.

Richter graduated from the German University of Prague in 1935, holding legitimate scientific qualifications, but appears to have been refused a doctoral degree after claiming to have discovered mysterious 'Earth Rays' emanating from within our planet's core, which supposedly had all kinds of wonderful effects, but turned out actually to be scattered X-rays, something he refused to accept. During the war Richter toiled for various military contractors, at one point working on a type of particle accelerator called a Tokamak. Perón, hoping to kick-start his failing economy with cheap nuclear power, smuggled a Tokamak into Argentina, but needed someone able to operate it.

Having already recruited various ex-Nazi fugitives to manage his domestic industries, Richter came to Perón's attention, and was illegally given Argentinian citizenship himself. Isla Huemul, an island in a remote Patagonian lake, was given over to Richter to build an experimental nuclear reactor based upon his highly aberrant theories about how such a thing might work, and hundreds of millions of pounds in today's money were wasted on building him giant structures so large they caused a nationwide cement and brick shortage.

In 1951, Richter announced he was the first person in the world to achieve nuclear fusion using something termed a 'Thermatron', although the global scientific community proved reluctant to believe him, probably because he gave few details of his work, and because those he did give were borderline incomprehensible. Some thought him a genius, others crazy, but Perón himself gave him a medal. And yet, the nuclear milk bottles failed to appear. Perón now appointed a committee to investigate, who found Richter a fraud; some of his expensive equipment on Isla Huemul hadn't even been connected up to power units. In 1952, Perón terminated the project, and the phrase 'It smells like Huemul', or 'It smells like a con', entered the national lexicon.

Following Perón's removal from power in 1955, Richter was briefly arrested for corruption, though it appears he was more a fantasist than a fraudster, who really did believe he had developed some new means of power generation, although sceptics suspect all he really did was explode hydrogen in an electric arc, cracking his reactor. During the war, Richter had made proposals to German officials about causing nuclear fusion by inducing shock waves within compressed deuterium plasma, but his idea was rejected. However, Perón had purged Argentina's universities of many opposition-supporting scientists after winning power, leaving him vulnerable to being personally talked into thinking similar methods could work by Richter, a bit like some Nazi bureaucrats once feared Viktor Schauberger might do to the similarly scientifically illiterate Hitler.

Even so, Richter does have his champions today, who argue that whilst his experiments may have failed, he did conceive some innovative notions, like that of ion-acoustic plasma heating, and that every scientific theorist has the right to be mistaken sometimes. Other pundits, however, prefer to argue that the media and scientific exposure of Richter as a self-dupe was simply a scam in itself, a US-led plot to hide the man's magnificent discoveries away from the world. One such pundit, naturally, is Henry Stevens. Although never actually Paperclipped, Richter had a Paperclip file anyway, which Stevens read through. Richter explained his ideas to US officials post-1945, but was never imported to the US like Braun et al. You might guess this was because his ideas were deemed useless. Stevens was not so sure.

Another plan of Richter was to use shock waves as a catalyst in aircraft ram jets, which Stevens views as possibly having applications for nuclear powered VTOL planes, something 'which brings UFOs to mind'. Richter seems to have been using the term Zero-Point Energy from 1957 onwards, thus being acclaimed by Stevens as the coiner of this term. According to him, Richter deserved credit, because his 'method was [practical] experimentation, not merely conducting "research" by scribbling mathematical babble on a chalkboard then insisting on a Spinozian [Baruch Spinoza being a Dutch-Jewish philosopher] set of definitions of exactly what the physical universe actually is'. In other words, he practised good old 'German Physics', not its inferior 'Jewish' rival – Stark and Lenard would surely have approved.

For Stevens, Richter's findings give us 'a glimpse into a probable post-war world [of free energy] if the Nazi government had survived and Dr Richter had gone on with his work, in Germany, without breaks in funding' – which rather ignores that he didn't get funding from the Nazis to perform fusion research, because they thought his ideas unworkable.[49] The cautionary example of Ronald Richter shows us that Viktor Schauberger was not Nazi Germany's only Viktor Schauberger.

* * *

In spite of his various eccentricities and unlikely explanations for how his repulsines may have actually worked, of all the purported Nazi saucer inventors, Viktor Schauberger is easily the most plausible, just so long as you don't misinterpret his work as meaning he literally built a full-size, fully operational UFO. Perhaps he really did make a small electromagnetically charged metal plate spark off and crash into a factory roof one day. In the years since, other inventors claim to have performed similar feats, most notably a Russian engineer and expert in Materials Science named Dr Evgeny Podkletnov (b.1955), who in 1996 caused widespread controversy after purporting to have developed a technique of 'gravity shielding', which would cause objects placed within a special electromagnetic field generated by a rapidly spinning ceramic superconductive disc to lose a small proportion of their weight.

Podkletnov's initial trials were not aimed at making Sir Isaac Newton weep at all, simply at developing new and better forms of superconductor. Yet someone in his lab was a pipe-smoker, and it was noticed that this man's tobacco fumes rose up in a vertical column above the superconducting disc being played about with, leading the scientists to investigate why. Performing tests, it was found that any object or substance placed above the disc, even on higher floors above the lab itself, lost as much as 2 per cent of its weight. If you suspended one gravity defying device over another, this effect apparently doubled.

Podkletnov was careful not to use the specific sci-fi label 'anti-gravity' in relation to any of this, but the media gleefully did, and his career was ruined, at least in the short term. The London-based journal to which Podkletnov had successfully submitted a paper summarising his findings leaked word to the *Sunday Telegraph*, who printed a rather sensationalist story implying that one day lifts could be removed from tall buildings, with people being enabled to simply float balloon-like up the now-empty shafts instead, imitating the rising pipe smoke of Podkletnov's assistant.

Expelled from his position performing superconductor research at a Finnish university, things got worse for Podkletnov when his co-author on the paper was seemingly pressurised by his superiors into removing his name from it, with face-saving claims being made that Podkletnov had performed his experiments entirely alone, not in collaboration with any other university staff. In the end, a demoralised Podkletnov simply withdrew his document from pending publication. When mention was then made of his discoveries in an episode of *The X-Files*, Evgeny's humiliation was complete, the implication being his findings were fit to be believed in only by FBI Special Agent Fox Mulder.

Podkletnov has since asserted that separate groups of experimenters in Sheffield and Toronto have successfully replicated his findings but refuse to reveal this fact to the general public due to fear they would be, as one journalist put it, 'ridiculed and ruined by the gravity establishment', just as their mentor had been. According to the BBC, engineering teams at Boeing were less small-minded and considered utilising Podkletnov's ideas as part of a clandestine scheme called Project GRASP, or 'Gravity Research for Space Propulsion', although Boeing themselves later denied this.

Undaunted, our old friend Nick Cook followed this report up for *Janes Defence Weekly*, writing that Boeing were indeed trying to exploit Podkletnov's data at their Phantom Works R&D facility in Seattle. According to Cook, Boeing had imitated Operation Paperclip and invited Podkletnov to fly over to the US to join them, something Russian authorities refused to allow, due to strict national security laws against the transferral of advanced technology to rival powers. More public about their interest were NASA, who also encouraged Podkletnov to become their next Wernher von Braun, on the grounds that, as one interested scientist explained, 'NASA has a responsibility to overcome gravity.' Rival aerospace firms Lockheed Martin and Britain's own BAE Systems also sniffed around Podkletnov, to no avail.

What, precisely, were these giants of the West's military-industrial complex interested in? Whilst never claiming he had literally managed to create anything which counteracted gravity, so much as developing a technique for shielding objects from it – 'we don't absorb the energy of the gravitational field', he once clarified, 'we [are] simply controlling it, as a transistor controls the flow of electricity' – Podkletnov later admitted that, if his ceramic disc was spun rapidly enough, it actually took off into the air itself, rather like Schauberger's reported repulsine prototype once did, back in Nazi Germany.

In a 1997 interview, Podkletnov claimed to now be working at an unnamed research centre in Moscow, where he had managed to create some new device based upon related but reversed principles, which he said would 'reflect gravity-waves and be small, fast and light, like UFOs'. In other words, some kind of super high-performance drones which worked via what physicists euphemistically term 'propelentless propulsion' – that is, floating aerial free-energy devices in which, for instance, gravity shielded craft, enjoying a 2 per cent weight reduction in a tall vertical column of air above them, would levitate, buoyed up by the heavier air below like a boat on the ocean.

According to a Boeing briefing document unearthed by Nick Cook, Podkletnov, despite his apparent pacifist principles, had been further speculating about the creation of some kind of anti-gravity death-ray device, or 'impulse gravity generator', which could 'exert an instantaneous force of 1,000G on any object – enough, in principle, to vaporise it' into atoms. Allegedly, a Russian lab had already demonstrated such a death beam's capacity to repel a target a whole kilometre away, lending it great future potential as an anti-satellite weapon or ballistic missile interceptor. Even more interestingly, Podkletnov's father was himself a noted Soviet-era scientist, and had actually owned some of Viktor Schauberger's original papers, which he had showed to his son many years beforehand. Is this what gave Podkletnov his inspiration to experiment in the first place?[50]

Remember, if any of this story is actually true – and some may feel that this is a big if – then it basically means that Vladimir Putin now has a fleet of what can only be termed real-life, miniature, anti-gravity UFOs at his disposal. The foo-fighters of the Second World War were surely not solid mechanical devices. But that doesn't necessarily mean the foo-fighters of any forthcoming Third World War beginning over in Ukraine might not be . . .

Chapter Six

Lightning Warfare: Renato Vesco, the Flying Tortoise, Feuerball and Kugelblitz

Another central figure in promoting the specific fantasy that foo-fighters were thoroughly solid in form was Renato Vesco (1924–99), whose book *Intercept – But Don't Shoot* (later retitled *Intercept UFO*) appeared in English in 1971, although his findings had sat gathering dust in a desk drawer since 1956. Vesco's conclusions were publicised in the August 1969 issue of popular US men's magazine *Argosy* where he enjoyed a substantially fake biography implying he worked in Alpenfestung German-Italian research installations for Fiat at Lake Garda during the war, and had spent the 1960s as an 'undercover technical agent' investigating UFOs for the Italian Air Ministry.

By the time of his 1971 book's later dust jacket, Vesco had acquired an alternative life as a general aerospace specialist and writer, together with the outright lie that, in 1944, he had also 'commanded the technical section of the Italian Air Force', at which point, given his listed birth year of 1924, he could have been no more than 20 years old. He also appeared to have attended university in Rome and studied at the German Institute for Aerial Development, all before the tender age of 15.

Doubting this incredible life story, an earlier British student of the Nazi UFO field, Kevin McClure, contacted Maurizio Verga, the knowledgeable Italian ufologist, seeking advice. Did Vesco even exist? Verga knew him personally. Vesco was a genuine aerospace engineer and journalist, who, during the 1950s, became rather disgusted by the idea of UFOs being alien spacecraft, something now known as the Extra-Terrestrial Hypothesis (ETH). Thinking the ETH an 'absurd . . . myth' which 'clashes with the most elementary horse-sense', Vesco set out to prove so in his writings, which were supposedly based on classified military files and interviews with unnamed 'important persons' whose identities he refused to reveal.[1]

Vesco's true method was to read popular articles about foo-fighters, list the things their pilot witnesses and fraudulent inventors said they could do, and then arbitrarily invent a wholly hypothetical device, christened Feuerball, or 'Fireball', with the capability to perform them. The end result was that, in Vesco's imagination, the Germans – and thus, definitely not aliens – had somehow managed to build a jet-powered flying metallic tortoise which possessed the ability to down Allied aircraft before magically escaping from the scene, thus accounting for their silvery shells' absence from aerospace museums. What could Vesco's SS-built Feuerball do, then? Quite a lot, really:

> It was circular and armoured, more-or-less resembling the shell
> of a tortoise, and was powered by a special turbo-jet engine, also
> flat and circular . . . which generated a great halo of luminous
> flames. Hence it was named Feuerball. It was unarmed and
> pilotless. Radio-controlled at the moment of take-off, it then
> automatically followed enemy aircraft, attracted by their exhaust
> flames, and approached close enough without collision to wreck
> their radar gear.[2]

As well as making it look like a giant Catherine-Wheel, the 'very rich fuel mixture' (including 'chemical additives') of the circular halo-producing jet engine had the helpful effect of 'overionising the atmosphere in the vicinity of the [enemy] plane' like Thor's Hammer, rendering the foo invisible to on-board radar, something helped by the presence of 'large klystron radio tubes protected with special anti-shock and anti-heat armour' beneath the tortoise's shell. As most readers won't have the faintest idea what klystron radio tubes are, this technical-sounding detail makes it sound as if Vesco really knows what he is talking about, as befits a man who once commanded the entire technical section of the Italian air fleet at the age of 20.

According to Vesco, the SS made great headway in producing electro-magnetic aeroplane disruptors during the war – and yet we have already seen how Elemag-Hildesheim's 1944 proposal to produce just such a thing was explicitly dismissed by that very same body as likely to take years to develop. Not so, says Vesco, who argues the Nazis' Alpenfestung Wunderwaffen factories were further along in development than many historians would care to admit, the complex as a whole being used as 'a sort of dry-land aircraft carrier' to launch them from. The Germans even managed to manufacture ground-based versions of the Feuerball, the Feuermolch ('Fire Salamander') and Feuerland ('Fire Land'), to jam Anglo-American communications with, thus ensuring all was quiet on the Western Front.

A sure sign Feuerball was invented not by the SS but inside Vesco's own post-1947 head comes in his statement that 'during the day it looked like a shining disc spinning on its side, and during the night it looked like a burning globe' when, as we have seen, disc-shaped foos were not described by witnesses except retrospectively, after the war had ended. If Allied airmen did see silver daytime objects, they resembled globes or Christmas-tree baubles, not saucers. As for why they often flew in formation not solo, Vesco explained there were several Alpenfestung foo-factories in operation, and those from some were 'not as perfect' as those from others, meaning the drones, used operationally before they were truly ready, had to fly out in twos and threes just in case one was faulty – whatever happened to that famous precision German engineering?

Hermann Goering took a close interest in Projekt Feuerball, personally inspecting its development labs 'a number of times', and no doubt came away particularly impressed by its James Bond-style method of self-escape and self-destruct. It was possible for SS drone operators to trigger on-board explosives and destroy them from the ground (so why not do this when they were hovering alongside Allied planes?), but just in case enemy gunners hit them, the Space-Age mutant Nazi turtles came with special switches concealed beneath their shells which, when shot by bullets, closed an electrical circuit, triggering a 'maximum acceleration device' and causing the foo to zoom away vertically, explaining why no downed Feuerballs were ever recovered by ground troops.

Thus, the real foo-fighters' apparent non-physical nature becomes instantly reconfigured as sure-fire evidence of the exact opposite. Blueprints for them were then captured by British raiders after the war's end, said Vesco, before being back-engineered. But, if post-war UFOs were thus caused by repurposed Nazi tortoise tech, how to account for most saucers being rather larger than the average shell-bearing pet reptile was?[3]

* * *

Vesco explained that Germany had soon developed an even better new foo-craft named the Kugelblitz, or 'Ball Lightning'. Confusingly, Daimler-Benz did indeed develop a deadly Wunderwaffe called Kugelblitz towards the war's end – but it was a mobile anti-aircraft twin-cannon 30mm flak gun, mounted on the chassis of a Panzer IV tank where the usual cannon turret would go, not a UFO, hence its fuller name, Flakpanzer IV Kugelblitz. Curiously, photographs of this very rare device's unusual spherical turret, taken from its tank-chassis and placed on display in military museums, do greatly resemble a self-contained and weaponised *Sputnik* Soviet space satellite of the 1950s. Viewed out of context, you could easily pass it off as a real, close-up image of a solid, metal SS foo-fighter, especially with its easily abused display label name tag.[4]

Unlike the Feuerball, Vesco's imaginary Kugelblitz, just like the real Daimler-Benz one, could down enemy aircraft, not simply ruin their radar. As many more people will have read the promotional article than the book, as all disappointed authors know, let's deal with the specific Kugelblitz account Vesco provided in his 1969 *Argosy* piece. Late in the war, 'the Special Air Research Corps of the SS' had created 'an amazing improvement' on the Feuerball by messing about with their spanners underneath the Alps, the Italian wrote:

> By combining the principle of the aircraft with a round, sym-metrical plane, with direct gyroscopic stabilisation, employing an ejector-gun using grisou and a gelatinous organic/metallic fuel for a total reaction turbine, adding remote-control, vertical take-off, infrared seeking equipment and electrostatic firing-systems, the harmless 'Fireball' became the lethal Kugelblitz! . . . The whole thing formed one compact, round mass which had absolutely nothing in common with any flying object ever produced before [except the Feuerball, presumably] . . . The incredibly fast and disc-shaped craft . . . was used only once. As the Allied forces crossed the Rhine, the only craft of its type was destroyed by the SS on instructions from Berlin.[5]

But this thing had already been used, even if only once? What did it do? Amazingly, it had downed an entire group of twelve US bombers over Dresden, 'without using firearms' (Vesco's later book also provides an additional account of 'a circular German fighter without wings or rudder' setting US planes aflame over Würtemburg). Kugelblitz possessed some special cannon that squirted unknown 'gaseous explosives' of a blue cloud-like appearance, derived by SS chemists from grisou or 'fire damp', a combustible methane-based gas sometimes found in mines. When enemy exhausts came into contact with this gas it exploded, ensuring certain doom. Vesco got this info from spy reports filed by 'a French diplomat' stationed in Switzerland who spoke in awe-struck terms of some 'strange hemispherical object which flew at fantastic speeds' towards the Dresden bombers, spewing out volatile vapours, apparently targeting the planes autonomously.[6]

The most obvious actual source for this story would have been left-wing Italian newspaper *Il Lavoratore*, whose 13 May 1952 edition featured the first appearance of this legend in print. Further inspirations may have included the Nazi spy-ring leader Nils Christian Christensen, who we met earlier offering to build Brazil a saucer fleet of its own in return for early release from prison. Christensen became a regular feature in the Brazilian press, making as many false promises about space travel as Richard Branson does today, and on 18 March 1950 he surfaced once more to pledge his initial aerial recon saucer could now act as an anti-aircraft device too. Once it reached a certain altitude, the disc would become an 'aerial torpedo', discharging flammable liquid over enemy jets.

Possibly Vesco got further inspiration from the *Kasseler Zeitung* for 7 June 1957, where the self-styled Austrian Wunderwaffen engineer H. Fister spoke of how he had once developed V-weapon anti-aircraft rockets equipped with a special 'rotating part' which emitted 'luminous gases' at 'very high temperatures', which would literally slice enemy planes to pieces like metal salamis. Fister's idea was so good that, a mere three months after proposing it, his design stood ready to be produced in full-size prototype form, before the invading Allies ruined everything. The USAF had since back-engineered Fister's rockets, before disseminating the popular lie they were piloted by ETs to confuse witnesses.[7]

Unlike Herr Fister, Signor Vesco alleged it was the British who won the back-engineering race from the Feuerball and Kugelblitz blueprints, sensibly making captured German scientists continue their work in Hitler's Alpenfestung factory labs at gunpoint to save time. The Nazis were only later Paperclipped off to England, Australia and Canada, where the revolutionary propulsion systems were stripped out from their foos, improved and used to power full-blown flying saucers with 'a half-moon-shaped crescent along the fuselage', thereby explaining Kenneth Arnold's 1947 sighting of 'bat-wing' craft.

They were not Martians flying over Washington State that day, revealed the ET-phobic Italian, but the British and their loyal Commonwealth Canadian co-conspirators, as proven by the later AvroCar affair. As further evidence, Vesco claimed 'the otherwise oh-so-eminently careful' BBC had accidentally announced the existence of these vehicles during a 1946 radio broadcast, proudly announcing Britain would 'soon have aircraft capable of speeds well over 1,000mph, that . . . could circumnavigate the globe several times because they needed only fuel for take-off and landing', not their actual flight – RAF suction saucers!

That Britain had indeed built suction vessels was shown by the 1954 experience of a Tehran businessman who had nearly been sucked into an RAF saucer whose pilot had 'a head like an elephant' due to his helmet and attached trunk-like oxygen tube. Annoyed that Washington had refused to gift her atom-bomb secrets after the war, London had ordered the construction of underground saucer hangars beneath 'the primeval forests of [British] Columbia' in the country next door, so retaining 'one major [military] trump-card which, one day, may become invaluable'.

However, the US and Britain still remained the closest of Cold War chums, and so the USAF, by now wise to England's industrial success, knew the RAF's saucers 'mean no harm', hence 'the long-standing order' handed out to all US fighter pilots should they ever come across one in US air space: 'Intercept – but do not fire upon.' Otherwise, you might cost Douglas Bader yet another one of his limbs.[8]

* * *

It is Renato Vesco alone who is responsible for inventing the Feuerball and Kugelblitz. But, like every weapon, once invented they could not be uninvented, and the consequences just have to be lived with by us all. A UFO enthusiast named Rob Arndt now runs a comprehensive website cataloguing the many different types of imaginary German air weapons, including Feuerball derivatives. According to Arndt, the very first Feuerballs, delivered in 1944, were 'simple, small, jet-powered silver discs launched off catapults and radio-controlled from the ground', intended purely as 'psychological test weapons' to gauge Allied pilots' reactions to seeing 'strange machines that defied all explanation'. If they were shot down, 'it was no loss', but if the SS preferred, they could bring them back home for recycling and re-use. Eventually, the Feuerballs were fitted with incendiary attack substances and

Messerschmidt-manufactured electrostatic field weapons that caused enemy engine-ignition systems to fail, 'one by one'.

To help the Feuerballs out, a range of other foos were launched alongside them, says Arndt, like the Seifenblasen, or 'Soap Bubbles', silvery metallic weather balloons, acting both as Feuerball-aping decoy targets and additional radar disruptors. Intended 'to add even more confusion' were AEG Kugelwaffen ('Ball Weapons'), small spherical devices 'roughly the size of a medicine ball' which flew in small groups and carried miniaturised Messerschmidt engine scramblers. Tested unarmed, these Kugelwaffen were responsible for the initial December 1944 reports of silvery Christmas-tree baubles hanging pointlessly over Germany.

The Kugelwaffen were powered by a plasma-based engine first developed for use in the SS' most advanced time-travel spaceships. By 'spinning containers of mercury at fantastic speeds within a ceramic bell-shaped object' charged with 'tremendous voltages', a 'mercury plasma gyro' was created, allowing the Kugelwaffen to defy the laws of gravity. As the Kugelwaffen could perform impossible manoeuvres, they naturally required impossible engines.

By splitting the foos into several separate sub-species, Arndt is able to account for the many discrepancies between their appearances and capabilities as reported by contemporary aircrews. Arndt further explains the wartime appearance of foos over Japanese skies by saying the Nazis transferred some Feuerballs and Kugelwaffen to their Asian Axis allies by U-boat, albeit with limited success. After using them to destroy a few US aircraft, the Japanese still didn't understand how the damned things worked, misinterpreting their incredible anti-gravity powers and fiery appearance as meaning that, rather than being purely technological items, they were supernaturally piloted, perhaps even possessed by devils.

Decrying them as 'Demon Things', Hirohito's hordes piled all their remaining Feuerballs in a big pit one day and dynamited them straight back to Hell. Covering up the whole affair, US intelligence preferred to write off any Pacific foo attacks as test-outs of the new Japanese Funryu-2 surface-to-air missile, not exported Nazi Wunderwaffen. (Arndt has apparently misunderstood the fact that the Japanese did indeed dynamite all their remaining Funryu stocks at the war's end, but only so the US couldn't get their hands on them, not because they were diabolically possessed.)[9]

Hating the 'inconclusive ravings' of ETH-believing ufologists, Vesco may have been equally as appalled to find that some, like Rob Arndt, apparently believe in time travel too.[10] Even worse, by helping spread the notion of Nazi UFOs, Vesco may only have accidentally opened another door for alien spotters to push their beloved ETH. A one-armed Swiss gentleman named Billy Meier (b.1937) has long claimed to be in contact with a beautiful Nordic-looking blonde from the Pleiades star cluster named Semjase, who inspired him to create his own personal New Age UFO philosophy. Ever since, he has produced many photographs of alien 'beamships', and even a time-travel one of an actual pterodactyl, images to make Vesco vomit.

Meier enjoys psychically channelling messages from other Pleiadian ETs with Scrabble-friendly names such as P'Taah, who in 1995 explained in his '254th contact conversation' that Luftwaffe 'flying tops' and foo-fighters were not created independently, but 'telepathically transmitted' to receptive German technicians by P'Taah's colleagues. Just like Alfred Nobel inventing dynamite, the Pleiadians naively hoped giving Germany such undefeatable Wunderwaffen would guarantee world peace, so terrible were they. When they realised the Nazis intended to actually use them, the ETs sabotaged the test flights.[11]

By disingenuously writing an entire fake book pretending the foos were solid, nuts-and-bolts German-built craft to debunk the Extra-Terrestrial Hypothesis, Vesco ironically empowered ETH believers to turn his thinking on its head by presenting Nazi UFOs as just more proof of alien visitation. Some new online folklore says the only reason the Nazis managed to build any saucers at all is because an ET one crashed in the Black Forest in 1936, or Mussolini's Italy in 1933, thus giving yet more back-engineers extensive overtime. Some say the UFO fell in Poland in 1938, causing Hitler's invasion that next year so he could steal it, meaning the trigger for the biggest conflict ever known to man was a kind of Nazi Roswell.[12] Studying English Literature at university many moons ago, I recall endless talk of something called 'The Death of the Author', which basically meant you could read whatever you wanted into any text, irrespective of its writer's actual intentions. Renato Vesco was not on the lecturers' rather post-modern curriculum, but he really should have been.

Chapter Seven

Some Bolts, Mostly Nuts: From Genuine German Jets to the Painted Plastic Pretender of Roswell

Is there any evidence foo-fighters were bona fide nuts-and-bolts Nazi craft, as Renato Vesco argued? Not really, but some at the time conjectured what was actually being seen were misperceived rear view glimpses of the burning exhaust jets of early German jets and rocket fighters. In retrospect, it appears some initial US newspaper reports about foos came inadvertently disguised as reports on these authentic new Nazi Wunderwaffen which entered active service during 1944. The following AP story appeared in various outlets on 7 November 1945, around a month prior to the sightings of giant Christmas-tree baubles dangling over the Reich:

Nazis Use Jet, Rocket Planes

Other New Gadgets Being Hurled Against Allied Night-Fighters
Paris, Nov 7 (AP): The Germans are using jet and rocket-pro-
pelled planes and various other new-fangled gadgets against Allied
night-fighters, Lt. Col. Oris B. Johnson, Natchitoches, La., com-
mander of a P-61 Black Widow group, said today. 'In recent nights
we've counted 15 to 20 jet-planes,' Johnson said. 'They sometimes
fly in formations of four but more often they fly alone.'[1]

Lieutenant Colonel Johnson's men were not unique. One 1945 article on the topic contains a description of 'A glowing red object shooting straight up, which suddenly changed to a view of an aircraft doing a wing-over, going into a dive and disappearing', which certainly sounds like a jet fighter.[2] This cannot generally have been the case, however.

The Messerschmidt Me-262, the sole such workable jet plane available to the Luftwaffe in reasonable numbers, only had one operational unit capable of night flying – night being when most foos were seen – and this was limited solely to defending the Berlin area, upon personal orders of Adolf Hitler. This unit, 10/NJG/11, didn't begin operations until December 1944, and until as late as February 1945 had but one pilot, the celebrated dare-devil Kurt Welter (1916–49), actually flying any missions after dark. The similarly uncommon Me-163 Komet rocket fighter also possessed a mere single active Combat Wing, JG-400, operating around Leipzig from July 1944 onwards, and during daylight hours only. This doesn't fit with the innumerable nocturnal foo reports emanating from right across Europe and Japan, over a much longer timescale. Shortage of aircraft, munitions, fuel, trained pilots and spare parts rendered German jets an impossible mass solution to the foo conundrum.[3]

These jets also did not behave terribly like jets. One US intelligence officer spoke of his unit's pilots encountering such 'jets' during late 1944:

> At first we thought they were seeing things . . . while I was on duty, they did not identify a jet as such. But I think that was the only conclusion we could reach . . . It could not have been a Will-o'-the-Wisp . . . these guys seemed to play around with them. They . . . never shot at them, and I can't recall whether the radar observer actually saw them on the screen. It was mostly visual in other words.[4]

When faced with a close-up view of a strange and possibly hostile object in the sky over enemy territory, the mind sees what it wants to see. Such was perhaps the case when, on the evening of 26 April 1944, RAF Flight Lieutenant Arthur Horton of 622 Squadron led a Lancaster bomber on a sortie over the Ruhr Valley, only to be tailed home by four orange balls of light, the size of large footballs, two on either wing.

Never having heard of foos, Horton thought it best to leave them alone; possibly they were some flying booby trap which, if fired upon, would unleash an aerial explosion. In the darkness, one gunner thought he could see 'small stubby wings' and an exhaust glow emerging from the rear of the things. The foos tailed the Lancaster like flaming shadows until, reaching the Dutch coast, they simply 'burned themselves out' and disappeared. Back at base, Horton guessed the Germans had deployed high-altitude radio-controlled anti-aircraft missiles, hence the supposed fins and exhausts. His debriefing officers just ridiculed him. Presumably they thought that, with the lamps out over Europe, he and his crew had only observed precisely what they had feared they may observe.[5]

At other times, however, it appears impossible to see something as being anything terribly comprehensible at all, if you possess no pre-existing frame of reference to place it within. Historian Dr David Clarke unearthed a prime example of this truth in action, receiving a 2003 communication from Ronald Claridge, a radar operator in another Lancaster bomber, who was returning from a mission in 1944 when he saw 'an enormous string of lights' which 'were circular, rather like portholes in a ship' and coloured 'a very bright yellow changing to intense white', about 1,000yd away in the night sky. They 'stretched fore and aft to what seemed like infinity'. After 30 seconds of open-mouthed staring, Claridge realised the lights were 'part of an enormous disc'.

Claridge later produced a drawing for Clarke's inspection. It is a classic flying saucer, three whole years before Kenneth Arnold. The entire crew were stunned by its presence, almost hypnotised, with the gunners feeling curiously unable to open fire; they 'all sensed we were being watched by another force outside our knowledge'. Yet this still cannot be taken as definite evidence for the existence of saucers prior to June 1947. For one thing, Claridge said the crew were ordered not to record the sighting in their logbooks, so there is no documentary proof it actually happened. Presuming it did, by 2003 the airman had nearly sixty years to reframe his puzzling experience into an encounter with a flying saucer, rather than merely a more uncategorisable sighting of odd lights in the sky.

He could not have reported to superiors that he had witnessed a flying saucer at the time, because there were not yet such things as flying saucers available for him to report. When the craft – for such it since became, in Claridge's mind – zoomed away at an impossibly high speed and vanished, it melted away into the clouds forever.[6] Today, though, in some bizarre compensatory fashion, the foo-fighter, that ineffable Will-o'-the-Wisp of the mid-1940s stratosphere, has, like cement in an imaginative mould, set itself into an actual, solid physical object in an increasingly non-solid media world. Today, there is even one on display inside a museum.

***

On a remote ranch at Roswell, New Mexico, in the first week of July 1947, something very interesting happened – a flying saucer did not crash there.

Despite this fact, mere weeks beforehand Kenneth Arnold had made his headlines and (to adopt, for the sake of simplicity, the standard sceptical line upon the whole affair), due to a complex series of misunderstandings involving the descent of an experimental high-altitude military weather balloon and its associated advanced instrument package, many people came to think one had done so.

Today, a non-museum stands near the site of this non-event, commemorating its non-occurrence with a series of curious non-exhibits – one of which is a plastic, camouflage-painted Airfix-type model of a gun-toting Nazi flying saucer within a glass display case, surrounded by toy German soldiers, the whole diorama bearing the label 'Nazi Foo-Fighter? (1945)'. This saucer is big enough to be piloted and its Flugkapitän has climbed on top with the aid of a small ladder, where he seems to be busily tying his jackboot. One soldier down below is feeding a kitten, fitting in with the well-known fact that Nazis were always kind to animals (it was humans they sometimes had a problem with). Appropriately enough, Roswell's International UFO Museum and Research Center is located inside an old cinema.

Most visitors will take note of the question mark on the model's display label and draw the obvious conclusion: this is another one of those fascinating historical questions to which the answer is 'no'. Others will take it more literally, as a legitimate issue being currently disputed by military historians within the halls of academe. Did the Nazis really develop such a craft? Puzzled tourists might go online and visit Wikipedia, typing in 'foo-fighter' to see what comes up. There, they will be immediately confronted with a large photograph of the very same diorama taken direct from the Roswell Museum.[7] If they don't bother to read beyond the first paragraph of the accompanying article, as many won't, they might be led to conclude that the Nazis did indeed develop their own combat-ready solid saucers during the Second World War, these being called foo-fighters.

Where did the Roswell Museum get hold of such a thing? It was hardly an Unobtainable Flying Object. Several military model manufacturers will today happily sell you kits containing dozens of fiddly Nazi saucer parts for you and your kids to fail to stick together properly with superglue. These are actively pushed as if once flown by daring Luftwaffe pilots for real, in 1939–45; in some parallel universe, perhaps they are even now busy bombing Legoland?

Most manufacturers would argue their models are intended purely as novelties, that it is blatantly obvious the Nazis had no flying saucers, and that nobody normal could ever think otherwise. Others may disagree. In 2018, German toy manufacturer Revell drew flak for its release of a model German UFO, or 'round aircraft', which was supposedly 'the first object in the world capable of flying in space' at a speed of 6,000kmph. Emblazoned with Nazi military emblems, Revell implied the saucer had enjoyed a successful test flight in 1943, but could not be mass-produced due to the deteriorating war situation.

The German Children's Protection Association and various historians quickly heaped scorn on Revell's new item. Jens Wehner, of Dresden's Military History Museum, complained that, as 'it was technologically impossible to build something like this' during the war, a toy maker saying otherwise might enable neo-Nazis to 'use this as a strategy to cast doubt on what we know today about National Socialism', thus making naïve, saucer hungry kids question whether Hitler was all bad after all. Chastened, Revell immediately withdrew the product from shelves. The Nazi UFO was 'in fact a legendary, extraordinary aircraft which cannot be proven in terms of its existence . . . unfortunately, our product-description does not adequately express this and we apologise for it' a penitent spokesman said. The company desired to glorify neither war nor Nazism, Revell added, saying any criticism received was 'absolutely justified' – but were such critics just being oversensitive?[8]

Maybe not. Revell has many non-German rivals in the model Nazi UFO market who, for as little as £26.07, or as much as £138, will gladly step in to flog you their own scaled down self-construction kit of another 'factual' class of Nazi saucer, dubbed the Haunebu II. Advertisements of such kits deliberately make them sound like actually extant craft of Nazi-era vintage, as with the Squadron toy company's following marketing spiel, listed on amazon.co.uk:

> According to some, Nazi Germany's scientific capabilities were so advanced that they began work on a series of secretive spacecraft. Known as Haunebu, these flying saucers were built upon specialised engines developed by the Third Reich and, again according to some theorists, remain in underground bases around the world. A newly-tooled replica of the otherworldly Nazi spacecraft, this

1:72-scale plastic kit features a well-equipped interior (with three main operating consoles, nine crew seats, and a grated floor), a three-piece upper exterior, forward bunker housing, two-piece bottom disc, a retractable entrance ramp (with extension), a main turret (with detachable roof), two 110mm cannons, optional-position landing-gear, four rotating ball-turrets (with 80mm guns), and one clear sprue (with injection-moulded windows). Assembly required. 125 pieces. Skill Level 3.[9]

If you want to know more about 'the infamous German WWII Haunebu II project', head towards Squadron's website, where you can view a video of an SS man inspecting a full-size computer generated saucer in its hangar, and learn that you get a free 'brief history' of the craft included in its instruction booklet. Squadron's slogan is 'SQUADRON: BRINGING HISTORY TO LIFE', but what if such 'history' was never actually lived in the first place?[10]

An even more detailed history of the Haunebu II appears on the website of Anigrand Craftswork, a Hong Kong-based firm who prefer making kits of 'unusual, experimental and conceptual aircraft and spacecraft' rather than boring old Spitfires and Hurricanes. Forming part of Anigrand's 'German experimental aircraft of the Second World War' range, the Haunebu II possessed the following highly specific statistics, so they say:

- Type: Heavy-Armed Flight Gyro
- Purpose: To explore the VTOL flying-disc
- Span (dia.): 32m
- Height: 11.20m
- Engine: 1xThule Triebwerk EMG engines
- Max speed: 6,000kmph
- Crew: 9
- Armament: 6xMG-131 machine-gun/2x3.7 Flak 43 cannon

How did Anigrand know all this? They must have bought one of Squadron's competing kits and read the free instruction booklet. A full production history for the $98 model (you could add $2 for extra swastika stickers, bringing it to a round $100) was also provided by Anigrand in broken Chinglish:

In 1935, a mysterious group, Vril, was found in Northwest Germany that was to develop a series of flying disc. The disc crafts were to be installed by a revolutionary electro-magnetic-gravitic engine that powered the rotating disc wing or internal disc blade. In 1939, A several of prototypes were said to be tested at Arado Brandenburg aircraft testing field. Stable and control problems were revealed during flight tests. In 1943, the SchutzStaffel [SS] manoeuvred to take control of the weapon from the German Army. One of the tasks was researching the alternative energies and fuels. The SS took over the most completed models, the Vril RFZ-5 and RFZ-6, redesigned it as Haunebu I and II. The armament was planned the KSK strong ray cannon but was installed existing KG gun and tank cannon instead. In 1944, the SS had intended to produce the Haunebu II with tenders for both Junkers and Dornier but in early 1945 Dornier was chosen. However, the end of the war prevented Dornier from building any Haunebu production.[11]

Never mind – now you can build your own instead! But, if you did buy one of Anigrand's kits, what would you actually be making? Pathetic faked photographs of these Haunebu on the company's website show what is quite clearly something known in ufology as an 'Adamski Scoutship', a class of saucers photographed by a notoriously dubious US alien Contactee named George Adamski (1891–1965) during the 1950s, and generally dismissed as showing something like car hubcaps or parts from electric lamp lights suspended in mid-air rather than true spaceships from Venus, as George claimed. Onto these have then been superimposed German military insignia.

Thus, the Haunebu II, allegedly developed prior to 1945 by the SS, has its actual paradoxical origins in two later inventions: Kenneth Arnold's original 1947 flying saucer and George Adamski's subsequent 1950s Venusian Scoutship rip-off of it. Another model Haunebu II available online comes from Pegasus Hobbies, who more honestly list their toy as part of their 'Sci-Fi Range', labelling the craft a purely 'theoretical 1940s-era German spaceship'. Despite this, one satisfied amazon customer had the following five-star review to offer: 'There are many trustworthy, mostly USAF crew, witnesses of "foo-fighters" during the latter months of WWII who described such "saucers". The model seems to be accurate when compared to the few not HD original photos . . . McDonald's are right:

I'm loving it!'[12] I don't know which 'few not HD original photos' of foos he means; presumably the doctored Adamski Scoutship ones you can find all over the Internet. Thus, the models are authentic physical manifestations of authentic Photoshopped fakes. Further proof such intellectual junk food is bad for you comes when you realise that the Roswell UFO Museum's purported foo-fighter on display is actually itself most likely a modified web-bought model Haunebu II, but with the characteristic Adamski-esque domed top left off so a toy Nazi can crouch there tying his bootlaces. It may sound a bit pedantic to say curators have accidentally placed the wrong variety of fictional saucer on display, but it is highly illustrative of the profoundly twisted chronology of this whole subject.

* * *

The Roswell International UFO Museum didn't open until 1991, as the Roswell UFO crash itself, despite ostensibly taking place in 1947, didn't really happen until 1980 when a best-selling book, *The Roswell Incident*, by Charles Berlitz (1913–2003) and William Moore (b.1943) appeared, based upon interviews with a key man on the scene back in the day, the fantasy prone military intelligence officer Major Jesse Marcel (1907–86). Marcel spun a most sellable yarn about indestructible super metals inscribed with ET hieroglyphs raining down upon the New Mexico ranch in question, but said nothing about now-familiar later additions to the tale, like alien corpses being found. He didn't even specifically mention any structured craft, just fire-proof, hammer-proof sheets of tinfoil-like metals.

These supplementary ideas only bloomed in the wake of Berlitz and Moore's book. The Roswell affair had been largely forgotten prior to this text's appearance, so the subsequent 'witnesses' to alien autopsies we associate with Roswell today were reacting more to a recent 1980s publishing event than to any original nuts-and-bolts saucer crash of 1947. Had the book never appeared, presumably they would have kept quiet, because it was the events in the book, not down on the ranch, they were really claiming to have seen.[13] Had the Roswell UFO Museum tried to open back in 1947, it could have had no exhibits. Headlines specifically said a flying disc had crashed there at the time, but this was quickly debunked by the military as being an error of interpretation and almost everyone accepted the fact. Nobody opens a museum devoted to something that didn't happen . . . until, that is, the thing that didn't happen suddenly does come to have happened, not in physical reality, but in the public mind. Curiously, in a certain sense the nuts-and-bolts enthusiasts of ufology thus have more faith in the power of the imagination than do their less literally minded psychosocial counterparts.

Fast forward to today, and the Roswell International UFO Museum still has no proper alien exhibits, but it does have a popular myth, created in 1980, to sustain it, and so can invent whatever displays it needs to fit in with it. And so, we end up with the mind-bending spectacle of a museum opened in 1991 to commemorate the reinvention of an event which didn't occur back in 1947, but was said to have done, retrospectively, from 1980 onwards, containing a plastic model of a Nazi Haunebu II flying saucer, invented by online fantasists during the 1990s, but modelled physically upon the appearance of a car hubcap promoted as being a different model of flying saucer, an Adamski Scoutship, during the 1950s, being used to represent a different form of flying saucer, known as a foo-fighter, witnessed for real during the years 1939–45, but never in the form of an actual flying saucer, because flying saucers didn't even exist themselves until 1947, when Kenneth Arnold didn't even see one before another one then quickly didn't crash at Roswell – except, weirdly, the saucer actually crashed at Roswell *before* Arnold had seen his saucer. It's just that, at this point in time, the Roswell wreckage could not yet have been seen as being a saucer, because Arnold himself had yet to not see one. I trust that all makes sense.

Tellingly, even the date of the Roswell Non-Incident itself is highly disputed. It is generally dated to early July, but original press accounts cite the ranch's operator, W.W. 'Mac' Brazel (1899–1963), as having stumbled across 'a large area of bright wreckage made up of rubber strips, tinfoil, a rather tough paper and sticks' on 14 June, a week or so before Kenneth Arnold's experience. At the time, Brazel 'did not pay much attention' to it, because it was just a pile of rubbish. On 5 July, however, Brazel first heard about these flying saucers of Arnold's whizzing around, with cash rewards of up to $3,000 for anyone who found one, and it was only now he visited his local sheriff, who in turn contacted Roswell Army Air Force Base saying he thought a disc might have come down nearby.

But had he not seen media reports of Arnold's sighting, Brazel might just have left the biodegradable-sounding 'saucer' there to rot. Brazel had found downed weather balloons before and, whilst 'sure what I found was not one of these' – it was, after all, a novel advanced one designed for detecting signs of Soviet nuclear tests in the atmosphere – it seems unlikely he would have considered it anything truly special had he not then read about Arnold in the papers.

Soon, Brazel could read about himself there too. The *Roswell Daily Record* for 8 July 1947 ran with the front-page headline 'RAAF [Roswell Army Air Field] Captures Flying Saucer On Ranch in Roswell Region', but by the next day, in the wake of official denials, preferred the less sensational 'Harassed Rancher Who Located "Saucer" Sorry He Told About It'. Below was the following description of what precisely Brazel found on his land, and later helped collect for military analysis:

> When the debris was gathered up the tinfoil, paper, tape and sticks made a bundle about 3 feet long and 7 or 8 inches thick, while the rubber made a bundle about 18 or 20 inches long and about 8 inches thick. In all . . . the entire lot would have weighed maybe five pounds. There was no sign of any metal in the area which might have been used for an engine and no sign of any propellers of any kind, although at least one paper fin had been glued onto some of the tinfoil . . . Considerable Scotch tape and some tape with flowers printed upon it had been used in the construction.[14]

That doesn't sound like the construction materials likely to have been used in either an alien spacecraft or any back-engineered Nazi Wunderwaffen to me. Aviation geniuses Rudolf Schriever and Wernher von Braun may have been, but not in the field of paper aeroplanes.

* * *

Further mutation of the Roswell myth came in 2011, with the release of *Area 51: An Uncensored History of America's Top Secret Military Base* by investigative journalist Annie Jacobsen (b.1967). The majority of her book is a sensible enough exploration of life in the titular base in question, located near the dried-up Groom Lake in the Nevada Desert outside Las Vegas and used for testing out new top-secret military technologies, from the U-2 spy plane to the B-2 stealth bomber. Opened in July 1955, 'Dreamland', as it is also known, gained notoriety during the late 1980s when self-claimed physicist Bob Lazar (b.1959) began promoting his story of having worked there on craft with anti-matter engines. The US military had dragged crashed saucers back to Dreamland from places like Roswell before harvesting their technology to create new items for use on Earth. Lazar's story made Area 51 a pop-culture icon, with groups of binocular wielding tourists being bussed out towards its perimeter for nights of guided UFO spotting. Some might even see something worth the ticket price.

Area 51 is a potentially profitable meme, then. Unfortunately, many of its genuine secrets are now so old they are no longer secrets any more. As a result, the majority of Jacobsen's 523-page book, whilst doubtless interesting to military aviation enthusiasts, was not going to garner any headlines. The final chapter, however, was different, successfully creating a media firestorm; in its first week of release in June 2011, *Area 51* entered straight in at number seven on the *New York Times* non-fiction hardcover bestseller list. This last section rather risibly reveals that the Roswell saucer was not an alien space-craft at all, but a special futuristic-looking stealth-fighter, back-engineered by Russia from a jet-powered aircraft with a single swept-back wing, the Horten Ho-229 (also known as the H-IX), developed by pioneering German aerospace siblings Reimar (1915–94) and Walter Horten (1913–98) near the end of the war. In reality, the US bagged the only remaining Ho-229 prototype as spoils of battle, but Jacobsen implied Moscow had somehow managed to get their hands on one too.

In Jacobsen's telling, Soviet dictator Joseph Stalin (1878–1953) had surprisingly teamed up with fugitive Nazi war criminal Dr Josef Mengele (1919–79), former chief physician at Auschwitz death camp, whose inmates he had infamously exploited for various totally inhumane medical experiments. After the war, Mengele had been located by the Kremlin and offered a deal: Stalin would provide him with a new laboratory, if only he would use it to engineer via plastic surgery a new race of deformed sub-humans who looked so bizarre they could be taken for alien beings.

Mengele agreed, kidnapping 12-year-olds to sculpt a crew of 'grotesque, child-size aviators' of 'alien-like' appearance, with 'oversized heads and abnormally-shaped, oversize eyes', to be locked inside back-engineered Horten Ho-229s. Such Horten 'flying wings' would then be further modified to look like futuristic alien ships, with a whole fleet of them being launched and flown over the US via remote control, before landing in public places. As the hideous bulbous-headed kids emerged, these would be taken for invading ET dwarfs, sparking mass panic, as is meant to have occurred in 1938 when Orson Welles' (1915–85) notorious radio play version of H.G. Wells' *The War of the Worlds* had been mistaken for a real-life news report by certain credulous listeners.

Stalin's plan was scheduled for that truly action-packed year of 1947. However, the Russians' remote-control broadcasts went seriously wrong, one Horten crashed at Roswell, and the 'alien' corpses found amongst the wreckage were recognised to be simply mutilated human children. US intelligence covered up the incident, transported the corpses (and two 'comatose but still alive' infants) and the downed Horten itself away to what is now Wright-Patterson Airforce Base in Ohio prior to it all then being sent on to Area 51 and placed within a sealed-off facility-within-a-facility named S-4 for further research and back-engineering.

Another reason for keeping the crash secret was that US President Harry S. Truman privately knew that 'we were doing the same thing' as the Russians behind closed doors anyway! His plot rumbled, Mengele fled to South America, where he hid out until his death in a swimming accident in 1979. As a responsible professional journalist, Annie Jacobsen of course did not make this story up herself. Instead, she relied upon someone else to do it for her, accepting the testimony of a single unnamed source, a retired engineer from the now-defunct US defence company EG&G, a private contractor with business inside Dreamland.

When the book was released, several genuine former Area 51 military engineers, pilots and technicians Jacobsen had interviewed for the main text were outraged, such as electronics expert T.D. Barnes, president of the ex-employees' group Roadrunners Internationale. For decades, the Roadrunners had kept quiet about their classified work at Area 51 during the 1950s and 1960s but now that their fine but long-since superseded inventions were no longer a matter of pressing national security, they wished to get their side of the story down.

Jacobsen had provided this opportunity, but by then going and writing a completely mad final chapter without asking them about any of it, Barnes' friends felt betrayed by her. The fiendish Mengele-Stalin plot never happened, they said, making the Roadrunners 'up in arms over the book'. It had 'its good points', Barnes added, but 'the last chapter just . . . totally destroyed the purpose of us talking and being in the book because all the [publicity] focus is on that'.

'She warped the history to fit her theme,' Barnes complained, making one final suggestion, 'I'm not telling people not to buy the book – I'm just asking people not to read the last chapter.' Fat chance of that. The final chapter is the only one designed to actually be read by the average purchaser, the rest is just filler. Remember that biography of David Cameron which nobody bought other than to flick quickly to the page where he supposedly rapes a dead pig in the mouth at university, as endlessly trailed in newspaper extracts prior to its publication? Jacobsen's book follows the exact same publishing model, it should really have been called 'Fakes on a Plane'. Stalin's sinister scheme has since popped up in the equally attention-grabbing form of a shocking plot twist in series two of sci-fi drama series *Project Blue Book*, broadcast on something presuming to call itself 'The History Channel'.[15]

Problems with Jacobsen's narrative are obvious. Popular accounts of the 1938 Orson Welles' *War of the Worlds* scare are greatly exaggerated, with reports of millions of panicking citizens creating chaos across the land bearing little relation to the much more limited unease actually elicited amongst a certain proportion of more excitable listeners. In light of inflated media reports about Welles' prank, many had since become ultra-sceptical of such announcements. When another of Welles' shows was interrupted in December 1941 by a genuine newsflash declaring Pearl Harbor had just been bombed by Japan, some presumed it was another joke. Instead of provoking hysteria, Stalin's plot may only have elicited cynicism.[16] Plus, if Stalin had truly back-engineered precious stealth aircraft from any captured Horten, he would hardly wish to hand over a working example to Washington for free, just to create short-term public alarm.

Anyway, in 1947 Walter Horten himself had contacted the US defence contractor Northrop and volunteered to be Paperclipped to work for them on a flying wing design, hearing they were investigating the possibility of such a craft; the US' B-2 stealth bomber was ultimately based on Horten's Wunderwaffe vehicle. Northrop said they would gladly give Walter a job, if only he could get permission from the correct authorities. Presumably, therefore, if Walter ever saw any footage of his modified plane landing on the White House lawn and being passed off as a spaceship, he would have been straight in touch telling the US what it really was and asking for a free passport. Walter had already been contacted after Kenneth Arnold's sighting and quizzed whether the Nazis had ever had plans to make any saucers. He said no. Worse, according to Jacobsen, instead of strange ET hieroglyphs being present on the Roswell wreckage, as had been claimed by Major Jesse Marcel, the Horten had foolishly instead come complete with 'letters from the Cyrillic alphabet'. What did this Russian writing say? 'Made in Moscow'? The whole story makes no sense at all.[17]

It also bears unusual similarity to an earlier scenario presented by UFO researcher Nick Redfern's 2005 book *Body Snatchers in the Desert*, which laid out the equally unlikely possibility that what really crashed at Roswell was a modified Horten, supported by a giant balloon, and filled with disabled Japanese people as part of some bizarre aerial medical test. According to Redfern's own anonymous sources, those involved were one-time prisoners of the Japanese Imperial Army's infamous Unit 731, a band of oriental Dr Mengeles who had also tortured live human subjects in the name of 'research' in Japanese-occupied Manchuria during the war, performing vivisections on resources described in official documents merely as 'logs' (re: innocent Chinese people). Although Unit 731 may have poisoned, burned, dissolved, infected and sliced to death up to half a million people, some of their officers, too, were given immunity from prosecution by the US in return for sharing their knowledge about biological and chemical weapons, just as with the moon-shooting Nazis of Operation Paperclip – that's Cold War realpolitik for you.

Like Mengele, Unit 731's doctors had a particular interest in unusual human specimens suffering from genetic conditions such as Progeria Syndrome and Ellis-van Creveld Syndrome, which lead to children being born with short-limbed dwarfism, oversized bald heads and non-standard numbers of fingers – just like the slant-eyed alien bodies supposedly found at Roswell, which were thus truly 'alien' only in the sense of being foreign. It is implied by Redfern's informants that Unit 731's leading lights, once Paperclipped to the US, united with their Nazi death-camp counterparts to continue experimenting upon their disabled wartime prisoners, who had been imported as human cargo too, thereby avoiding any US lives having to be sacrificed in the post-war scientific arms race. Perhaps this is what President Truman meant when allegedly acknowledging the US was up to the same tricks as the Soviets? Or maybe Annie Jacobsen's informant had just read Redfern's earlier book and decided to create an unofficial sequel?[18]

Not long after *Area 51*'s release, Florida-based ufologist Tony Bragalia outed her anonymous source as an 89-year-old former EG&G scientist named Alfred O'Donnell (now dead), formerly involved in nuclear weapons research for the US military. Tracking him down, Bragalia asked point-blank if he was Jacobsen's informant, but a surprised O'Donnell more-or-less refused to comment, although he did let slip that 'I do know Annie'. Bragalia is a champion of the ETH, and saw O'Donnell as both telling the truth and not telling the truth simultaneously. The yarn about Mengele and Stalin was obvious garbage, but it was one O'Donnell had been fed by military authorities.

Invited to view alien bodies at Area 51 before being misinformed that they were dead Japanese dwarfs, O'Donnell's misleaders had one of two motives. Maybe they just wanted to see if he blabbed about the amazing sight before entrusting him with any truly top-secret work out at Dreamland. Alternatively, if O'Donnell did blab, then the cover story they had fed him was so obviously insane that, the more it was spread around, the more people would become sceptical anything had really happened at Roswell at all. Thus, for Bragalia, the clear untruth of O'Donnell's story proved it was in fact clearly true . . . at least from O'Donnell's own too-trusting perspective. Considered in a wider sense, it was actually a lie . . . but a lie which, inadvertently, told the actual truth, namely, that an alien saucer really had crashed at Roswell after all. Whenever the US reveal any of their latest tech to the world, Bragalia says, they have to explain where they got the idea from. Instead of admitting 'from the aliens', they usually just say 'from the Russians', hence the absurd dead give-away Cyrillic letters reported by O'Donnell as being visible on the craft.[19]

* * *

A similar Roswell-type legend is that of the Spitsbergen saucer crash, first mentioned in a German newspaper on 28 June 1952, which is both after a weather balloon crashed at Roswell in 1947, but before it turned into a full-blown alien craft in 1980, providing an interesting intermediate case study. The *Saarbrücker Zeitung* alleged that a squadron of Norwegian jet-planes had been performing training routines over the Svalbard Islands, about 930km north of Norway, a remote and sparsely populated region covered in ice and snow.

One of the islands is called Vest Spitsbergen, and whilst passing over this area, the jets' radios malfunctioned. Looking down, one pilot realised why; he saw 'a metallic, glittering, circular disc of between 40 and 50 meters in diameter, which was brighter than the icy snow', from which 'an apparently partly destroyed cockpit protruded'. Within hours, investigating Norwegian troops had found the saucer was unmanned, made of 'an unknown metal', bore 'Russian symbols' on its measuring instruments, had a ring of forty-six propulsion jets on its base and appeared designed to transport high explosives, possibly even atom bombs; carrying 'a radio-detection finder equipped with a plutonium core', it was certainly radioactive.

When the *Saarbrücker Zeitung* put this description to someone they called 'the German V-weapon designer Riedel' – presumably Walter Riedel (1902–68), a one-time V-2 engineer who was actually rather a saucer sceptic – he supposedly responded, 'That's a typical V-7 on whose serial production I have worked myself', no doubt alongside Richard Miethe. Indeed, in 1955 an obscure book, *Flying Saucers Over South Africa*, was published in that country by one Edgar Sievers, specifically claiming it was one of Miethe's V-7 designs which had spluttered its last on Spitsbergen.[20] In fact, the entire event was invented wholesale, under a journalistic non-name. Enquiries have since demonstrated that no other newspapers reported the story at the time, not even in Norway itself, where you may have thought it would have been big news. None of the names of the pilots or scientists listed have proved traceable and records show all Norway's early generation military jets were stationed too far south for the Svalbard Islands to be within their flight range at the time. When Project Blue Book asked the Norwegian Air Force about the incident, they replied it was 'definitely false'.

The idea the Soviets had captured a Nazi disc and then back-engineered it to carry atom bombs over Scandinavia just didn't shift enough copies, though, so on 26 July 1954 another German rag of low editorial standards, *Hessiche Nachrichten*, decided to resurrect and re-jig it somewhat, riding on that year's pan-European saucer wave. By this stage, the idea UFOs contained ET beings was very firmly lodged within the public mind, so *Hessiche Nachrichten* simply claimed, quoting a Norwegian Air Force colonel with a made-up name, that 'a misunderstanding developed, some time ago' that the downed saucer was of Soviet-Nazi origin. It was not a Wunderwaffe at all, but something that 'has – this we must state emphatically – not been built by any country on Earth'. Instead, extraterrestrials had a secret base somewhere at the North Pole, from whence they were buzzing Europe in their circular vessels. This, it was explained, was why Swedish TV reception had been so poor of late!

If German newspapers could report upon a fake saucer crash taking place on a remote Norwegian island, then why should not Norwegian newspapers gain revenge by reporting upon a fake saucer crash taking place on a remote German island? On 19 December 1954, Norway's *Verdens Gang* shamelessly relocated the Spitsbergen saucer to Heligoland, a small German possession in the North Sea. Now the Soviet-Nazi saucer was a definite spaceship, controlled by special 'push buttons' which enabled it to fly via manipulation of 'the magnetic forces that hold the planets in their position in space' – forget the crashed UFO, *Verdens Gang* should really have been reporting on the disproval of the theory of gravity!

Onboard were found navigational books written 'in completely unknown writing', special water 'three times as heavy as normal water' and 'a few pills which were taken to be food'. There were also seven bodies, of general humanoid appearance, but 'burned beyond recognition' – all except for their 'perfect sets of teeth'. The theory of investigating scientist Hans Larsen Løberg, a 'one-time winner of the Hungarian Physics Award' – both scientist and honour alike appear to have been equally fictional – guessed the ship had been blown from the atmosphere by a US hydrogen bomb test, which had fried its occupants but left the machine itself unharmed, made as it was from special indestructible alien metals (like IMPERVIUM, maybe?). Even better, there was 'a beam-gun which used magnetic rays' aboard too, which Løberg bizarrely linked to a local spate of vandalised car windows. From here, the story of the Spitsbergen/Heligoland crashes entered into the more general UFO literature, where they were often passed off as having been a pair of real events, perfect alien smiles and all.[21]

The entire legend demonstrates clearly how fashions change. Back in 1952, the idea of a Nazi-Soviet V-7 Wunderwaffe saucer was thought likely to sell newspapers. By 1954, when landed humanoid aliens were being reported by the media as having been seen all over the place during that year's great pan-European UFO wave, the idea of ET craft crashing was deemed more likely to boost sales. Far from being solid, nuts-and-bolts craft, this fact alone is highly suggestive of the fact that these things are but products of the mind, just like Macbeth's famous dagger, hardly as sensible to feeling as to sight. That is one reason why writing a full history of Nazi UFOs is such a peculiar task; because, in the end, it amounts to a history of nothing much at all.

Chapter Eight

In My End is My Beginning: The Back-Engineering of Nazi Narrative Lego Sets

The Nazi UFO mythos we enjoy and endure today is wholly ahistorical in more than one way. It is not just that none of this stuff ever actually happened. It is also that the chronology of the entire narrative doesn't make any sense, with the Nazis developing saucers during a period when there wasn't any idea of saucers for them to develop, for instance. As was once said, 'This is not a story with a beginning, a middle and an end' – or, if the silly symphony does have all these notes, they are not necessarily being played in the right order.[1]

To its observers, the supersonic V-2 rocket appeared to possess a kind of reverse causality to it too. Being faster than the speed of sound, the device's explosive warhead hit the ground before the noise of its path through the air could reach the ears of its victims, as famously depicted in Thomas Pynchon's absurdist 1973 novel *Gravity's Rainbow*. A V-2 thus appeared to somehow detonate before it had even arrived. The legend of Nazi flying saucers is constructed upon similar temporal principles. This was once inadvertently summed up very well by Henry Stevens:

> The German flying disc programme built upon itself, each innovation retaining something from a previous design yet incorporating a new innovation. This progressed through several steps until the original had seemingly nothing in common with the original design. At each step a saucer project, or at least a saucer design, seems to have been spun off. Each of these spin-offs was not an independent, stand-alone project, but . . . if viewed out-of-context, the multiplicity of designs and spin-offs have led to confusion concerning the whole. Proponents of each design or spin-off have championed the project with which they were familiar as THE German Saucer project.[2]

Stevens means this literally, in terms of physically built craft; I mean it less so, in terms of the whole hoax story's overarching narrative structure. If someone comes along and points out these things can't fly, someone else can always just add a new element to the blueprint, rectifying the initial design flaw. Stevens himself gives the example of the French engineer René Leduc (1898–1968), whose designs for a saucer engine were supposedly stolen and then fitted to Belluzzo and Miethe's craft to make it work properly. Yet this is a more modern suggestion, intended to account for the original designs' non-viability.[3] Like Lego, these narratives can always gain new bricks added to them, altering the grand narrative's superstructure in unpredictable ways, just as a child can always change their original Lego airport into a Lego spaceport, with enough spare parts and imagination.

Exhibit A might be the latest brick in the wall of the Schweinfurt Raid narrative, one laid down by Eric Ouellet, a Professor of Defence Studies at the Royal Military College of Canada, in his interesting 2015 saucer book *Illuminations*. Ouellet's basic thesis is that UFO waves are really psychic precognitions of future social tensions; Russia had one prior to the collapse of Communism, for instance. With reference to Schweinfurt, Ouellet proposes the saucerian mini-discs seen by pilots might have been some form of technologically disguised banshees, or supernatural death omens, foreshadowing the tragically huge number of losses suffered by US pilots during the raid – over 300 B-17s flew out to Germany that day, but only 197 came back.[4]

It's a novel idea, but, yet again, one only possible to propose in retrospect, once the theory of UFOs being paranormal in origin had come into vogue many years after the events involved, and also relies upon ignoring the much more plausible explanation of the case being down to unusual Nazi flak devices. Nonetheless, if you wanted to apply Ouellet's general suggestion to the reported upsurge in foo-fighter reports over Germany heading into 1945, then maybe you could speculate the foos represented the psychic anxieties of the German people, fearing imminent defeat. Or they could have been psychic projections of Allied airmen expressing their own worry about being killed by some new Nazi air defence technique just when it looked as if they might get out of the war alive. It is easy to project whatever shape you like onto those pesky foos, with the false perspective of hindsight.

* * *

Exhibit B is even odder. In relation to Renato Vesco's total pack of lies, there is the confusing fact that a genuine scientific concept for a new form of wonder device called a 'Kugelblitz Engine' does today actually exist. In a 1955 paper, John Wheeler (1911–2008), a founder of the theory of black holes, used the pre-existing equations of German physicist and astronomer Karl Schwarzschild (1873–1916) to propose that, if enough pure energy could be focused into a truly tiny area of space, smaller than a sub-atomic proton, it would generate a microscopic black hole christened a 'Schwarzschild Kugelblitz'.

In 1974 English physicist Stephen Hawking (1942–2018) demonstrated that, the smaller a black hole, the larger its possible maximum radiation energy emitted, thus potentially making a Schwarzschild Kugelblitz the best battery ever. If the radiation shed by one were to be surrounded by a special shield, this shield could operate in a similar manner to a ship's sail, providing directional thrust to push a spaceship ever onwards, basically forever, with the energy waves acting like gusts of wind. This concept has since explained how the vessels of *Star Trek* can just keep on going boldly where no foo-fighter has gone before without having to regularly stop off at the next interstellar petrol station for fuel. Puny humans can't yet make these things, but the Romulans can – it specifically says so in a 1993 episode of *Star Trek: The Next Generation*.[5]

Vesco published before Hawking's theory was made public, so he cannot have known about it. But some people could use the subsequent development of Hawking's ideas, and the pure coincidence of the Kugelblitz name, to propose Vesco was right all along, and the RAF saucers hidden in Canada must have been powered by such means, having been back-engineered from SS Kugelblitz saucer tech. This would be why, as the BBC had once so carelessly announced, RAF super planes of the future would need no refuelling after take-off, just like Romulan space-fighters.

When such wishful-thinking persons consider the further curious coincidence that, in later versions of the Nazi UFO story, German craft sometimes began to come emblazoned with a Black Sun on their sides, they may pause again. Is this Black Sun really just a symbolic depiction of the tiny black hole which powers such Kugelblitz craft? Some conspiracy theorists honestly believe NASA's Paperclipped Nazis have, since the war, been deliberately seeding sci-fi shows with significant imagery to slowly mentally prepare the public for their forthcoming official announcement of the reality of both alien life forms and the original German creation of UFOs. Considered in this light, are *Star Trek*'s Kugelblitz-powered starships another telling indication Vesco was actually right? Maybe for 'Romulan' we should really read 'Rommel'?

And what would such total disc-heads make of the third uncanny coincidence that, in 2008, researcher Nick Redfern published several official documents he had unearthed in which US authorities spoke of attempts by Paperclipped Nazis to harness ball lightning – that's Kugelblitz in German, remember – as a potential weapon? One file, from 1950, proposed that 'the theoretical incendiary applications' of ball lightning 'might be useful to the several German projects at Kirtland', this being an Air Force base in New Mexico, the same state where Roswell lies.

Another document, from 1965, has the telling title 'SURVEY OF KUGELBLITZ THEORIES FOR ELECTROMAGNETIC INCENDIARIES'. The paper features much talk of the theoretical physics surrounding the still-controversial and poorly understood phenomenon of ball lightning, and speculation about how, using laser direction, it could perhaps be deployed against specific targets to burn them up, declaring 'the high-energy Kugelblitz' to be a potential 'weapon of importance'. Himmler would have loved this – a true Thor's Hammer!

Suddenly, the situation becomes more complex. Presumably, the military were going down this avenue starting from scratch, on a purely speculative basis – Redfern's files nowhere say anyone ever succeeded in weaponising ball lightning – and the Kugelblitz name was just adopted because that is what the Paperclipped German scientists working on it would naturally have called the phenomenon, rather than as a nod to Vesco's claimed Nazi flying tortoises. But all the same, if the original real-life glowing wartime foo-fighters were just some variant of ball lightning, as some might say, and the Americans were truly trying to weaponise such a thing, then doesn't this mean foo-fighters were potential Wunderwaffen, after all? Or . . . not? You could abuse semantics to argue the case either way.

Nick Redfern tentatively chose to speculate perhaps the US did later succeed in controlling ball lightning, that this is what many subsequently sighted UFOs really were, and even that an encounter with such a top-secret thing lay behind the famed UFO encounter in Suffolk's Rendlesham Forest in December 1980, near to the RAF Woodbridge airbase, since dubbed 'Britain's Roswell'. Here, one Colonel Charles Halt (b.1939) of the USAF witnessed 'a red sun-like light' after dark, which 'moved about and pulsed', before it 'broke into five separate white objects and then disappeared'.[6] Sound familiar? As late as December 1980, almost fifty years after Europe had been liberated, American airmen posted abroad were still seeing foo-fighters.

* * *

This never ending rain of ufological documents, photos, testimonies, intelligence reports and even full-blown physical artefacts, of debatable ontological status and veracity, strike me as nothing but so many 'hrönir'. A 'hrön' is a concept introduced by the great Argentinian writer Jorge Luis Borges (1899–1986) for his typically labyrinthine 1940 short story *Tlön, Uqbar, Orbis Tertius*, about a secret society who create an all-encompassing encyclopaedia relating to the history of a fictional world named Tlön, and then plant suggestive textual evidence of its supposed literal existence within genuine printed reference works, thus creating a seed within the human mind that such a place might actually be real – these days, they would be creating fake websites.[7]

On Tlön, objects do not exist physically in space, so much as subjectively in time, within the fleeting moment-by-moment perceptions of them by individual citizens. As such, within Tlönite tongues there are no nouns; as the moon is not conceived of as an objectively extant object, independent of its observers' momentary perception of the thing, you can't speak of 'the moon' rising as such, but would need to use a verb to say that 'it mooned' in the night sky. When nobody is there to see it, the moon does not exist – and, when it does, there are many moons, as many as there are people currently looking at it. Tlön is a world of radical subjectivity which destroys all idea of objective facts, of a collectively agreed-upon nature.

The basis of Tlönite mathematics is the notion of 'indefinite numbers', holding that the very act of counting things alters their physical quantity, thus meaning one man could count a pile of sweets and arrive at the number ten, another man count the same pile as numbering eleven, and both be correct. Extreme solipsism is abroad, making the very notion of science, with its need for universally agreed-upon formulas and standard measurements, impossible – and yet this does not mean there are no sciences on Tlön. Instead, there are infinitely many sciences, as citizens compete to devise the most unusual, entertaining or aesthetically pleasing ones, best suited to their own tastes. For them, writes Borges, 'metaphysics is a branch of fantastic literature', not a search for truth.

Eventually, the Tlönites realise such principles can apply to history too. Via the methodical fabrication of fake objects dubbed hrönir and the planting of them within dig sites, just like Himmler's SS Ahnenerbe pseudo-scholars once did during many of their own fraudulent historical excavations, archaeologists find they can manufacture their own past, 'which is now no less plastic and docile than the future'. The past becomes not an objective thing, but formed of memories. Once forgotten, the past disappears, as all objects (if defined as being purely objects of perception) do; Borges describes a doorway which only remained standing because a beggar used to sleep beneath it at night, and which dissolved at the moment of his death. The past becoming plastic in this way, combined with the manner that a second generation of hrönir can be manufactured from a previous one, before this second generation itself then gives birth to a new cohort of hrönir, and so on ad infinitum, has peculiar consequences.

Ultimately, the difference between fact and fancy becomes so confused that apparently genuine objects and artefacts called 'ur' turn up which appear to authenticate the faked hrönir which simultaneously preceded and succeeded them depending upon which perspectival time frame you wish to examine the whole situation from – so, for us, the flying saucers of Kenneth Arnold are hrönir which subsequently begat further generations of themselves, like the 1950s Nazi saucers of Schriever, Miethe and Belluzzo, which then in some reverse-chronological sense somehow managed to begat the original ur of solid 1940s foo-fighters which preceded them in the historical record.

Suddenly, these newly minted ur artefacts then appeared within the memories of people like Leonard H. Stringfield, as strange, solid alien machines trying to down their planes from Japanese skies several years beforehand, back when such things didn't even exist to their percipients. Foos really were seen by wartime pilots, but, as on Tlön, they were in some sense not really physical objects existing consistently throughout time, but subjective temporal perceptions of what might be termed 'foo-ness', whose precise nature has since proven to shift endlessly between different observers, much like the number of sweets in a pile, or the precise essence of the moon, on Tlön.

This ur can then produce further hrönir, however, such as the Haunebu II craft of the 1990s, models of which then end up being placed on display within rather Borgesian pseudo-museums and inaccurately labelled as 'Nazi Foo-Fighters'. In Borges' original fiction, the forged encyclopaedias of Tlön are a form of literary hrönir so compelling they slowly become the objects of mass belief amongst human beings until such a point that 'a fictitious past occupies in our memories the place of another, a past of which we know nothing with certainty – not even that it is false'. Once the beggar is dead, the direct first-person memory of his sheltering doorway disappears, and the doorway along with it.

It is likewise with the events of the Second World War, such as the death camps, the formerly widely agreed-upon accounts of which are today coming under increasing revisionist pressure from neo-Nazi Holocaust-deniers, now their original witnesses are rapidly dwindling in number. As society fragments and becomes less homogenous, disguised by the never ending repetition of that truly Orwellian term 'diversity', our online era of culture wars is proving an ideal environment within which to incubate new and ever more exotic ranks of hrönir. Ours is an age growing steadily as solipsistic, relativistic and subjective in nature as that of Tlön, in which extremists like Ernst Zündel can use lies about Nazi UFOs to argue Auschwitz didn't happen, or Henry Stevens can claim, like a typical Tlönite, that different, competing versions of science might exist, and that the Black Sun SS might have had access to some hitherto-secret one allowing them to power their saucer ships.

No matter how obviously fake your hrönir, they can still help manufacture new narratives of alt-history. In 2018, President Donald J. Trump announced the creation of a new US military Space Force, to counter Chinese interference with satellites. But online conspiracy theorist Art Greenfield thought it more likely Trump needed to combat alien lizards than Chinese taikonauts. For Art, the US already had anti-gravity spacecraft, reverse-engineered from the Nazis – and the Nazis themselves had probably reverse-engineered them from UFOs which had previously crashed over Germany, Roswell-style.

'Hitler himself had written' that, during the First World War, he had been captured by extraterrestrial lizard men and marched off to an underground base, there to be implanted with a mind-control chip to make him help out in a secret alien 'logistical human meat-harvesting operation', something which left him 'VERY scared', said Greenfield – do ponder the meaning of the phrase 'Hitler himself had written' in that sentence. He wrote no such thing, but simply by saying he did, yet more fake artefacts for wholly baseless claims are conjured from the ether. You don't even have to produce the relevant documents anymore, just say they exist and hope someone will either believe you, or else helpfully forge you some copies.

Then as final 'concrete proof that the Nazis REALLY had anti-gravity craft' derived from lizard folk, Greenfield produces images of a set of obviously fraudulent Nazi commemorative stamps, showing paintings of their 'secret' saucer weapons for every fascist philatelist to see . . . most of which are Haunebus, which, at the time the stamps were purportedly printed in 1939–45, hadn't yet been invented even as fictional concepts. Worse, these images have been floating around online for years, the Haunebu originally being superimposed onto other scenes, like Nazi airbase hangars. The forger simply re-superimposed the already superimposed Haunebus onto the basic design template of old German postage stamps. Logically, the next step would be to superimpose these stamps themselves onto a letter, and super-impose this letter into the hand of Adolf Hitler, before claiming the envelope contains his account of having been abducted by the lizard people.[8]

* * *

'The contact and the habit of Tlön have disintegrated this world', wrote Borges, as our reality 'longed to yield' to theirs. Reality may have an innate order to it, but such divine laws are, Borges perceives, by definition 'inhu-man laws', impenetrable to the mind of man, and thus our existence appears chaotic, in some sense unknowable. The philosophy of Tlön, with its radical subjectivity, solves all such problems. If every man has his own reality, then this means there is no coherent, underlying reality to existence at all – but, paradoxically, the very fact there is no underlying reality then itself becomes the single explicatory fact underlying reality! The only truth is that there is no truth. Thus, every false belief, just like every shade of ufology, partici-pates within a wider truth – that there is no truth – simply by virtue of its being demonstrably untrue. This is the confusing world of online conspiracy theory and endlessly competing belief systems in which we live today.

And, once the hrönir of these competing 'truths' gain hold and our previously agreed-upon reality melts away to be replaced by that of Tlön, the next stage is the appearance of apparently genuine physical artefacts of this alien world within our own. In his story, Borges' narrator finds 'a cone of bright metal the size of a die' which, in the palm of his hand, feels impossibly heavy for something so tiny; a child could not even lift it from the floor. All who hold it feel it is horribly 'wrong', somehow not of this Earth – it is an artefact of Tlön.

So, you might say, were the IMPERVIUM-like indestructible 'alien met-als' supposedly handled by Major Jesse Marcel out at Roswell. In a world of objective truths, these tinfoil-like materials were just that . . . tinfoil, from a weather balloon. Once the hrönir eat into your head, however, the tinfoil becomes part of a ship from Planet Tlön, a tangible artefact of a new reality.

The USAF could get hold of some of this tinfoil, analyse it in a lab and say 'Look, we told you – it's just tinfoil, here, make a new hat out of it', but as, for the Jesse Marcels of this world, the 'mysterious metals' in question have already become not simple physical objects, consistent in space-time, but wholly subjective mental objects, like a Tlönite moon, such crudely objective results would seem antiquated, outmoded and irrelevant.

It is an amusing coincidence that the other object which seeps into being straight from Planet Tlön in Borges' story is a special compass bearing letters from the Tlönite alphabet, which suddenly turns up uninvited within a jewellery box one day. In his own books, Henry Stevens mentions another pair of Nazi Wunderwaffen, this time both defensive in nature, the Magnetofunk ('Magnetic Radio') and Himmelskompass ('Heavenly Compass'). Incredibly, it transpires that some Nazis may have survived the war in a far-flung Arctic fastness called Point 103, using their Magnetofunk contraption to 'deflect the magnetic lines of force in the instruments of Allied aircraft ever so slightly' which, over the 'vast tracts of the Arctic' would be just enough to steer them off course, thus preventing the Germans from being detected, Stevens argues.

If the Magnetofunk fooled compasses into thinking the magnetic North Pole was somewhere else, though, then how did Nazi saucers find their way back home? By use of the Himmelskompass, which oriented itself northwards not via magnetism, but by sensing polarised light from the sun, even when the sun was not visible in the sky, so sensitive was the thing (maybe it really detected the Black Sun?). By measuring the amount of polarised sunlight, a simple calculation could be performed by Nazi aviators to establish their position in relation to the real magnetic North Pole, allowing them to navigate with full accuracy, unlike their pixie-led US counterparts.

Stevens' source here is a 1971 neo-Nazi novel written by an unrepentant Austrian SS officer named Wilhelm Landig (1909–98). The novel implausibly purports to be based on fact and, like the original encyclopaedia entries about Tlön, has since been taken as an authentic account of another world by those who want to believe in miracles. Also like Borges' Tlön, Point 103 has since begun to generate physical artefacts of its own existence, even though it has none.

Stevens unearthed references to both 'an artificial horizon' and a 'Mother Horizon' within US interviews with German POWs, taking these as coded references to Landig's Himmelskompass, even though mention is made in these same documents of such aerial aids functioning via gyroscopes, not polarised sunlight. Artificial horizons are not compasses, being intended to allow aviators to maintain their planes at a level axis with the ground during flight, like dashboard spirit levels, not to direct them towards magnetic North. So, Stevens must describe these references as 'brief and rather cryptic', as such 'references' are not truly references to the Himmelskompass at all. Still, he reproduces photocopied transcripts, which function ably as hrönir for those willing to view them as such.[9]

The next step, according to Borges' model, would be for a faked physical Himmelskompass to appear somewhere – maybe in a little glass box inside the Roswell International UFO Museum. Such a hrön couldn't be that hard to manufacture, could it? Maybe one day, with a bit of luck, it might even produce its own ur? Maybe it already has . . .

A navigational device known as a 'sunstone' appears in medieval Icelandic manuscripts, which, when held up to natural light, allowed Viking sailors to determine the location of the sun even when totally obscured by cloudy skies. The texts which speak of sunstones may or may not be allegorical, but in recent decades it has been proposed Nordic sailors exploited the obscure mineral Iceland spar, which has the ability to polarise light, making it possible to determine the approximate location of the sun in otherwise unfeasible conditions, as with the Himmelskompass.

In 2016, a lump of this magical sounding mineral was found in a wrecked sixteenth-century English warship off Alderney. Was this proof sunstones were real, and the English inherited their use from their Norse ancestors? Not necessarily. The mineral was found near other navigational aids, but for all we know it could have been used as a mere decoration, or a paperweight to hold down maps.[10] Nonetheless, as good Nordic types, perhaps the polar Nazis of Point 103 had themselves also rediscovered the wisdom of their hardy, war loving ancestors. Retrieving an ambiguous artefact from a shipwreck and passing it off as high technology definitely has certain parallels with narratives of the Roswell type.

Another promoter of compass-related hrönir is William Lyne, American author of *Space Aliens from the Pentagon*, who argues like Renato Vesco that the ETH is baloney, used to cover up how saucers are actually 100 per cent man-made. Lyne thinks the US is an unfree dictatorship in disguise, as shown by the process of 'CANNIBALISTIC FASCIST LITIGATION' he was subjected to by 'judicial turds' between 1986 and 1992, when the courts ruined his life and destroyed his family, following a lawsuit relating to his purported invention of some fantastic new solar voltaic cell. Innocently filing a patent application after ten years' hard work, Lyne was disgusted to have it stolen by a Paperclipped Nazi, with the profits shared between the German scientist, the CIA and the military-industrial complex.

Lyne now perceived the entire US Patent Office was a scam, intended to steal naïve inventors' ideas for the undercover 'IllumiNazi' State. By employing 'illiterate or semi-retarded' patent clerks, it proved easy for CIA front corporations to exploit the Office's 'weird rules' and claim the blueprints for themselves, undermining the basis of the free-market economy and intellectual property rights. Several attempts were made to murder Lyne to keep him quiet, such as having children infect his food with salmonella, so in 1993 he released his book-length investigation into what other evils the Paperclipped Wunderwaffen men had perpetrated in cahoots with 'the local trash . . . [of] small-time toadies, drug-dealers, money-grubbers, property-thieves, trashy and crooked realtors, title examiners and insurers, yeggs and socialist bureaucrats' who had ruined him. To help readers identify such 'giant evil spiders', Lyne provided a helpful illustration of policemen and judges transformed into uniform-clad were-monkeys, surrounded by bizarre occult symbols.

Hoping to promote his self-published text and 'punish the elite', Lyne posed in a local newspaper, complaining about persecution by homosexual spies and holding a giant compass, bigger than a man's head, with a fluorescent dial and swastika in the middle. It appears genuine, presumably having its origins in some mundane German machine or vehicle, but Lyne boasted it came straight from a Nazi saucer. Lyne and his parents had personally encountered UFOs in Texas, one of which was 'egg-shaped' and caused his father's car to stall.

Via intense research, Lyne discovered such ovoid CIA 'Flying Turtles' had been back-engineered from Nazi Wunderwaffen like the Kugelblitz spheres, which were not remote-controlled after all, but piloted by tiny Hitler Youth members who steered them from within, which 'must have required a lot of dexterity, like a videogame or a skateboard'. Lyne provides an amusing cutaway illustration of a small foetal-position child inside such a ball-lightning craft; their electromagnetic ability to make enemy plane engines fail was proved by his dad's dead car.

The Nazis also had larger Kreisel Teller, or 'gyrating plate' saucers, one of which had rescued Hitler from his bunker in 1945 and ferried him away to a waiting giant cigar shaped flying aircraft carrier called the Graf Zeppelin, which could also function as a submarine or spacecraft. From here, Hitler and his girlfriend could control a U-boat fleet armed with nuclear missiles which had surrounded the US, ensuring a tense stalemate situation. If Washington didn't let Hitler and his lover return to live in a 'cosy and secure' house in Germany in peace under covert US military protection, the country would be nuked. Lyne thought this plausible because he had met Hitler himself at the 1967 World's Fair in Texas. Then an artist, Lyne was painting pictures, one of which Adolf took an interest in, before the Führer was recognised and 'whisked away by security agents'.

Lyne had long been interested in UFOs, having childhood connections to Roswell, whose disued POW camp his father had bought and demolished, repurposing its materials to build a family home. In 1947, inspired by a neighbour's tall tales of human saucer inventors, the 9-year-old Lyne had used iron bars from the prison's windows to conduct electromagnetic experiments, eventually developing a 'Triax System' which implied the universe was an invisible battery from which you could gain a free source of inexhaustible Green energy, like Viktor Schauberger.

Throughout the 1970s, Lyne frequented scrap dealers, seeking bits and bobs for a perpetual motion machine, buying his giant Nazi compass in an Albuquerque junk yard in 1979 for only 'a handshake, a smile and $7.50'. Stolen from a US military base where Wunderwaffen had been back-engineered, Lyne found it was marked Peiltochterkompass, which he interpreted as meaning 'Polar-Slave-Compass' (it really indicates something more like 'daughter compass', apparently being linked to some controlling 'father compass' master device termed a Meisterkreiselkompass or 'Master-Spinning-Top-Compass'). He thought it must have been used aboard a Nazi saucer as a 'celestial or inertial guidance system'; its serial number 'KT-p2' stood for Kreisel Teller.

But was it really likely Wunderwaffen components could be bought in a junk shop for less than $10? 'In retrospect,' wrote Lyne, 'I have decided that the Peiltochterkompass and other items may have been clues placed there intentionally, and that perhaps someone expected me to interpret their use' – these men must have been agents from Tlön. Or did they really hail from Point 103? Following Lyne's media appearances, his colossal compass has been acclaimed by some as proof the Arctic-set neo-Nazi novels of Wilhelm Landig must have had some nuts-and-bolts basis in truth after all.[11] Landig's Himmelskompass, although entirely fictional, thus turns out to have had its impossible ancestors; proof positive every hrön has its ur. If Borges were alive today he would surely have loved books like those of Bill Lyne and Henry Stevens.

* * *

Personally, I do think pilots of the Second World War were, in an objective physical sense, seeing something strange flitting over German skies, albeit of a strictly non-Nazi, non-ET, non-paranormal nature, perhaps weird atmospheric plasmas of some kind. If I can put it in this deliberately paradoxical fashion, foo-fighters seem to have been real. They just don't seem to have been foo-fighters. And they certainly weren't flying saucers, Feuerballs or Kugelblitzes. Both Smokey Stover and Kenneth Arnold were in the fire-safety business, but each accidentally ended up proving that, sometimes, there can be at least some smoke generated without much of an initial feu after all – the whole story so far resembles nothing but a giant smokescreen.

The more metastasised the legend grows, and the more hrönir it develops, the more difficult it can become to perceive that there is almost nothing at all behind it, especially at first glance. Even detailed exposés like my own will be incomplete and disputable in nature. Believers will examine what I have outlined above and, safe in the knowledge there are innumerable variant versions of the entire myth, set out to debunk my own debunking. Maybe it could be said that my account includes mistakes, which doubtless it does . . . but, as there is no canonical version of the whole meta-narrative available, it becomes highly debatable what a mistake within such a context even constitutes, just as the nature of truth became debatable upon Tlön.

As the legend is constantly being made up by the people who write it as they go along, no final debunking is in fact possible. New ways around any criticism can always be found, more fake documents can easily be unearthed, more cryptic re-interpretations of wholly non-cryptic statements be advanced, more false witnesses interviewed, and if all else fails you can just say I'm working undercover for the CIA (although I actually work for Mossad). And, if you think this whole maze-like affair is rather too Borgesian in its nature already, then I do warn you that it only gets worse with each passing year.

To quote that early enemy of Nazi saucer pilots Sir Winston Churchill: 'This is not the end. It is not even the beginning of the end. But it is, perhaps, the end of the beginning.' Or is it? In conclusion, we probably need to step into a more advanced SS saucer of the time-travel variety and take a quick trip back through the decades – or is it in fact a trip forwards? As ever, it is rather hard to say . . .

Conclusion

Saved by The Bell? The Nine Lives of Dr Hans Kammler and Nazi Time Travel

'Life must be lived forwards, but it can only be understood backwards.'

Søren Kierkegaard, pioneering Danish ufologist of the early psychosocial school

One final figure central to Nazi UFO mythology today is SS Obergruppenführer Dr Hans Kammler (1901–45?), who has increasingly become the implausible mastermind behind the entire German UFO programme. He either appears as a specific character, or is named in passing, in various Nazi UFO-related novels and movies, as well as meriting mention in many supposed non-fiction titles like those of Ernst Zündel and Renato Vesco.

In Henry Stevens' Wunderwaffen books, he is presented as a super villain super genius, operating within an Ernst Stavro Blofeld-style Alpenfestung lair of doom surrounded by early Nazi computers, the Z3 and Z4, real-life devices created by Dr Konrad Zuse (1910–95), which Stevens inflates into something they were not. Protected by 'a triple wall of security', Kammler and Zuse developed the world's first 'software computer languages and magnetic-tape storage devices' of a kind not developed elsewhere until the late 1960s, he says. Handling computer development with 'the excellence for which he was known', Kammler's machines proved so advanced that, when the invading Allies found them, they didn't even understand what they were.[1]

Not a medical doctor, but a Doctor of Engineering, Kammler was a Class-A war criminal whose true place in history was to have designed the architectural layout of the death camps; by claiming his greater role was actually to have co-ordinated the creation of Nazi UFOs, Kammler's genius thus becomes redeemed. As Kammler had charge of millions of slave labourers,

Henry Stevens admits that 'I think we can all agree this was probably illegal', but points out Kammler did not stand trial at Nuremburg, whereas other top Nazis were hanged for far lesser crimes.

The standard explanation as to why Kammler was not charged is that, by the time of the Nuremburg Trials, he was dead – and yet, recent research suggests otherwise. Hans Kammler definitely is a man of mystery. Stevens says he managed successfully 'to pull Albrich's Cloak of Obscurity [a magical device from Wagnerian opera] over himself', which is indeed true.[2] This is what has made him so ideal to fill the role of the overall Nazi UFO *éminence grise*; a man with so many gaps in his life story is just begging to have them filled in by fantasists.

What do we know for sure about Dr Kammler? His early administrative career was in the German Civil Service, acting as a municipal building supervisor in Berlin from 1924, before working in the German Ministry of Labour from 1928, where he made many useful contacts and became known for his efficiency in streamlining construction processes. Had it not been for the election of the Nazis in 1933, Kammler would surely have remained an even more little-known figure than he is today.

However, in March 1932, cannily anticipating Hitler's success, Kammler became a Party member, reflecting equal parts cynical ambition and natural sympathy with Nazi rhetoric, particularly that of an anti-Communist nature. Joining before Hitler assumed office, Kammler could now exploit his status as one of the loyal 'old guard' when jostling for future promotion. That same year, he gained a Doctorate in Engineering from the Technical University of Hanover. On 30 May 1933, Kammler joined the SS Cavalry Corps Waffen-SS sub-division as Black Order Knight #113,619. Kammler then rose to be Chief Government Surveyor at the Air Ministry, building hangars and barracks, giving him experience in military construction projects as well as civilian ones.

In 1941, Himmler grew so impressed with Kammler's organisational capabilities that he asked him and his team to transfer across directly to SS logistics services; in 1943, he became SS building supremo, in ultimate charge of construction projects and their related materials across the Reich. Most notably, he assumed responsibility for expanding and repurposing concentration camps into full-blown death camps once the final decision had been made to exterminate all Europe's Jews. Kammler it was who dramatically enlarged Auschwitz, installing its gas chambers and crematoria and adding its sub-camp of Birkenau.

To save money and ensure more efficient mass-murder, Kammler stream-lined and standardised camp designs, administrative regimes and building materials, thus ensuring an all-encompassing economy of scale. For exam-ple, to increase camp holding capacity without spending any more money, he gave orders the number of prisoners to be housed in each already over crowded barrack should be increased from 550 to 744, basing this on the average space each inmate would take up in a coffin, as each was essentially a walking corpse anyway. He was also involved in the infamous decision to use Zyklon B as the most effective gas to kill prisoners with.

Yet Kammler did not wish to eliminate all Jews immediately – that would make no economic sense. Instead, he separated out those too old, young, ill or weak to work for immediate gassing, and used the more able-bodied as slave labour within his massive construction empire. In his ultimate plans for reconstructing seized Eastern territories like Ukraine, Kammler estimated he would need to work around 29 million forced labourers to death over the course of two decades, to give Aryan settlers their necessary homes, trans-port and sewage networks and other such amenities.

In the meantime, he rented out his slaves to German industry, with firms like BMW and Siemens getting 12-hour shifts for less than 10 Reichsmarks a day, with the consequent huge sums of cash helping the SS gain financial independence as a 'State within a State'. Such developments eventually allowed Himmler and Kammler to seize control of much arms production and research as the war reached its end; one of Kammler's final promotions was to the grandly titled role of Special Plenipotentiary of the Führer for Jet Aircraft.

Having around 40 per cent of the Reich's slaves under his direct control at any given time, Kammler was assigned the task of evacuating V-2 facilities away from Peenemünde once they had been discovered and bombed by the RAF. His solution was to use forced labour to dig out and staff blast-proof Alpenfestung-style tunnel complexes beneath the mountains near the town of Nordhausen, where assembly plants for V-1s, V-2s and jet-fighter Wunderwaffen were located in a sort of actual subterranean Hell christened 'Mittelwerk'. To save time, the prisoners lived below surface like human moles during excavation work, which continued in shifts around the clock.

Conditions underground and in the attached Mittelbau-Dora concentration camp were arguably worse than in Auschwitz, but to prevent rebellions or sabotage, Kammler personally ordered the slow public execution of troublesome slaves by hanging them from cranes, leaving their corpses on display as a warning, methods he later boasted about as once again improving efficiency, which really was his watchword. Even Wernher von Braun and the other Nazi rocket scientists whom he took control of thought Kammler a most unpleasant individual, Braun calling him 'the greatest rogue and adventurer I have ever seen' – and he knew plenty, including himself.[3]

* * *

Given the magnitude of his crimes, you would think Kammler would be better known, but outside of Nazi ufology he is an obscure figure to say the least, not meriting a single stand-alone entry in standard textbooks like Louis L. Snyder's (1907–93) *Encyclopaedia of the Third Reich*. Yet during the war itself, the Allies definitely knew about him. In February 1945, Kammler was included in a British list of ten key targets for assassination due to the operational role he had recently taken on blasting V-2 rockets against London from typically innovative mobile launching units.

Part of the problem may be that, unlike those war criminals captured and put on trial at Nuremburg, Kammler just disappeared. Officially, on 9 May 1945, he committed suicide like Hitler and Himmler, an assessment based largely on the testimony of his driver, Kurt Preuk, who claimed to have performed his impromptu roadside burial near a forest crossroads close to the Czech village of Jílové u Prahy. In July 1945 Kammler's wife Jutta petitioned authorities to have him officially recognised as deceased on this basis. German courts agreed, and in September 1948 Frau Kammler got her death certificate – and her widow's pension.

According to Preuk, following an argument with a fellow SS Obergruppenführer, Kammler had gone into the forest and never come back, shooting himself through the head with his service pistol. Preuk consequently took up a shovel and buried Kammler in a shallow woodland grave, which he could never subsequently relocate. However, the narrative of Preuk conflicts with that of another of Kammler's drivers, Heinz Zeuner, who claimed the suicide was actually by means of cyanide, not bullet, and took place on a different date, in a different place.

Preuk subsequently recalled contradictory details about Kammler's suicide himself, apparently becoming confused. In one later interview, Preuk broke down and admitted he had lied, leading some to speculate the whole narrative was a scam intended to ensure Hans' wife got her pension money. Kammler appears to have had more lives than the average cat, with as many as thirteen different accounts of his demise existing. Other alleged first-hand eyewitnesses have him falling in a hail of Czech Resistance bullets in Prague, whilst others had him being shot by a fellow SS man to prevent him falling into enemy captivity; yet others prefer to say the Russians took him alive after all, or have him living in a monastery disguised as a monk, or on a farm disguised as a labourer. Maybe he just had plenty of doppelgängers.[4]

The most tantalising option is that Kammler was Paperclipped to the US, maybe even being the first individual to be treated this way, but that, due to the incredible magnitude of his crimes, this fact had to be covered up completely, unlike with the recruitment of skilled scientists like Wernher von Braun whose Nazi-era careers could be more easily sanitised. If Kammler remained listed as dead or missing, then the sins of Wunderwaffen rocketeers at Nordhausen could be conveniently pinned on him, not the others.

Shortly before his death in 1997, US Counter-Intelligence Corps (CIC) veteran Donald W. Richardson (1917–97) confessed to his sons that he had personally arranged for Kammler's transfer stateside and then interviewed him, being subsequently obliged to stay silent about the matter for reasons of national security. Kept under custody in strict isolation, Kammler decided he was better off dead and hanged himself in 1947, said Richardson; if he had only delayed tying the noose until that June, Kammler would have just had time to read about Kenneth Arnold's sighting of his alleged greatest creation in the skies over Washington State. An alternative version has it that Kammler was murdered in US custody in 1947, however.

Richardson's specific testimony is essentially unsupported, yet declassified documents from the CIC and other organisations uncovered in recent years do appear to confirm that Kammler did not die at the war's end after all, and did indeed languish in US custody for a certain period. One, dated 7 May 1945, two days before his officially recognised death, specifically states Kammler had surrendered to US forces on 6 May, carrying documents 'which may prove to be of considerable value'. Kammler had then been interviewed, and tasked with writing a full report on German Wunderwaffen and Alpenfestung facilities, as he was by this stage in overall control of them.

This fits in with a statement from Albert Speer that Kammler had previously confessed his intention to surrender to the Americans and bargain away rocket and jet-plane research in return for his life. It has even been speculated Kammler's decision to move V-2 production to Nordhausen was partially made with the suspicion this area was more likely to be reached by invading US forces first rather than the Russians, with the anti-Communist Kammler very much preferring to surrender his men to the capitalists, not the Reds.

Other CIC documents show Kammler was still in US hands in 1946, when officials from the Nuremburg Trials were still seeking his whereabouts for prosecution. Certain elements in US intelligence seemingly sought to put prosecutors off his scent by spreading disinformation he was in Soviet custody, not their own. Some dodgy dossiers imply Kammler had been arrested by US forces but had then supposedly escaped into the hands of the Communists, which is most unlikely given his hardline anti-leftist political leanings. The British seemed to know this was a bluff, as they contacted CIC to request his extradition into their own hands, though no record of what came of this plea is known to exist. It looks very much like there really was a Paperclip cover-up.[5]

Kammler must have had something worth trading to have been worth all this bother. From August 1943 onwards, Himmler had appointed Kammler head of Sonderstab Kammler, or 'Special Staff Kammler', giving him authority to take charge of basically whatever he liked in terms of weapons-production facilities. Amongst the greatest prizes of his new empire were the Škoda factories and HQs in Pilsen and Prague, to which he made visits right at the end of the war, immediately prior to his disappearance, risking his life in the face of rapid enemy advance. There must have been something there requiring his immediate attention.

During Soviet times, Škoda became best known as a manufacturer of cars which, when exported to the West, were derided as being of comically low quality, but prior to Russian expropriation of its factories and designers, Škoda was in fact one of the world's leading engineering companies. The second largest munitions manufacturer in all of Europe, Škoda's Czech plants hosted one of Kammler's chief armaments-related think-tanks, whose researches were tightly guarded by SS counter-intelligence agents.

What was Kammler doing in Prague in the war's dying days? The best book-length investigation into Kammler's life, Dean Reuter's *The Hidden Nazi*, published in 2019, tentatively concludes he may have been gathering up files about his team's attempts to create some kind of V-2-mounted radiological dirty bomb, the blueprints for which obviously would have been of paramount interest to US security forces. Reuter's guess is that, in return for providing these plans, together with helping facilitate the transfer of von Braun and the remains of the V-2 programme across the Atlantic, the CIC ultimately promised to arrange for Kammler's safe future passage to Juan Perón's Argentina, there to start a new life amongst all the other ex-Nazis Perón sheltered.[6]

Yet we will recall Prague's Škoda factory was the very same location Rudolf Schriever and his assistants had supposedly test-flown their V-7 saucers in, thus raising another dubious possibility: that Kammler was actually in Prague in May 1945 to retrieve evidence of the secret Nazi saucer programme to trade for his life with the Americans. It is interesting to note that, whilst Reuter's book, being printed by the major US publisher Regnery, nowhere mentions UFOs, one of its assistant co-authors was none other than Keith Chester – whom we named earlier as being the writer of the best book about foo-fighters, in which he was a literal nuts-and-bolts believer.

Under the influence of Leonard H. Stringfield, Chester felt aliens were responsible for foos, not Nazis, but it seems reasonable to presume the reason he became interested in Hans Kammler in the first place was because of his earlier researches into Nazi ufology (or 'aerial phenomena reported by Allied military pilots during the Second World War', as his flyleaf mini-biography more coyly puts it). As it was Reuter, Chester and their other co-author Colm Lowery who did most to unearth evidence of Kammler's apparent post-war survival, it appears digging into the subject of Nazi UFOs can occasionally unearth some genuinely worthwhile information after all.

In the end, nobody knows for sure what happened to Dr Hans Kammler. Perhaps the only thing we can be certain about is that he isn't living in a giant UFO base beneath Antarctica, as some have since tried to claim online. Nonetheless, to the terminally gullible, another intriguing possibility does present itself – is the real reason Kammler disappeared so completely at the end of the war simply that he managed to escape in his own personal Wunderwaffe time machine?

* * *

In 1950, US intelligence agent Charles Wolkonowski reported the intriguing testimony of a former inmate of Darmstadt POW camp, maintained by US forces after the war. This ex-prisoner, Georg Stalling, spoke about in-camp lectures he had attended about V-2 rockets and V-7 flying saucers in 1948, once Kenneth Arnold's discs had made the German media. The prisoners giving these talks, delivered under the false pretext of being harmless Verein für Raumschiffahrt-style sci-fi lectures about men journeying to Mars and the moon, had been ex-SS officers and scientists who had developed such secret Wunderwaffen during the dying days of the Third Reich.

The name of the chief lecturer was unknown to Stalling, but was described by him as being 'approximately forty years of age, 6' 2" tall, oval face, dark hair', and came equipped with the title 'Doctor'. This tall, dark stranger was foolishly released from the camp by the Americans free of all charges in May 1948, and seemingly never seen again. Was this Kammler in disguise? No further action was taken upon Wolkonowski's report, and we can reasonably dismiss this as an informant just trying to prove his worth to an intelligence agent by exploiting modish contemporary newspaper headlines about saucers.[7]

Yet Stalling's yarn shows how, as early as 1950, the evil SS saucer building genius was already emerging as a potential stock character in the script of the self-writing, live-action Nazi UFO b-movie which was soon to appal and delight audiences worldwide. The first specific attribution of the name 'Hans Kammler' to this previously generic figure is uncertain, but the source of his modern day infamy as a builder of exotic anti-gravity – and, soon, time-travel – craft lies squarely with the prolific Polish writer of Wunderwaffen books Igor Witkowski (b.1963).

The hard-working Witkowski edited two military history magazines whilst also producing full-length normal texts like *Tanks of the World*, but in 1996 came a sudden fringe book, *Visits from Heaven: Was von Däniken Right?*, a reassessment of the career of Europe's leading ancient astronaut guru, the former Swiss hotelier Erich von Däniken (b.1935), who argued age-old structures like the Pyramids had actually been built by aliens, not by humans. Titles like *Super-Secret Weapons of Islam*, published in 2001, and *Japanese Wonder-Weapons*, published in 2010, now became a speciality, together with other oddnesses like *Christ and UFOs*. Witkowski soon learned books with Nazis on the cover sold well, hence *Hitler's Underground Kingdom*, *Wewelsburg: [Himmler's] Castle of the Holy Grail*, *Hitler in Argentina* and *Hitler's Werewolves* ('werewolves' in this context disappointingly referring to partisan guerrilla resistance units).

Most of Igor's output remains Polish-language only, but his most notable translated effort, *The Truth About the Wunderwaffe*, published in 2000, proved remarkably influential, capturing the attention of aerospace journalist Nick Cook, Aviation Editor of defence industry bible *Janes Defence Weekly*, whom we met earlier investigating Viktor Schauberger.[8] As we have seen, Cook was writing his own opus, *The Hunt for Zero Point*, about alleged attempts to master the art of anti-gravity, which detailed the history of the Canadian AvroCar and German repulsine devices. When he heard Witkowski possessed evidence the SS had successfully tested an anti-gravity craft called The Bell, Cook was eager to listen.

If Hans Kammler had been Paperclipped to safety by the Americans in spite of being a Class-A war criminal, then he must have possessed some knowledge so valuable, so awesome, that it was worth the colossal reputational risk in stealing him away. What could it have been? Was it something even better than a V-2-mounted atom bomb? When writing his Wunderwaffen books, Witkowski had been particularly interested in German military scientific activities in and around the city then called Breslau, since subsumed into Polish territory after the war and now renamed Wroclaw.

He found evidence of various underground Alpenfestung-style labs and factories in the Lower Silesia region, becoming particularly interested in activities at the disused Wenceslas Mine outside the remote village of Ludwigsdorf/Ludwikowice near the Czech frontier, which was equipped with its own power plant. Wenceslas Mine was part of a huge subterranean complex code-named Riese, or 'Giant', excavated by forced labourers from Gross-Rosen concentration camp, with attempts being made to connect the mine to a larger body of factories by a 10km-long tunnel, as part of Kammler's underground kingdom. Witkowski claims his investigations came to the attention of an 'impeccable' but unnamed source within Polish officialdom, who allowed him to read some classified documents and take notes, but not make any photocopies. Here, he found tantalising mention of The Bell.

Nobody else has ever seen these files, though. Furthermore, all the Wunderwaffen scientists directly involved in whatever was going on down Wenceslas Mine had purportedly been taken out and shot by the SS near the end of the war, leaving nobody to contradict Witkowski's narrative. Thus, the whole story of The Bell rests on whether you believe Witkowski or suspect him of following the model of Major Rudolf Lusar by inserting something sensational into an otherwise fairly sober Wunderwaffen book with the aim of boosting sales.

Witkowski said these files revealed post-war Soviet interviews with SS Obergruppenführer Jakob Sporrenberg (1902–52), who led a section of the SS' Special Evacuation Kommando corps, tasked with spiriting away Wunderwaffen from the path of Allied advances. Captured by the British in 1945, Sporrenberg was handed over to the Poles due to his role in helping run that country's death camps, being executed in 1952, following interrogation. Amongst the items Sporrenberg had been tasked with evacuating, he said, was something called 'Die Glocke', or The Bell, together with all its supporting components and paperwork. Although, like Kammler, Sporrenberg was no scientist but a talented practical administrator, and thus did not fully understand the technical details behind the device, he did his best to explain what the thing was.

According to Sporrenberg's account – at least as relayed to Cook via Witkowski – Die Glocke was so named because it was bell-shaped, being cast from some 'hard, heavy metal' to dimensions of 5m in height and 3m in diameter at its widest point, then covered over with a thick ceramic casing during actual experiments (although descriptions in Witkowski's and Cook's books differ slightly in various respects, with Witkowski implying it was only half this size). Naturally, it came with a large swastika carved into its front.

Placed in a special pool chamber deep underground within the Wenceslas Mine, and fed with huge voltages of electricity via cables from the surface power plant, The Bell contained two separate cylinders which were filled up with a violet-coloured mercury like substance with a golden tint code-named Xerum-525, which was so toxic it had to be stored in a special lead-lined, metre-tall Thermos flask. This was then mixed with normal pure mercury and other substances termed Leichtmetall ('lightweight metals'), believed to include thorium and beryllium peroxide, both of which are used in nuclear reactors.

These cylinders, filled with the metallic mixtures, were then rapidly spun in opposite directions at incredible speeds for approximately 1 minute, causing The Bell to emit a 'pale blue glow' indicative of localised ionisation of the atmosphere or the presence of plasma fields, whilst any electrical devices in the vicinity suddenly stopped working or short-circuited. A sound like 'the humming of bees' was also heard, gaining it another nickname of 'The Hive' – similar sounds are often reported from contemporary UFO sightings.

Whatever this procedure actually did, it was highly dangerous. All personnel were kept at least 150m away from it, wearing special protective rubber suits and red eye-visors, but despite this several Wunderwaffen scientists died and many fell ill, with symptoms ranging from sleep problems, muscle spasms, memory loss, balance issues, ulceration and a permanent metallic tang in the mouth.

Following each experiment, disposable concentration-camp prisoners were brought in to douse the entire pool chamber with a pink brine-like liquid for 45 minutes straight, whilst the ceramic tiles layered with thick rubber matting with which the room was covered were removed, taken away and burned in a special furnace. As Dr Ernst-Robert Grawitz (1899–1945), a leading SS medical official, had also supposedly been involved with The Bell in some way, Witkowski speculated Josef Mengele-like trials had been conducted on deliberately exposing prisoners to the effects of The Bell to see what happened.

According to Witkowski's documents, the SS had certainly exposed various animals, like insects, lizards, frogs, mice and rats to The Bell's rays, together with plants, moulds, mosses, ferns and fungi, and organic substances like blood, milk, egg white and meat. All were destroyed by The Bell, with a 'crystalline substance' forming within animals' tissues, rotting them from within, whilst all bodily liquids, like blood, solidified into gels and separated away into distinct cellular units. Plants became completely white 4 to 5 hours after exposure like vegetable albinos, with all green chlorophyll simply disappearing, living on for a week before they suddenly decomposed into pools of scentless grease.

According to some descriptions, The Bell also had the additional property of transmuting mercury into gold, linking the whole thing back to alchemy. Supposedly, the inspiration for the machine's design came from a 2,000-year-old Hindu text, which said 'By means of the power latent in the mercury which sets the driving whirlwind in motion, a man sitting inside may travel a great distance in the sky in a most marvellous manner' – another triumph for the Ahnenerbe.

As Professor Walther Gerlach (1889–1979), a scientist associated with Germany's atomic weapons research, was also meant to be involved in the project, it may perhaps be assumed The Bell was a nuclear device of some sort, and the deaths, illnesses and disintegrations due to harmful radiation emissions. Witkowski disagreed. Professor Gerlach had interests in other fields too, like gravity and magnetic fields, sometimes using Viktor Schauberger-like terms such as 'vortex compression'. Admittedly, after the war, Gerlach never referred to such fields ever again, but maybe this was because he had been forbidden to do so?

Witkowski argued that, as the Nazis hated the 'Jewish Physics' of Albert Einstein, they had developed a radical new approach to gravity based upon quantum theory, several of whose leading lights, like Werner Heisenberg (1901–76), were pleasingly full-blooded Germans. As such, proposed Witkowski, The Bell was actually an experimental anti-gravity device, a scaled-up alternative to the repulsine of Viktor Schauberger.

Suggestive of this was a nearby structure today known either as Mucholapka ('The Flytrap') or 'Hitler's Stonehenge', a broadly circular concrete construction 30m wide and 10m high, consisting of 12m-thick columns linked by horizontal beams in a decagonal ring structure. The thing looks very eerie, and very striking. But that does not necessarily mean it was actually anything much out of the ordinary. In reality, Hitler's Stonehenge was probably nothing more than the skeletal base of an unfinished giant water cooling tower. How disappointing.

But wait! In the soil below the Mucholapka can be found some ceramic tiles, just as were supposed to be found within The Bell's underground pool chamber, and there are also strong steel hooks embedded within the tops of the concrete pillars, which Witkowski interpreted as meaning The Bell was tested outdoors within this structure, too. The anti-gravity machine was chained to the hooks on this test rig, he says, so it didn't just float away out of control like Schauberger's repulsine had once done. According to Witkowski, local residents had reported seeing mysterious 'flying barrels' acting in a VTOL fashion nearby during the war – evidently test flights of The Bell. When Witkowski later visited a Warsaw scientific institute and examined a contemporary plasma-trap chamber, he thought it looked remarkably similar to The Bell, meaning the Nazis had therefore obviously sought to create 'plasma vortexes' to facilitate such al fresco acts of levitation.[9]

* * *

Igor Witkowski himself did not actually claim The Bell was a time machine, although that is now what it is most famous as being. Instead, it was Nick Cook who introduced this thrilling idea to the world. In *The Hunt for Zero Point* Cook was keen to report the theories of his pseudonymous informant 'Dan Marckus', a physicist at a leading British university, about the implications of the two contemporary SS code-names for The Bell, Laternentrager and Chronos. The first meant simply 'lantern holder', but the second means 'time', which clearly indicated that, as Marckus put it, Kammler was 'trying to build a fucking time machine!'

Marckus hypothesised that, by spinning the Xerum-525 in its cylinders, Die Glocke generated something called a 'torsion field', a rather vague pseudo-scientific concept which in Marckus' interpretation could potentially bend space-time around The Bell's main body, thereby allowing the theoretical manipulation of time itself. Say the Nazis managed to slow time within The Bell's underground pool chamber by a rate of one-thousand by literally bending it to their will. If the Germans had sat in there for a year in 1945, then when they opened the hatch and emerged, it would have been 2945 outside, and they could have seen for themselves whether Hitler's promise of a Thousand-Year Reich had come true or not.

Furthermore, the creation of a torsion field could also have accounted for The Bell's anti-gravity properties. A torsion field, said Marckus, would be best imagined as an invisible 'whirlpool' created in the atmosphere which then manages to dip into the hidden Zero-Point Energy Field also once supposedly tapped by Viktor Schauberger. This would agitate the unseen energy like a whirlpool in a lake, stirring things up like crazy until the energy began to flood into our own world. Torsion fields stimulated not only the surrounding three dimensions of space, but also the fourth dimension of time, allowing access to a hypothetical fifth dimension dubbed 'hyperspace', where all the Zero-Point Energy hid.

Thus, when Nazi Bells or repulsines levitated, they were really doing so as a result of unobservable reactions taking place within the fifth dimension, not our own realm, so accounting for how they disobeyed the laws of physics – because the laws of physics in the fifth dimension were very different than those which applied within our own. What the SS had been trying to do was 'tune' Die Glocke's electromagnetically emanated waves into the correct resonant frequency to allow torsion fields of an appropriate nature to pass through into the fifth dimension and interact with these new, secret laws of physics lurking away there, thereby letting them levitate objects and control time.[10] With knowledge like that up his sleeve, it's no wonder the Americans wanted Hans Kammler!

* * *

Witkowski and Cook aren't the only ones with books to sell, and other authors have since added further spurious details to the history of Die Glocke, to make their own version of the narrative even more 'complete'. If The Bell's torsion fields could bend time, why should the device not also contain special concave mirrors allowing clever Nazis to peer into the past?[11] Or why shouldn't it merge with another popular Polish war legend, that of the top-secret Nazi gold train full of looted art treasures and bullion supposedly buried somewhere within the very same Alpenfestung complexes near where The Bell was tested? Maybe it is even on-board in a big crate like the Lost Ark in Indiana Jones?[12] And as for the mysterious, violet-coloured, mercury like Xerum-525 spun within The Bell's centrifuges, might this not be the fabled 'red mercury', a mythical liquid substance which was supposed to act as a catalyst in thermonuclear reactions, thus making atom bombs small enough to fit inside a terrorist's suitcase, a modern version of the miraculous 'red tincture' of alchemy?[13]

Sceptics may prefer to point out the curious superficial similarity between the myth of The Bell and the plot of the popular US horror writer Dean R. Koontz's (b.1945) 1988 thriller novel *Lightning*, concerning as it does wartime Nazi time-travel experiments involving an electricity emitting machine made up from rotating cylinders which creates tunnels between dimensions.[14] With the typical circular logic we are by this stage familiar with, The Bell also now makes specific named appearances in certain Nazi-related sci-fi films, which can thus be marketed as being 'based on real life', in precisely the same misleading sense films about Roswell can be – mere modern day versions of *Frau im Mond*. When Dean R. Koontz innocently invented his fictional Nazi chrono device back in 1988, did he know that one day he would end up not as a fiction writer, but a sort of accidental pseudo-historian instead?

Another authorial option is to reclaim The Bell not as being an impossible time machine or anti-gravity spaceship, but as some form of superficially more plausible prototype Nazi atomic weapon or uranium production unit. This was the path chosen by writer Michael Fitzgerald, whose own Wunderwaffen book, *Hitler's Secret Weapons of Mass Destruction: The Nazi Plan for Final Victory* appeared in 2019. The book is slightly reminiscent of Major Rudolf Lusar's own previous effort in this genre (albeit with no disturbing pro-Nazi subtext!) in that it mixes genuine Wunderwaffen data, which I have mined myself whilst writing this current book, with total twaddle, mostly about German-built UFOs. Fitzgerald thinks foo-fighters were probably real in a literal nuts-and-bolts sense, and falls for the fibs of Rudolf Schriever and his ilk more-or-less wholesale, devoting a third of his pages to re-telling their legend from a largely non-sceptical perspective, unwisely relying on the likes of Henry Stevens and Renato Vesco as sources.

When he finally comes to examine the story of The Bell, however, whilst personally feeling it was indeed a real, physically extant device, Fitzgerald dismisses the wilder interpretations of Witkowski and Cook, saying that Die Glocke was no floating UFO-like craft but some kind of particle accelerator intended not to transmute mercury into gold, but to transmute thorium (which he says was being mined nearby to the site where The Bell was tested) into weapons-grade uranium. If so, this would explain why all the people, plants and animals exposed to the Wunderwaffe's presence rotted away and died not long after – they were being subjected to radiation poisoning by cruel SS scientists as an entertaining side project during their efforts to create Hitler an atom bomb.

In this hypothesis' favour, the Nazis did indeed have various war-time atomic-research projects on the go, and it is obviously more likely they could have been trying to develop a nuke than attempting to build a time machine. But, on the other hand, Fitzgerald's speculation is just that – speculation, and relies overall upon the initial highly debatable notion that something like The Bell actually did really exist in the first place, a proposition which really just has to be taken on trust.

If you comb through the post-war testimonies and interviews of various captured Nazis, conducted many decades prior to Witkowski writing his 2000 Wunderwaffen book, as Fitzgerald has done, and look for instances of them talking about things which could be said to *sound* a bit like The Bell, at least if you really want them to, then this is actually possible. Yet such an exercise seems precisely akin to how Viktor Schauberger's wartime repulsine devices, whilst real, could only be interpreted as being flying saucers retrospectively, once said saucers had been later 'invented' by Kenneth Arnold in 1947. Without Witkowski likewise having 'invented' The Bell himself in 2000 by repeating his claimed source data in print, the words Fitzgerald cites issuing from the mouths of captive Nazis, even if describing genuine inventions, could not have been interpreted as being The Bell either.[15]

* * *

By far the most elaborate later addition to the tale of The Bell concerns the supposed Kecksburg UFO crash of 9 December 1965, another Roswell-style narrative of highly dubious legitimacy. There is absolutely no doubt that on the evening in question, a glowing fireball-type object was seen hurtling across the skies of several US states. Reports were received of it coming down to Earth from Michigan to Pennsylvania, although it actually seemed to disappear near Lake Erie on the US-Canada border. Astronomers tracked the object's path across the sky and said it was simply a fiery bolide meteor. The closeness or otherwise of such a thing is notoriously difficult to gauge with the naked eye, and when one disappears from witnesses' line of sight behind a building, tree or hill, they may naturally conclude it has landed quite nearby, whereas in fact it may be many, many miles away.

One location where this flaming phantom was said to have crashed was the small village of Kecksburg in Pennsylvania, about 30 miles south-east of Pittsburgh. Sonic booms, grass fires and rains of metal debris were attributed to the thing as far afield as Michigan and Ohio, whilst in Kecksburg itself reports were called in to emergency services of something landing in nearby woods, accompanied by blue smoke, vibrations and a loud 'thump' emanating from 'a burning star', all of which may not have been lies so much as misinterpretations. According to some witnesses, the object stopped still in the sky before deliberately changing direction towards the landing zone – but equally, according to other witnesses, it didn't.

Local radio station WHJB received a report of a 'huge fireball' in the Kecksburg woods, which were cordoned off by police and volunteer fire marshals, before USAF personnel and State troopers searched the location, only to find . . . absolutely nothing. But that is only if you choose to believe the USAF, police and newspapers of the day, which carried headlines like 'Searchers Fail to Find Object'. To conspiracy theorists, that headline really means 'Searchers Succeed in Finding Object, But Don't Want You to Know About It'.

In 2005, tying in with the Kecksburg Crash's fortieth anniversary, NASA released news that their scientists had examined metallic fragments from the area and determined they were from a Russian satellite which had fallen from orbit and disintegrated, but said their records proving this had sadly been lost, which only makes it all sound even more like a conspiracy theory. Backed by the Sci-Fi Channel, ufologist Leslie Kean sued NASA under the Freedom of Information Act, demanding they search again for the missing papers, which they did – but it turned out they were still missing, legal action couldn't just suddenly make them appear from nowhere. Some have suggested the Kecksburg fireball may have actually been a secret US spy satellite which failed, an embarrassment the powers-that-be were reluctant to reveal, but predictably others have preferred to claim it was an alien spacecraft.

NASA now admits the object was likely to have been a meteor after all, not a satellite, with a rather large administrative error having been made.

Just as the Roswell Incident didn't really happen until 1980, when a best-selling book was written about it, so the Kecksburg Crash didn't really happen until 1990, when prime-time NBC documentary series *Unsolved Mysteries* broadcast a show partly devoted to the event. Here, the story of local resident James Romansky, a 19-year-old volunteer firefighter back in 1965, was given its first widespread airing. According to Romansky, he had combed through the woods only to find a silvery gold object 'the shape of an acorn' with 'a kind of ring . . . [or] metal bumper' around the bottom, on which appeared what looked like 'Egyptian hieroglyphics, but without any animal-signs . . . [only] straight and broken lines, dots, squares and circles'.

After hearing Romansky, other witnesses came forward with further testimony which either confirmed Romansky's own, or else spuriously built upon it, depending on your viewpoint. Maybe the object in the woods actually resembled 'a big burned orange' which 'glowed, crackled and sparked'. Maybe the crashed item, about as large as that other timeless masterpiece of German engineering, a Volkswagen Beetle, was retrieved and placed beneath some tarpaulin on a military truck before being driven away to a USAF base. Personnel guarding it there were reputedly given strict orders to shoot and kill anyone who tried to enter.

Most telling was the word of a witness given the pseudonym 'Myron', who worked as a truck driver for his family owned cement factory in Dayton, Ohio, not too far from Wright-Patterson Air Force Base, from which establishment the firm received a large order for 6,500 specially glazed bricks two days after the Kecksburg Crash. Inexplicably, the official who ordered them needlessly let slip they were needed for 'building a double-walled shield around a recovered radioactive object'. Delivering these bricks to the base, Myron looked inside a hangar whose door had, equally inexplicably, been left open only to see 'the shadowy outlines of a large, bell-shaped object . . . about 9 feet wide and 12 feet high'. Was the Kecksburg Acorn really the Nazi Bell?

An acorn is a comparable shape to a bell, and both objects were supposed to be of similar dimensions, and to have given off radioactive field-type effects, whilst the glazed bricks used to shield personnel from the Kecksburg object recall the glazed ceramic tiles used to shield Nazi scientists from The Bell. Possibly those 'hieroglyphs' around the base were really ancient Nordic runes of the kind once researched by the Ahnenerbe, it has been guessed.

Some have drawn out the path of the fallen object as it invaded US skies back in 1965, concluding it actually emanated not from outer space, but from the icy northern wastes of Arctic Canada, somewhere near the North Pole . . . precisely where the saucer base of Point 103 was located in the former SS officer Wilhelm Landig's neo-Nazi novels, the basis for the myth of the Himmelskompass mentioned earlier.

Meanwhile, Roswell-aping claims that corpses were carried away from the thing under sheets, from beneath one of which a lizard-like arm with three fingers and scaly skin swung loose, suggest the Nazis may have been secretly allied with a race of ET lizard men called the Draconians. Thus, it now apparently becomes possible for The Bell to have been manned, something Witkowski and Cook never originally implied. Obviously, some have therefore speculated the reason Kammler's Bell disappeared in 1945 was actually because it shot forward in time away from the advancing Russians and landed in Pennsylvania in 1965 instead; maybe it even had him in it? As with Roswell, the narrative mutates and metastasises more rapidly than the tissues of a lab rat exposed to a cylinder full of spinning Xerum-525. Yet perhaps the Kecksburg Acorn most truly came not from outer space, Point 103 or another time frame but, once again, straight from the uncanny realm of Tlön.

Kecksburg now hosts an annual UFO festival to raise money for the volunteer fire department whose members were originally called out to the local woods to deal with the roast acorn, with a UFO store opening there in 2005, from which you can buy natty little 'space acorn' souvenirs. The town's primary tourist attraction for holidaying saucer heads, however, is a classic hrön. Mounted in front of the local fire station is a large replica of the famed space acorn, complete with carved hieroglyphics, something which never fails to be filmed by visiting documentary crews from TV series like *Ancient Aliens* – and yet such shows very rarely mention the statue's specific origins.

Simply to look at, viewers might assume it was commissioned by locals as a quasi-official recognition of the space acorn's reality. In truth, it was made as a prop for the 1990 episode of *Unsolved Mysteries* which launched the Kecksburg Roswell into the public eye in the first place, donated to the villagers by the show's producers as a sign of gratitude for their kind co-operation. So, the main piece of physical 'evidence' broadcast by contemporary documentaries about this total non-event is in fact proof only that somebody else made a similar documentary about this same total non-event themselves thirty or more years beforehand. In this sense, the Kecksburg Acorn-Bell really is a classic Nazi UFO after all: that is to say, something wholly imaginary made into something inappropriately solid by the powers of the human imagination, a brand new foo-fighter for the twenty-first century.[16]

And, with that, it is high time we brought this whole labyrinthine narrative to a final Bell-End. The celestial typewriter of the ghost of Jorge Luis Borges deserves a bit of a rest now, I think.

Notes

Introduction – Jerry-Built Saucers?

1. https://drvitelli.typepad.com/providential/2016/09/the-hitler-hoax.html; https://www.thedailybeast.com/the-kentucky-miner-who-scammed-americans-by-claiming-he-was-hitler-and-plotting-a-revolt-with-spaceships.
2. McGovern (ed.), pp. 545–6, 592, 698–9; https://www.nationalarchives.gov.uk/documents/briefing-guide-12-07-12.pdf; it is worth noting that the USAF was only founded on 18 September 1947, thus meaning flying saucers were born before it was.
3. Evans and Stacy (eds), p. 22.
4. Aldrich, Jan, '1947: Beginning of the UFO Era', in Evans and Stacy (eds), pp. 18–27; Arnold, Kenneth, 'What Happened on June 24, 1947', in Evans and Stacy (eds), pp. 28–34; Legrange, Pierre, 'It Seems Impossible, But There It Is', in Evans and Spencer (eds), pp. 26–45; Devereux and Brookesmith, pp. 13–14, 21–4; Evans and Bartholomew, pp. 177–80; McGovern (ed.), pp. 41–2, 231.
5. http://it.wikiufo.org/index.php?title=UFO_Nazisti.
6. Santos; http://it.wikiufo.org/index.php?title=UFO_Nazisti, pp. 5, 7, 16–17, 27.
7. Roberts, 2011; Good, pp. 18–19; Stevens, 2002, pp. 233–4; https://paraview.wordpress.com/2012/03/11/sonderburo-13-the-secret-nazi-ufo-squad/.
8. Strieber, p. 226.

Chapter One – No Foos Without Fires

1. https://www.456fis.org/FOO-FIGHTERS_INDEX.htm;http://www.faqs.org/rfcs/rfc3092.html.
2. Chester, p. 59.
3. Chester, pp. 52, 56; Clarke, 2011, p. 24; Lindell; http://www.saturdaynightuforia.com/html/articles/articlehtml/foofightersofworldwariipartone.html.
4. Roberts, 2011.
5. Clarke, 2011, p. 24.
6. *New York Times*, 14 December 1944.
7. Chester, pp. 96–7, 120–2; *Youngstown Vindicator*, 15 December 1944.
8. Chamberlin; http://www.project1947.com/articles/amlfoo.htm.
9. Lindell; other accounts say a pilot called Charlie Horne named the foos; see Chester, p. 100.
10. Chamberlin; Lindell; Chester, pp. 113–18.
11. *New York Times*, 2 January 1945.
12. *Time*, 15 January 1945; Chester, pp. 125–6, 207.
13. Redfern, 2007.
14. http://www.saturdaynightuforia.com/html/articles/articlehtml/foofightersofworldwariipartone.html.
15. York; Chester, p. 207.
16. Wilkins.
17. Lindell.
18. Chamberlin.
19. Wilkins.
20. https://www.clashmusic.com/news/foo-fighters-on-their-band-name.

21. Chester, pp. 38, 55, 281–96; Clark and Parish; https://en.wikipedia.org/wiki/Foo_fighter; http://www.saturdaynightuforia.com/html/articles/articlehtml/foofightersofworldwariipartone.html;http://www.saturdaynightuforia.com/html/articles/articlehtml/foofightersofworldwariiparttwo.html; http://www.saturdaynightuforia.com/html/articles/articlehtml/foofightersofworldwariipartthree.html.
22. http://www.saturdaynightuforia.com/html/articles/articlehtml/foofightersofworldwariiparttwo.html.
23. Chester, p. 122; http://www.saturdaynightuforia.com/html/articles/articlehtml/foofightersofworldwariipartone.html; to be clear, the term 'sticky spotlight' is my own, not the RAF's.
24. Chester, pp. 191–3, 209–11, 221; Clark and Parish; Stringfield, pp. 7–9; Redfern, 2007.
25. Clarke, 2011, p. 25.
26. Lindell.
27. http://www.saturdaynightuforia.com/html/articles/articlehtml/foofightersofworldwariipartone.html.
28. Clarke, 2011, pp. 27–9; Chester, pp. 3–4.

Chapter Two – Metal Gear Solid

1. http://it.wikiufo.org/index.php?title=UFO_Nazisti.
2. *New York Times Herald*, 8 July 1947.
3. Lubbock, Texas, *Morning Avalanche*, 8 July 1947.
4. *New York Times*, 20 February 1952.
5. Evans and Stacy (eds), pp. 21–2.
6. Jerome Clark, 'Meeting the Extraterrestrials: How the ETH Was Invented', in Evans and Stacy (eds), pp. 71–2.
7. Clark, in Evans and Stacy (eds), p. 72.
8. Santos.
9. http://it.wikiufo.org/index.php?title=UFO_Nazisti.
10. *Denver Post*, 9 November 1947; http://it.wikiufo.org/index.php?title=UFO_Nazisti.
11. http://www.saturdaynightuforia.com/html/articles/articlehtml/taleofthenazisaucer.html; http://it.wikiufo.org/index.php?title=UFO_Nazisti.
12. Clark and Parish.
13. Chester, pp. 67–8.
14. Clark and Parish; Chester, pp. 90–3.
15. Clark and Parish.
16. Roberts, 1990; Roberts, 2000; Snyder, pp. 316–17.
17. Chester, pp. 43–7.

Chapter Three – Discoid Inferno

1. The majority of this chapter is based on Italian ufologist Maurizio Verga's excellent summaries of German-, French- and Italian-language newspapers which I can't read; any unreferenced material, translations and summaries of all foreign-language newspaper reports and similar texts mentioned herein are thus taken from http://it.wikiufo.org/index.php?title=UFO_Nazisti, complemented by McClure and http://www.saturdaynightuforia.com/html/articles/articlehtml/taleofthenazisaucer.html.
2. Try https://www.manmade-ufos.com and http://discaircraftgreyfalcon.us.
3. Santos.
4. *Los Angeles Mirror*, 25 March 1950; Olean, New York, *Times Herald*, 25 March 1950.

5. Lima, Ohio, *News*, 2 April 1950.
6. *FranceSoir*, 7 and 14 June 1952.
7. McClure, pp. 59–60.
8. Harbinson, pp. 119–123; McGovern (ed.), pp. 51–2; Vesco and Childress, 1994, pp. 252–5, 257–62, 278–9; http://www.saturdaynightuforia.com/html/articles/articlehtml/taleofthenazisaucer.html.
9. Fitzgerald, pp. 64–7; http://discaircraft.greyfalcon.us/ARTHUR%20SACK%20A.htm; http://www.saturdaynightuforia.com/html/articles/articlehtml/taleofthenazisaucer.html.
10. Brookesmith (ed.), pp. 66–9; Harbinson, pp. 116–18; https://en.wikipedia.org/wiki/Vought_V-173; https://en.wikipedia.org/wiki/Vought_XF5U.
11. Moore and Nero, p. 176; https://en.wikipedia.org/British_Rail_flying_saucer; http://news.bbc.co.uk/1/hi/uk/4801928.stm; https://www.theguardian.com/science/2006/mar/13/spaceexploration.transportintheuk.
12. McGovern (ed.), p. 52; http://britishaviation-ptp.com/aesir.html; https://www.theengineer.co.uk/uk-team-unveils-innovative-flying-saucer-uav/.
13. Keyhoe, pp. 30–6.
14. *Welt am Sonntag*, 25 April 1953.

Chapter Four – V for Vengeance, F for Fake

1. https://www.oradour.info/appendix/dortmund/lusar01.htm; Lusar was not involved in the massacre himself, incidentally.
2. Compiled from Fitzgerald, especially pp. 26–9, 33–5, 59–60, 94–102, 238.
3. Lusar, pp. 165–6.
4. McClure, p. 56.
5. Kurlander, pp. 145–6, 153, 155, 181–2, 226–7, 272–3; Longerich, p. 266.
6. http://it.wikiufo.org/index.php?title=UFO_Nazisti.
7. Kurlander, pp. 263–70.
8. McKale, p. 136.
9. http://it.wikiufo.org/index.php?title=UFO_Nazisti.
10. Snyder, p. 268; Stevens, 2002, p. 16.
11. Stevens, 2002, pp. 86–7; McClure, p. 45.
12. Fitzgerald, pp. 88–9, 243–4; https://news.bbc.co.uk/1/hi/magazine/4443934.stm;https://skeptoid.com/episodes/4293;http://it.wikiufo.org/index.php?title=UFO_Nazisti.
13. https://www.livemint.com/Leisure/nANJmPojfquesREYWGNkoJ/Rewriting-the-past-Wunderwaffen-What-if.html; Fitzgerald, pp. 78–83; https://ethw.org/Spaceflight_in_Silent_Film.
14. Ley.
15. Kurlander, pp. 220–2, 271–2; Uwe Schellinger, Andreas Anton and Michael T. Schetsche, 'Pragmatic Occultism in the Military History of the Third Reich', in Black and Kurlander, pp. 157–80.
16. Kurlander, pp. 23, 133–4, 294.
17. Kurlander, p. 271.
18. Masters, pp. 135–6; McClure, p. 58.
19. Kingsepp.
20. Kurlander, pp. 267, 273.
21 Szöllösi-Janze (ed.), pp. 12–13.
22. Ford, p. 6; Fitzgerald, p. 79.

23. Evans and Bartholomew, pp. 497–8; Chester, pp. 7–10; Anders Liljegren and Clas Svahn, 'Ghost Rockets and Phantom Aircraft', in Evans and Spencer, pp. 53–6.
24. Evans and Bartholomew, 2009, pp. 487–94.
25. Evans and Bartholomew, 2009, pp. 208–11; http://it.wikiufo.org/index.php?title=UFO_Nazisti.
26. Clarke, 2011, pp. 12–13; David Clarke, 'Scareships Over Britain', in Moore (ed.), 1999, pp. 39–63.
27. Helmuth Trischler, 'Aeronautical Research Under National Socialism: Big Science or Small Science?', in Szöllösi-Janze (ed.), pp. 79–110.
28. Ford, pp. 9–17; Fitzgerald, pp. 53–6.
29. Zündel, pp. 17, 18, 19, 24–5, 40, 47, 55, 83.
30. Zündel, pp. 53–5, 99–100.
31. Zündel, pp. 102–3.
32. Zündel, p. 102.
33. Zündel, pp. 1–6.
34. Zündel, p. 42.
35. Zündel, p. 12.
36. Zündel, pp. 28–9.
37. Snyder, p. 48; Zündel, p. 79.
38. Zündel, pp. 30–1, 33, 38, 74.
39. Zündel, pp. 93, 94, 96.
40. Stevens, 2007, pp. 176–89.
41. Stevens, 2007, pp. 170–1.
42. Stevens, 2007, pp. 27–9.
43. https://de.m.wikipedia.org/wiki/Axel_Stoll; http://www.jasoncolavito.com/blog/more-on-anti-semitism-and-nazi-apologetics-on-h2-and-the-history-channel; https://www.vice.com/de/article/nnkaz7/stuff-zu-besuch-bei-den-ufo-esoterik-nazis; https://www.vice.com/de/article/jmnmy7/dr-axel-stoll-hat-den-strafplaneten-verlassen-aldebaran-hohlerde-835.
44. Stevens, 2007, pp. 37–41, 42–3, 92, 103–7, 134–6, 152–5.
45. Stevens, 2007, pp. 66, 72–3.
46. Stevens, 2007, p. 131.
47. Stevens, 2007, pp. iii, vii.
48. Stevens, 2007, pp. 122–30; https://sfdictionary.com/view/1727/impervium; https://starwars.fandom.com/wiki/Impervium.
49. Goodrick-Clarke, 2002, pp. 170–1; McClure, pp. 50–1; https://rationalwiki.org/wiki/Henry_Stevens; https://en.wikipedia.org/wiki/Five-Percent_Nation.
50. Stevens, 2007, pp. i–iii.
51. Stevens, 2007, p. 52.
52. Stevens, 2007, p. 334.
53. Stevens, 2002, p. 253.
54. Stevens, 2002, p. 13.
55. Stevens, 2002, pp. 233–6.
56. Stevens, 2002, p. 84.
57. Stevens, 2002, pp. 262–7.
58. Stevens, 2002, p. 267.
59. Stevens, 2002, pp. 261, 267–8.

Chapter Five – Little Green Germans

1. http://it.wikiufo.org/index.php?title=UFO_Nazisti, pp. 28–30; http://greyfalcon.us/restored/JOSEF%20ANDREAS%20EPP. htm; https://www.manmade-ufos.com/andreas-epp; *New York Times*, 22 May 1952.
2. Stevens, 2002, pp. 42–52.
3. http://it.wikiufo.org/index.php?title=UFO_Nazisti.
4. Stevens, 2002, pp. 86–113.
5. Stevens, 2002, pp. 90–2.
6. www.victoryfortheworld.net; https://www.ibtimes.com/do-aliens-exist-yes-some-look-just-like-us-says-paul-hellyer-former-canadian-defense-minister-video; https://mysteriousuniverse.org/2019/11/strange-disclosure-and-a-former-canadian-politician-who-really-really-likes-ufos/; https://en.wikipedia.org/wiki/Paul_Hellyer;http://www.share-international.org/magazine/old_issues/2011/2011-05.htm.
7. Gorightly and Bishop, pp. 9–11.
8. Kurlander, pp. 146–50, 240; Snyder, pp. 33, 61; Goldberg, p. 385; https://en.wikipedia.org/wiki/Blood-and-soil.
9. Zündel, pp. 21–4.
10. Vesco and Childress, insert between pp. 133–4; Fitzgerald, pp. 24–6; *New York Times*, 29 June 1945.
11. Cook, p. 210.
12. Alexandersson, pp. 11–12, 75; Bartholomew, pp. 11–12.
13. Goodrick-Clarke, 2002, pp. 163–4.
14. Alexandersson, pp. 88–9.
15. Cook, p. 210.
16. Kurlander, pp. 273–4.
17. Alexandersson, pp. 88–91.
18. Alexandersson, pp. 86, 126; Cook, pp. 211, 214.
19. Kurlander, pp. 274–5; Cook, pp. 205–6; Alexandersson, pp. 92–5.
20. Cook, pp. 211–16.
21. Alexandersson, pp. 92, 156.
22. Cook, pp. 217–20, 222; Alexandersson, pp. 92–5.
23. Cook, p. 220.
24. Alexandersson, pp. 17–23, 32–4.
25. Alexandersson, pp. 24–9.
26. Alexandersson, pp. 36–7, 39, 43–7.
27. Alexandersson, pp. 53–4, 72–3, 11–13.
28. Alexandersson, p. 125.
29. Alexandersson, p. 133.
30. Alexandersson, pp. 117–18.
31. Alexandersson, pp. 76–83; Bartholomew, Ch. 6.
32. Alexandersson, pp. 84–7.
33. Alexandersson, pp. 15–17.
34. Bartholomew, Ch. 8.
35. Bartholomew, Ch. 6.
36. Wilson, p. 253; Bartholomew, Ch. 2.
37. Alexandersson, p. 17.
38. Alexandersson, Ch. 18.
39. Cook, pp. 100, 108–14.

40. Zündel, pp. 48–9, 106–7; obituary in *The Times*, 26 August 2017; Goodrick-Clarke, 2002, p. 157; Alexandersson, p. 120.
41. Cook, pp. 224–6.
42. Alexandersson, p. 120.
43. Alexandersson, p. 125.
44. Stevens, 2002, pp. 121–9, 261–8.
45. Stevens, 2007, pp. 58–62.
46. Stevens, 2007, pp. 212–15; Fitzgerald, pp. 18–20.
47. Stevens, 2007, pp. 309–13, 322–4; Bartholomew, Ch. 2.
48. Ball, pp. 70–2, 83–90, 104–6, 265; Sagan, p. 261.
49. Stevens, 2007, pp. 258–305; https://www.iter.org/newsline/196/930; https://www.wired.co.uk/article/nuclear-island; https://en.wikipedia.org/wiki/Ronald_Richter; https://en.wikipedia.org/wiki/Huemul_Project.
50. Cook, pp. 101–7, 236–8; https://www.wired.com/1998/03/antigravity/; http://news.bbc.co.uk/1/hi/not_in_website/syndication/monitoring/media_reports/2159629.stm; https://web.archive.org/20020802222642/http://www.janes.com/aerospace/civil/news/jdw/jdw020729_1_n.sht; https://web.archive.org/web/20050314023910/http://www.telegraph.co.uk/htmlContent.jhtml?html=%2Farchive%2F1996%2F09%2F01%2F01%2Fngrav01.html.

Chapter Six – Lightning Warfare

1. McClure, pp. 15–20; Vesco and Childress, pp. x, 85.
2. Vesco and Childress, 1994, pp. 85–6.
3. Vesco and Childress, pp. 85–8, 113, 115–16, 158–9; McClure, pp. 15–18.
4. http://www.acthungpanzer.com/kugel.htm#kugel.
5. Vesco.
6. Vesco; Vesco and Childress, 1994, pp. 134–6, 144.
7. http://it.wikiufo.org/index.php?title=UFO_Nazisti.
8. Vesco; Vesco and Childress, pp. 177–8, 225, 229, 231, 248–69.
9. http://discaircraft.greyfalcon.us/WNF%20Feuerball.htm.
10. Vesco and Childress, p. xi.
11. McClure, pp. 48–50.
12. McClure, p. 42.

Chapter Seven – Some Bolts, Mostly Nuts

1. *Minnesota Evening Tribune*, 7 November 1945.
2. Chamberlin.
3. Lindell.
4. Lindell.
5. Clarke, 2011, pp. 22–3; Chester, pp. 64–6.
6. Clarke, 2011, pp. 30–1; Chester, 2007, p. 75.
7. https://en.wikipedia.org/wiki/Foo_fighter.
8. https://www.popularmechanics.com/military/research/a21750317/nazi-ufo-model-taken-off-shelves-for-historical-inaccuracy/; https://www.thelocal.de/20180619/toy-nazi-ufo-taken-off-market-after-criticism.
9. https://www.amazon.co.uk/Haunebu-German-Flying-saucer-model/dp/B01N33TZCB.

10. https://www.squadron.com/Squadron-Models-1-72-Haunebu-II-German-Flying-Sa-p/sqm0001.htm.
11. https://www.anigrand.com/AA4011_Haunebu.htm; https://www.anigrand.com/.
12. https://www.amazon.co.uk/Haunebu-Saucer-144th-Scale-Model/dp/B06W2GSGP8/.
13. Clarke, 2015, pp. 148–53; Devereux and Brookesmith, pp. 120–37; Dennis Stacy, 'Eight Days That Shaped Ufology', in Evans and Stacy (eds), pp. 6–8.
14. *Roswell Daily Record*, 9 July 1947.
15. https://www.telegraph.co.uk/news/newstopics/howaboutthat/ufo/8512408/Roswell-was-Soviet-plot-to-create-US-panic.html; https://www.huffingtonpost.co.uk/entry/area-51-ufos-aliens-annie-jacobsen-nazi-soviet_n_869706?ri18n=true; https://www.washingtondecoded.com/site/2011/07/area51.html.
16. Evans and Bartholomew, 2009, pp. 465–9.
17. https://mysteriousuniverse.org/2020/01/more-on-roswell-russia-and-project-blue-book/.
18. Redfern,2005;https://mysteriousuniverse.org/2020/01/more-on-roswell-russia-and-project-blue-book/.
19. https://www.ufoexplorations.com/area-51-book-exposed-source-for-ros.
20. Goodrick-Clarke, 2002, pp. 155–6, 329.
21. Braenne, 1992.

Chapter Eight – In My End is My Beginning

1. McClure, p. 4.
2. Stevens, 2007, p. 114.
3. Stevens, 2002, p. 60.
4. Ouellet, pp. 14–16.
5. https://www.space.com/24306-interstellar-flight-black-hole-power.html.
6. Redfern, 2008.
7. Borges, pp. 27–43.
8. *Fortean Times*, issue 373, p. 28; https://antigraywarning.webs.com/.
9. Stevens, 2007, pp. 52–7.
10. https://en.wikipedia.org/wiki/Sunstone_(medieval); https://www.smithsonianmag.com/smart-news/simulation-suggest-legendary-viking-sunstones-could-have-worked-180968710/; https://www.sciencemag.org/news/2018/04/viking-seafarers-may-have-navigated-legendary-crystals.
11. Lyne, pp. 30, 89–103, 207–10, 219–24; Farrell, 2005, pp. 257–9; *Albuquerque Journal North*, 6 January 1994.

Conclusion – Saved by The Bell?

1. Stevens, 2007, pp. 18–23.
2. Stevens, 2007, pp. 1–5.
3. Reuter, Lowery and Chester, pp. 13–14, 17–20, 25–6, 31, 35, 38, 43–8, 50, 55–6, 64–71, 104–5.
4. Reuter, Lowery and Chester, pp. 200–1, 205; Döbert and Karlsch; https://en.wikipedia.org/wiki/Hans_Kammler.
5. Reuter, Lowery and Chester, pp. 105, 133–5, 166–7, 169, 172–6, 219–20, 313; Döbert and Karlsch; https://en.wikipedia.org/wiki/Hans_Kammler.

6. Reuter, Lowery and Chester, pp. 108–9, 224, 263–4, 268, 272–3, 328; Döbert and Karlsch; https://en.wikipedia.org/wiki/Hans_Kammler.
7. http://www.saturdaynightuforia.com/html/articles/articlehtml/taleofthenazisaucer.html, p. 2.
8. https://igorwitkowski.com/English.html; https://pl/wikipedia.org/wiki/Igor_Witkowski.
9. Cook, pp. 182–97; Farrell, 2006, Part Two, Chapter Four; https://www.atlasobscura.com/places/mucholapka; https://periergeia.org/en/nazi-secret-weapons-part-2-die-glocke-the-antigravity-bell.
10. Cook, pp. 228–9, 232–4.
11. Kurlander, p. 273.
12. https://www.washingtonpost.com/news/morning-mix/wp/2015/08/28/a-frenzy-in-poland-over-the-latest-mysterious-nazi-gold-train/.
13. Farrell, 2005, p. 335.
14. Farrell, 2005, p. 234.
15. Fitzgerald, pp. 191–213.
16. Farrell, 2005, pp. 335–42; https://en.wikipedia.org/wiki/Kecksburg_UFO_incident; https://www.post-gazette.com/news/science/2015/12/06/50-years-later-the-Kecksburg-Westmoreland-County-UFO-is-identified-probably/stories/201512060146; https://www.space.com/7589-case-finally-closed-1965-pennsylvania-ufo-mystery.html; https://www.pabook.libraries.psu.edu/literary-cultural-heritage-map-pa/feature-articles/acorn-space-kecksburg-incident; http://www.debunker.com/Kecksburg.html; http://www.jasoncolavito.com/blog/review-of-in-search-of-aliens-s01e02-nazi-time-travelers.

Bibliography
The Sources of the Saucers

Note: Editions listed are ones I personally consulted, not necessarily those of the original publishers or publication dates. Some are online editions for which I have had to provide my own page numbers.

Books
Alexandersson, Olof, *Living Water: Viktor Schauberger and the Secrets of Natural Energy*, Gill Books, 2002

Ball, Philip, *Serving the Reich: The Struggle for the Soul of Physics Under Hitler*, Vintage, 2014

Bartholomew, Alick, *Hidden Nature: The Startling Insights of Viktor Schauberger*, Floris Books, 2003

Black, Monica and Kurlander, Eric, *Revisiting the Nazi Occult: Histories, Realities, Legacies*, Camden House, 2019

Borges, Jorge Luis, *Labyrinths*, Penguin Modern Classics, 2000

Brookesmith, Peter (ed.), *Marvels & Mysteries: UFOs*, Parallel, 1995

Chester, Keith, *Strange Company: Military Encounters with UFOs in WWII*, Anomalist Books, 2007

Clarke, David, *The UFO Files: The Inside Story of Real-Life Sightings*, Bloomsbury, 2011

Clarke, David, *How UFOs Conquered the World: The History of a Modern Myth*, Aurum, 2015

Cook, Nick, *The Hunt for Zero Point: Inside the Classified World of Anti-Gravity Technology*, Broadway Books, 2002

Devereux, Paul and Brookesmith, Peter, *UFOs & Ufology: The First 50 Years*, Blandford, 1997

Evans, Hilary and Bartholomew, Robert, *Outbreak! The Encyclopedia of Extraordinary Social Behaviour*, Anomalist Books, 2009

Evans, Hilary and Spencer, John (eds), *Phenomenon: From Flying Saucers to UFOs – Forty Years of Fact and Research*, Macdonald, 1988

Evans, Hilary and Stacy, Dennis (eds), *UFO 1947–1997: Fifty Years of Flying Saucers*, John Brown, 1997

Farrell, Joseph P., *Reich of the Black Sun: Nazi Secret Weapons and the Cold War Allied Legend*, Adventures Unlimited, 2005

Farrell, Joseph P., *The SS Brotherhood of The Bell: NASA's Nazis, JFK and MJ-12*, Adventures Unlimited, 2006

Fitzgerald, Michael, *Hitler's Secret Weapons of Mass Destruction: The Nazi Plan for Final Victory*, Arcturus, 2019

Ford, Roger, *Germany's Secret Weapons in World War II*, Spellmount, 1999

Godwin, Joscelyn, *Arktos: The Polar Myth in Science, Symbolism and Nazi Survivalism*, Adventures Unlimited, 1996

Goldberg, Jonah, *Liberal Fascism: The Secret History of the Left from Mussolini to the Politics of Meaning*, Penguin, 2009

Good, Timothy, *Above Top Secret: The Worldwide UFO Cover-Up*, Sidgwick & Jackson, 1988

Goodrick-Clarke, Nicholas, *Black Sun: Aryan Cults, Esoteric Nazism and the Politics of Identity*, New York University Press, 2002

Goodrick-Clarke, Nicholas, *The Occult Roots of Nazism*, IB Tauris, 2009

Gorightly, Adam and Bishop, Greg, *'A' is for Adamski: The Golden Age of the UFO Contactees*, Gorightly Press, 2018

Harbinson, W.A., *Projekt UFO: The Case for Man-Made Flying Saucers*, Boxtree, 1995

Keyhoe, Donald A., *The Flying Saucers Are Real*, Fawcett Publications, 1950

Kurlander, Eric, *Hitler's Monsters: A Supernatural History of the Third Reich*, Yale University Press, 2017

Longerich, Peter, *Heinrich Himmler*, Oxford University Press, 2012

Lusar, Major Rudolf, *German Secret Weapons of the Second World War*, Philosophical Library, 1959

Lyne, William, *Pentagon Aliens* (formerly *Space Aliens from the Pentagon*), Creatopia, 1999

McGovern, Una (ed.), *Chambers Dictionary of the Unexplained*, Chambers, 2007

McKale, Donald M., *Hitler: The Survival Myth*, Cooper Square Press, 2001

Masters, David, *German Jet Genesis*, Janes, 1982

Moore, James and Nero, Paul, *Pigeon-Guided Missiles: And 49 Other Ideas That Never Took Off*, History Press, 2011

Moore, Steve (ed.), *Fortean Studies, Vol. 6*, John Brown, 1999

Ouellet, Eric, *Illuminations: The UFO Experience as a Parapsychological Event*, Anomalist Books, 2015

Redfern, Nick, *Body Snatchers in the Desert: The Horrible Truth at the Heart of the Roswell Story*, Paraview Pocket Books, 2005

Redfern, Nick, *Contactees: A History of Alien-Human Interaction*, New Page Books, 2010

Reuter, Dean, with Lowery, Colm and Chester, Keith, *The Hidden Nazi: The Untold Story of America's Deal with the Devil*, Regnery History, 2019

Sagan, Carl, *The Demon-Haunted World: Science as a Candle in the Dark*, Ballantine, 1997

Snyder, Louis L., *Encyclopaedia of the Third Reich*, Wordsworth Military Library, 1998

Spencer, John and Evans, Hilary, *Phenomenon*, Macdonald, 1988

Stevens, Henry, *Hitler's Flying Saucers*, Adventures Unlimited, 2002

Stevens, Henry, *Hitler's Suppressed and Still-Secret Science, Weapons and Technology*, Adventures Unlimited, 2007

Strieber, Whitley, *Communion: A True Story*, Souvenir Press, 2016

Stringfield, Leonard H., *Inside Saucer Post . . . 3-0 Blue*, CRIFO, 1957

Szöllösi-Janze, Margit (ed.), *Science in the Third Reich*, Berg, 2001

Vesco, Renato and Childress, David Hatcher, *Man-Made UFOs 1944–1994: 50 Years of Suppression*, Adventures Unlimited, 1994 (revised edn of Vesco's earlier *Intercept – But Don't Shoot/Intercept UFO*)

Wilson, Colin, *The Occult* , Watkins, 2006

Zündel, Ernst, (AKA Mattern, Friedrich), *UFOs: Nazi Secret Weapon?*, Samisdat, 1975

Articles, Pamphlets, Magazines and Online Sources

Braenne, Ole Jonny, 'The Legend of the Spitsbergen Saucer', *International UFO Review*, November/December 1992 (1992), online at http://naziufos.greyfalcon.us/Legend%20of%20the%20Spitsbergen%20Saucer.htm

Chamberlin, Jo, 'The Foo-Fighter Mystery', *The American Legion Magazine*, December 1945 (1945), online with commentary at http://www.project1947.com/articles/amlfoo.htm

Clark, Jerome and Parish, Lucius, 'Foo-Fighters', n.d., online at https://www.465fis.org/FOO-FIGHTERS.htm

Döbert, Frank and Karlsch, Rainer, 'Hans Kammler, Hitler's Last Hope, in American Hands', CWIHP Working Paper #91 (2019), https://www.wilsoncenter.org/publication/hans-kammler-hitlers-last-hope-american-hands

Kingsepp, Eva, 'Scholarship as Simulacrum: The Case of Hitler's Monsters', *Aries: Journal for the Study of Western Esotericism*, 19 (2019), online at https://www.researchgate.net/publication/335886797_Scholarship_as_Simulacrum_The_Case_of_Hitler%27s-Monsters

Ley, Willy, 'Pseudoscience in Nazi-Land', *Astounding Science Fiction*, May 1947, online at http://www.alpenfestung.com/ley_pseudoscience.htm

Lindell, Jeffery A., 'A Historical and Psychological Perspective of the Foo-Fighters of World War Two' (1991), online at https://www.456fis.org/HISTORICAL_&%20PSYCHOLOGICAL_PERSPECTIVE.htm

McClure, Kevin, 'The Nazi UFO Mythos: An Investigation – SUFOI UFO Document #5' (2004), online at http://www.sufoi.dk/e-boger/The%20Nazi%20UFO%20Mythos.pdf

Redfern, Nick, 'Strange Company: Military Encounters with UFOs in World War Two' (interview with Keith Chester), *UFO Magazine*, July 2007, online at http://www.nicap.org/keithchester_ufo.pdf

Redfern, Nick, 'Project Kugelblitz', *Fortean Times*, issue 242 (2008)

Roberts, Andy, 'WWII Document Research: In Search of Foo-Fighters', *UFO Brigantia* No. 66 (1990), online at http://www.project1947.com/articles/arwwr.htm

Roberts, Andy, 'Schweinfurt: A Mystery Solved?' (2000), online at http://www.project1947.com/articles/foosolv.htm

Roberts, Andy, 'Foo History: The Story So Far . . .', *Phenomena Magazine*, issue 22 (2011), variant also online at http://www.project1947.com/articles/foo.htm

Santos, Rodolpho Gauthier Cardoso dos Santos, 'Flying Saucer Inventors in Brazil – Science and Imagery at the Beginning of the Cold War, 1947–1958', *Electronic Proceedings of the 14th National Seminar on the History of Science and Technology* (2014), online at https://www.14snhct.sbhc.org.br/arquivo/download%3FID_ARQUIVO%3D1878&prev=search

Vesco, Renato, 'Aerospace Expert Claims Flying Saucers Are Canada's Secret Weapon', *Argosy*, August 1969, online with commentary at https://www.sacred-texts.com/ufo/vesco.htm

Wilkins, Harold T., 'The Strange Mystery of the Foo-Fighters', *FATE*, Vol. 4, No. 6 (1951), online at http://www.project1947.com/articles/foowilkins.htm

York, Max, 'Joe Thompson and the Foo-Fighters', *The Nashville-Tennessean Magazine*, 30 October 1966, online at http://www.project1947.com/articles/joethomp.htm

Index